BREAKING THE SILENCE

BREAKING THE SILENCE

SURVIVORS SPEAK ABOUT 1965–66 VIOLENCE IN INDONESIA

EDITED BY PUTU OKA SUKANTA

TRANSLATED BY JENNIFER LINDSAY

HFF HERB FEITH FOUNDATION

MONASH University Publishing

Breaking the Silence: Survivors Speak about 1965–66 Violence in Indonesia
Editor: Putu Oka Sukanta
English translation by Jennifer Lindsay

Monash University Publishing
Building 4, Monash University
Clayton, Victoria 3800, Australia
www.publishing.monash.edu

Monash University Publishing brings to the world publications which advance the best traditions of humane and enlightened thought. Monash University Publishing titles pass through a rigorous process of independent peer review.

www.publishing.monash.edu/books/bs-9781922235121.html

Design: Les Thomas

Cover image: Salim M.

National Library of Australia Cataloguing-in-Publication entry:

Author: Sukanta, Putu Oka, 1939–

Title: Breaking the silence: survivors speak about 1965–66 violence in Indonesia / Putu Oka Sukanta.

ISBN: 9781922235121 (paperback)

Series: Herb Feith translation series.

Subjects: War victims--Abuse of--Indonesia--Personal narratives.
Indonesia--History--Coup d'état, 1965--Personal narratives.
Indonesia--History--Coup d'état, 1965--Social aspects.
Indonesia--Politics and government--1950-1966.

Dewey Number: 59.8036

Printed in Australia by Griffin Press an Accredited ISO AS/NZS 14001:2004 Environmental Management System printer.

The paper this book is printed on is certified against the Forest Stewardship Council ® Standards. Griffin Press holds FSC chain of custody certification SGS-COC-005088. FSC promotes environmentally responsible, socially beneficial and economically viable management of the world's forests.

Contents

About the Herb Feith Translation Series vii

Foreword ix

Editor's comments xiii

Glossary xv

1. Asman Yodjodolo 1
   Never-ending struggle

2. Beny 19
   The search for healing

3. I Ketut Sumarta 34
   Guilty until never proven innocent

4. Lambatu bin Lanasi 49
   Demanding rehabilitation of his reputation

5. Leo 61
   Surviving New Order oppression

6. Lestari 82
   My ideals for my country

7. Luh Sutari 95
   Plaiting stories

8. Nadue 103
   Always loyal to my country

9. Niko 114
   Clarity at last

10. Permadi 125
Life in painting

11. Rahim Marhab.. 145
History will reveal the truth

12. Rukiah 157
Undying loyalty

13. Sutarni 169
A story of family survival

14. Ibu Tachrin.. 190
Triumph over oppression

15. Wardik 214
New Order survivor

About the editor .... .233

About the Herb Feith Translation Series

The Herb Feith Translation Series publishes high-quality non-fiction manuscripts not yet available in English, which enhance scholarship and teaching about Indonesia. Published by the Herb Feith Foundation in conjunction with Monash University, the books are available 'open access' or for free download.

The Herb Feith Foundation was established in 2003 to commemorate the life and work of Herb Feith (1930–2001), volunteer, scholar, teacher and peace activist. Its mission is to promote and support work of the kind to which Herb Feith devoted his life, including the study of Indonesia, through a range of educational activities including research and teaching and in the publication and promotion of such work.

Series Board

Translating accounts of the 1965–66 mass violence in Indonesia

Series co-ordinated by Dr Kate McGregor and Dr Jemma Purdey

Until recently there have been very few accounts available in Indonesian or English of the 1965–66 mass violence as told by witnesses, survivors or perpetrators. Today an increasing number of memoirs and short testimony collections are available in Indonesian, however, very few are yet available in English language. This has prevented a greater understanding outside Indonesia of how this violence continues to impact on Indonesians and of how they now understand this traumatic period of their nation's history.

These translated works are valuable resources for all who seek to understand Indonesia today, and especially for undergraduate students of Asian history and the history of mass violence and genocide. This book is the second in this series of translated accounts of the 1965–66 mass violence in Indonesia.

Foreword

Like other sixth graders in primary school in Jakarta at the time, my class was taken on a 'study tour' to Lubang Buaya – an important site for the New Order. We crowded together to listen to the stories about the shallow well where the bodies of the generals were thrown, and with our limited imaginations we tried to make sense of the diorama that depicted the extermination of people who were said to have wanted to destroy our country. We were told about the heroism of Soeharto who rescued our nation. But because we were still children, we could not take in much of it other than fear, because indeed the whole idea was to make us frightened. I stared open-eyed at the relief depicting women dancing with their scarves while, as the story went, the generals were being tortured and then murdered. My teacher whispered. 'Move along now. Don't spend time here. These are bad women'. We hurried on, turning back to take a peek.

It was only later in my teens that I began to understand the truth that had been hidden all this while. This truth was not taught in schools or universities, not broadcast on television, nor was it to be found in history books. This truth one had to search for oneself had to dig up from a snippet here, a snippet there. We heard vaguely about the blood that had flowed and the suffering of our fellow citizens. There before our eyes were the living witnesses who were still silent and silenced.

The Reformation era that began in 1998 opened up the opportunity for Indonesia to acknowledge the evils of the past and restore a social order based on truth and justice. But this has not been done, still to this day. In 2004, parliament passed a law to form a Truth Commission. But this law was weak and controversial. The law offered the victims reparations, but only in return for amnesty for the perpetrators. In the end, rather than fix it or strengthen it, in 2006 the Constitutional Court cancelled the Truth Commission. And so there was a vacuum, where the leaders did not dare to take firm steps to acknowledge their past wrongs, as though they were just glancing back. They did not care.

Telling the truth

This book is a compilation of stories from 15 people whose lives were forged by a holocaust in Indonesia. The word 'holocaust', which is used to refer to Nazi barbarity in exterminating the Jews, and meaning 'destruction or slaughter on a mass scale', is fitting to describe what happened in Indonesia in 1965–66. This book is written by a group of people – senior and emerging writers – who have been involved with 1965 issues for a long time or who are only now learning about what happened. The questions in their hearts were: 'what did it feel like to be in the midst of this wave of evil towards humanity? How could someone salvage their own humanitarian sense at a time when the entire value system that had been nurtured for centuries had been completely overturned for the interests of the 'power of the moment'?

Fifteen people, representing all points of the compass, were engulfed by the political storm that completely changed their lives. The following short extracts show just how terrible the events were that attacked the lives of those who became victims:

Leo, the young artist from Yogya: A young artist in Yogyakarta, charged with youthful enthusiasm, joins an art group on campus with ideals for change. He is invited to the capital city to make posters and banners for Indonesian independence day. When he returns to Yogyakarta, the world is upside down. Two weeks later the police take him to a 'safe place'. He does not realise that he will be 'held safely' for 14 years. His experiences are amazing – he is moved from cell to cell in Java, to Nusakambangan and finally to Buru island. Before he boards the ship taking him to Buru, Leo is given an identity number, 3041, written in ink on the pillow he has just been given, like all the other prisoners. The island of Buru becomes his home for the next ten years. While on Buru, the prisoners are visited by the Red Cross, and someone smuggles a letter to them, written in English. Because the letter is discovered, everyone is punished. After a visit by the Attorney General Ali Said, their lives improve a little. They are allowed to organise sports and arts events. They are given a television set, but are not allowed to hear the news. They can only watch the pictures without sound – a silent drama that continues until today.

Benny, the policeman from West Timor: Even now, decades after his experiences, Benny is still disturbed by his memories. He finds it difficult to wipe the memories, difficult to leave them behind, the victims who had to die at the point of the gun he held. When he and his wife had difficulties having children, he was haunted by the thought that this might be Divine retribution. A generation later, Benny's children have to interpret their own inner worries: was my father a murderer? Was he also a victim? Or both? Should I have to bear the burden of the sins of my father?

Nadue, a teacher on the island of Sabu: 'It turns out that I am still someone, that there are still people who want to listen to this bitter history, who believe in me.' She never imagined that her suffering on a small island in the remote southern islands of Indonesia was also that of thousands, even hundreds of thousands, of others. As a young teacher, Nadue wanted to serve her nation and was the only female who could teach algebra and English on the whole of the island of Sabu at that time. She joined the Indonesian women's movement, Gerwani, and her husband, who was also a teacher, joined the Communist Party because he thought it cared for the interests of the people. Nadue was arrested when she was heavily pregnant. It was also said she carried a bomb in her trousers, even though she never wore trousers. She was permitted to give birth at home, but immediately afterwards was taken back into prison. There she heard that her husband had been murdered. A soldier roughly cut her hair off short. 'Even today, a woman with short hair is often called Gerwani.' After her imprisonment, Nadue eked out a life as a farmer. She was no longer permitted to teach – even though she had contributed so much to the nation. And hundreds of schoolchildren on the island of Sabu missed out on the opportunity to study with her.

Rukiah, a young activist yearning for equality: There is a memory that haunts Rukiah, a Gerwani official from Makassar, from the time when she was finally captured with her baby in East Java. She saw a woman prisoner being tortured, stripped to the waist. The woman's small child was tied to her legs and crying because it could not reach its mother's breast. Without giving it much thought, Rukiah approached a friendly female prison guard and offered her small daughter to her for adoption. She had to surrender her child so her daughter could get a better life. Fifteen years later, Rukiah looked for her daughter, going from house to house until she found her. This is love that was not severed when struck by the wave of history.

And there are so many more stories: *Lambatu* from Bau-bau, Sulawesi, opened a school in his neighbourhood, but was later arrested and tortured. He spent time in a cell measuring 3 x 3 metres that held 22 other prisoners, witnessed 15 people die in prison, and experienced forced labour. Others who experienced forced labour were *Asman* and *Rahim* in Central Sulawesi, and *Wardik* in North Sumatra, who all did heavy work with little to eat, and were basically slaves for development projects. On the island of Buru, the prisoners also had to work just to stay alive, including *Permadi*, a famous artist who had represented Indonesia overseas. Then there are the women who held ideals of improving the lot of their gender; *Lestari* in East Java and *Ibu Tachrin* on the run, were arrested and sidelined. *Luh Sutari* from

Bali was said to be a Gerwani member because her family were members of the Communist Party and killed. *Sutarni*, also on the run in Jakarta, had to raise her children and was then imprisoned and forced to give her children to various relatives. *Ketut*, a young artist in Bali, was arrested, released, then arrested again, and wrestled to get his life back on the rails. *Niko* in Kupang still starts when he hears the rumble of trucks, recalling the trucks that took away people who never returned.

These fifteen stories are just a fraction of the hundreds or thousands of stories still unrecorded. We are racing against time because the number of living witnesses is decreasing. These testimonies depict holocaust-like situations: slaughter; concentration camps; giving numbers to replace identities; prisoners organising their own food, health and arts; families torn apart; female prisoners having their hair cut short. This is our very own Indonesian holocaust. Probably we need to find the right name to describe what happened. Perhaps these stories will be the key to the liberation we yearn for.

Telling stories: breaking the silence, opposing indifference

These stories from living witnesses are our bridge. They allow us to look back, to take stock of the wrongs and tyranny of the past, and step towards the future to arrange a better life. It is time for us to reject silence, to demand the truth, and to change the ways we learn and teach history. Elie Wiesel, holocaust survivor, writer and Nobel Peace Prize winner, said:

> The opposite of love is not hate, it's indifference. The opposite of art is not ugliness, it's indifference. The opposite of faith is not heresy, it's indifference. And the opposite of life is not death, it's indifference.

The dream of those etching stories in this book is to oppose indifference. We hope that readers are moved and spurred to give support to the voices of truth. No longer just taking a peek.

Galuh Wandita

Human rights worker and expert on transitional justice

Jakarta, 11 August 2011

Editor's comments

This book, originally published in Indonesian in 2010, titled *Memecah Pembisuan: Tuturan penyintas tragedi '65–'66*, is the product of collaboration between the interviewees, interviewers, writers, illustrators, commentators, writer of the foreword, those who inspired us, those who initiated the project, and the funders.

Together, we felt the need to publish this book so as to erode Indonesia's mono-faced history which represents the interests only of those in power. We want to build a history that represents diversity and includes the experiences of those actors categorised as 'the defeated'. In the particular case of the humanitarian tragedy or 1965–1966 in Indonesia, the New Order (namely the military and Golkar) succeeded, through various formal and informal media, in indoctrinating people with history that was full of lies, discriminative and fictive; a history that the government has, to this day, still never clarified.

'The defeated' are now termed the survivors, namely those who managed to survive oppression and succeeded in their fight to restore themselves, even though their civil rights have still not been fully restored. The project began with the interviewees telling their experiences to the interviewers, who made transcripts of the recorded interviews. Some of the interviewers then wrote narratives based on the transcript. Others handed the transcript to the Lembaga Kreatifitas Kemanusiaan (LKK, Institute for Human Creativity) to be written up by others. LKK then invited a few writers – mainly young people with some writing experience – to write narratives based on the transcripts. The end product is 15 narratives from source interviewees in Medan, Palu, Kendari, Yogjakarta, Jakarta, Bali, Kupang and the island of Sabu.

In the editing process, I made very few changes, especially as far as writing style is concerned, so that the different approaches in the book would be maintained. There were many considerations we had to take into account in writing up all the data clearly, because even today the survivors still experience discrimination. But the narratives in this book are entirely based on the life experiences of the resource interviewees. Our hope is that their voices will help push the government and all parties involved to become wiser, more humane and fair in treating the survivors as fellow human beings.

The Lembaga Kreatifitas Kemanusiaan (LKK) would like to express its gratitude to the Tifa Foundation and the International Center for Transitional Justice (ICTJ) who entrusted us with coordinating this program. LKK also wishes to thank Bung Budi Setiyono from *Historia*, Sri Lestari Wahyuningroem and Dody Yuniar from ICTJ for running the writing workshop for young writers, which was the start of the program. Thank you too to Galuh Wandita, Director of Asia Justice and Rights (AJAR) – an NGO promoting accountability and human rights in the Asia region – who agreed to write the foreword; Samuel Gultom from TIFA, and other colleagues. LKK also wishes to express its deep respect and gratitude to the interviewees, some of whom preferred not to have their real names cited, also to the interviewers and to the writers: Akhmad Zakky, Alice, Amangku Bumi, Anandito Reza B., Dorkas Nyake Wiwi, Fati Soewandi, Nancy, Ilham Dayawan, Ika Mustika, Mery Kolimon, Paoina Ngefak-Bara Pa, Puti Yassmina, Rini Prastnawati, Roro Sawita, and Tachrin Ny. Thank you to the illustrators, Salim M, Adrianus Gumelar and Kuncoro A.Broto, and JAKER which helped with the printing of the original Indonesian book. LKK also expresses its gratitude for the support of the Goethe Institute in Jakarta.

There still remain many people living in towns and outlying regions all over Indonesia prepared to talk about their experiences, whom we have not been able to include in this book. This is why similar projects of documentation and writing up the life stories in the popular media are still very much needed. We hope that LKK does not rest on its laurels, but continues its work and to inspire others.

I would like to express my gratitude to the Herb Feith Foundation and editors of the Translating Accounts of the 1965–66 Mass Violence in Indonesia Series, Dr Jemma Purdey and Dr Kate McGregor, for their willingness to publish *Memecah Pembisuan* in English language translation. I hope that this book will supplement existing documentation about the humanitarian tragedy of 1965–66.

With deep respect,

Putu Oka Sukanta

Editor and coordinator

poskanta@indosat.net.id

Glossary

3 Bersama (or Tiga Sama)	Bekerja bersama, makan bersama, tidur bersama; '3 togethers', work together, eat together and sleep together; a Communist Party slogan for working at the grassroots (see turba)
3 M	a Communist Party slogan: Merangkul (Embrace), Membatasi (Limit) and Menggunakan (Utilise)
AD	Angkatan Darat (Army)
Agresu	Aliansi Gerakan Reformasi Sumatera Utara (Alliance of the North Sumatran Reformation Movement)
Aspri	Assisten Presiden (Assistants to the President)
ASRI	Akademi Seni Rupa Indonesia (Indonesian Academy of Visual Art)
Babinsa	Bintara Pembina Desa (police or army neighbourhood watch)
BAKOKSI	Badan Kontak/ Koordinasi Organisasi Kethoprak Seluruh Indonesia – (All Indonesia Ketoprak Organisation)
BAP	Berkas Acara Pemeriksaan (interrogation report or dossier)
BAPRERU	Badan Pelaksana *Resettlement* dan Rehabilitasi Buru (Body for the Administration of Buru Resettlement and Rehabilitation)
Babinsa	bintara pembina desa (Non-Commissioned Officer for village control)
Berdikari	Berdiri di Atas Kaki Sendiri (Stand on one's own two feet)
BKTN	Bank Koperasi Tani dan Nelayan (Cooperative Bank for Farmers and Fishermen)

BMB	(Bagaimana Masyarakat Berkembang). How Society Develops (a course in Marxist ideology)
BPUP	Badan Pelaksana Urusan Pangan (Administrative Body for Food Affairs)
Brigmob	Brigade Mobile (police mobile brigade)
BTI	Barisan Tani Indonesia (Indonesian Peasants Front)
Bulog	Badan Urusan Logistik (Body for Logistic Matters)
Bung	term used for 'Brother', especially for the President, Sukarno (Bung Karno)
Bupati	head of regency or district (kabupaten)
Buterpra	now known as KORAMIL, komando rayon Militer (Military district command)
Camat	head of kecamatan, subdistrict
CGMI	Consentrasi Gerakan Mahasiswa Indonesia (Indonesian Student Movement Concentration)
CHTH	Cung Hua Tjung Hwee
CPM	Corps Polisi Militer (Military Police Corps)
FPN	Front Pemuda Nasional (National Youth Front)
Gerag	Gerakan Reformasi Agraria (Movement for agrarian reform)
Gerwani	Gerakan Wanita Indonesia (Indonesian Women's Movement)
Gerwis	Gerakan Wanita Sedar (Movement of Alert Women)
GMIT	Gereja Masehi Injil di Timor (The Evangelical Christian Church in Timor)
GESURI	Genta Suara Republik (The Pealing Bell of the Indonesian Revolution)
GMNI	Gerakan Mahasiswa Nasional Indonesia (Indonesian National Students Movement)

GSNI	Gerakan Siswa Nasional Indonesia (Indonesian National High School Students Movement)
G30S	Gerakan 30 September (Thirtieth of September Movement)
HMI	Himpunan Mahasiswa Islam (Association of Moslem University Students)
HSI	Himpunan Sarjana Indonesia (Association of Indonesian Graduates)
Ibu	polite term used to address women. Literally 'mother', but also meaning 'Mrs'
IKOHI	Ikatan Keluarga Orang Hilang Indonesia (Indonesian Association of Families of the Disappeared)
Inkopal	Induk Koperasi Angkatan Laut, (Master Navy Cooperative)
IPAS	Ikatan Pelajar Anak Seberang (League of high school students from over the water)
IPPI	Ikatan Pemuda dan Pelajar Indonesia (League of Indonesian Youth and High school Students)
Inrehab	instalasi rehabilitasi, 'rehabilitation post' (detention camp)
JAREK	Jalannya Revolusi Kebangsaan (the progress of the national revolution)
JPIT	Jaringan Perempan Indonesia Timur (Women's Network of East Indonesia)
Kabupaten	regency or district
KAMI	Kesatuan Aksi Mahasiswa Indonesia (Union of Indonesian Student Action)
Kampung	neighbourhood, either urban or semi-rural
Kamsing	Kamp Pengasingan (Camp of Exile)
KAPPI	Kesatuan Aksi Pemuda Pelajar Indonesia (Indonesian Youth and High school Student Action Union)

KASI	Kepala Seksi Satu, Kepala Inteligen (Head of Intelligence)
Kecamatan	sub-district (below kabupaten)
KGP	Kursus Guru Partai ([Communist] Party Teacher Training Courses)
KKGSP	Kursus Kilat Guru Sekolah Partai (short course for teachers in [Communist] party schools)
KODAM	Komando Daerah Militer (Regional Military Command)
Kodim	Komando Distrik Militer (Military District Command)
Komdak	Komando Daerah Kepolisian (Regional Police Headquarters)
Komnas HAM	Komite Nasional Hak Asasi Manusia (National Commission on Human Rights)
Komnas Perempuan	Komite Nasional Perempuan (National Commission on Women)
Komsek	Komando Sektor Kepolisian (District Police Command)
KontraS	Komisi untuk Orang hilang dan Korban Tindak Kekerasan (The Commission for the Disappeared and Victims of Violence)
KOPKAMTIB	Komando Operasi Pemulihan Keamanan dan Ketertiban (Command for the Restoration of Security and Public Order)
KORAMIL	Komando Rayon Militer (Military District Command at the kecamatan level)
KOREM	Komando Resort Militer (Military Area Command, i.e. the army command between the Kodam and the Kodim)

Lekra	Lembaga Kebudayaan Rakyat (The Institute of People's Culture)
Letda	Letnan dua (Second Lieutenant)
Letkol	Letnan Kolonel (Lieutenant Colonel)
Lettu	Letnan Satu (First Lieutenant)
LKN	Lembaga Kebudayaan Nasional (Institute of National Culture)
Lurah	head of village (below kecamatan level)
Malari	Malapetaka Limabelas Januari (15th of January [1974] disaster')
MDH	Materialisme, Dialektika, Historis (Marxist theory of dialectical and historical materialism)
MPP	Mantri Pamong Praja (Civil Service Police at Kecamatan level)
Non Vak Sentral	(Teachers Union not affiliated to any political party)
NU	Nahdlatul Ulama (Revival of Islamic Scholars)
OSIS	Organisasi Siswa Intra Sekolah (Inter High School Organisation)
Pancasila	Five guiding principles of Indonesian Republic
P4	Pedoman Penghayatan Pengamalan Pancasila, (Guidelines for Understanding and Implementing Pancasila)
PANGKOPKA-MTIB	Panglima Komando Pemulihan Keamanan dan Ketertiban (Commander for the Restoration of Security and Order Operations)
PBH	Pemberantasan Buta Huruf (Banish Illiteracy program)
Pelda	pembantu lieutenant kedua (deputy second lieutenant)
Peltu	pembantu lieutenant satu (deputy first lieutenant)

PKI	Partai Komunis Indonesia (Indonesian Communist Party)
PNI	Partai Nasional Indonesia (Indonesia National Party)
PNS	Pegawan Negeri Sipil (Civil Servant)
POMAD PARA	Polisi Militer Anggota Angkatan Darat
PP SGA	Persatuan Pelajar SGA (SGA high school students' union)
PR	Pemuda Rakyat (People's Youth)
PSI	Partai Sosialis Indonesia (Indonesia Socialist Party)
PSII	Partai Sarekat Islam Indonesia (Indonesian Islamic Union Party)
PUSPOM ABRI	Pusat Polisi Militer, Angkatan Bersenjata Republik Indonesia (Centre of Military Police, Indonesian Armed Forces)
PUTERPRA	(now KORAMIL)
RK	Rukun Kampung (neighbourhood level unit)
RPKAD	Resimen Para-Komando Angkatan Darat (Army Para Command Regiment)
RRI	Radio Republik Indonesia (Indonesian national radio)
RT	Rukun Tetangga (sub-kampung/neighbourhood level unit)
Sarbuksi	Serikat Buruh Kehutanan Seluruh Indonesia (The All Indonesia Union of Plantation Workers)
SBKA	Serikat Buruh Kereta Api (Railway Workers Union)
SGA	Sekolah Guru Atas (senior high school for teacher training)
SKBD/BL	Surat Keterangan Bersih Diri dan Bersih Lingkungan: (certification that oneself and one's family was 'clean' of involvement with the 30th September Movement)

SOBSI	Serikat Organisasi Buruh Seluruh Indonesia (All-Indonesia Trade Union Federation)
SP	Sekolah Partai (Party School)
SPBU	Satuan Pengisian Bahan bajar Umum, (petrol station)
SPDP	Sekolah Partai Daerah Besar (Party School at Provincial level)
SR	sekolah rakyat (primary school)
STM	Sekolah Teknik Menengah (junior technical high school)
TAVIP	Tahun Vivere Pericoloso (The year of living dangerously [1964])
Tefaat	Tempat Pemanfaatan (location utilisation, euphemism for political prisoners' camp)
Teperda (also Tiperda)	tim pemeriksa daerah (local interrogation team)
Tonwal	peleton pengawal (platoon guard)
TPU	Tempat Penahanan Umum (general detention centre)
Turba	turun ke bawah (a slogan of the Communist Party and Lekra), 'go below', work at the grassroots level
URECA	Universitas Republika
UUBH	Undang-undang Bagi Hasil (Laws for Produce Distribution)
UUPA	Undang-undang Pokok Agraria (Agrarian reform laws)

Chapter 1

Asman Yodjodolo

Never-ending struggle

A person of dignity is someone emulated for their attitudes and their deeds, not someone smothered with esteem and praise for their sweet talk. Asman Yodjodolo has upheld this belief throughout his fight for liberation of his fundamental rights, as a person and as a citizen, from narrow-minded culture, politics and power. And this is what he has continued to fight for in his days living with the stigma of being an 'ex political prisoner'.

> I was born to a normal kind of family, there was nothing unusual about us, you know, we were just like most *kampung* (neighbourhood) families. When I went to primary school which was called SR (peoples' school, *sekolah rakyat*) back then, I went to live with my grandmother in Tawaeli, Central Sulawesi. My parents stayed on in Tomoe, because it turned out that my grandmother was unusual, she loved me more than my mother did. So that was my life, with a grandmother loving me more than my mother, and I went to school here in Tawaeli.

In 1957, Asman finished primary school. He worked hard so he could further his schooling. He went to the junior high school (SMP) at Donggala and graduated in 1960. Still not wanting to end his education, he went on to the senior high school for training teachers (Sekolah Guru Atas, SGA) and graduated in 1964. He was then qualified to teach in junior high school.

Asman was a high-achieving student. He considered poverty as no reason to be lazy, let alone to squander opportunities. Nonetheless, like many other youth, Asman liked to fool around. The difference with him, though, was that when he played up, he stood out compared to his friends. 'At school, I was one of the naughty ones, stubborn, and opposing the teachers', Asman explained.

> Punishment at school back then was much worse than today. For instance, I got punished for making a noise when the school next door

was in session. The headmaster told me to go outside and hammer a plank of hardwood. I was not allowed to stop for the entire lesson time. Back then, headmasters did not have classes of their own to teach, they only did relief teaching. So he kept checking to make sure I did not stop. After a while, I threw the hammer up on the roof. And sure enough, out he came, '*who* threw that ...? It turned out he had been watching through a hole in the wall. When I threw the hammer away again, out he came, very angry. I was called into the office. He went to hit me with his bag, but because I ducked, the bag hit a pole and the strap broke. He got even madder. But something positive came out of all that, because from that point on I was branded as extremely naughty, so I was even more singled out. Before that, I always sat at the back of the class, but now I had to sit in the front. No one wanted to sit in the front, probably because they were afraid of being near the teacher. So it was a punishment, but it was a good one, because I was then able to focus on learning, whereas before when I was at the back I would just annoy my friends. I was also one of the high achievers at school. But if the teacher said something I did not agree with, I would speak up.

No rest

Higher education has never been easy, and this was particularly the case back then. Even though Indonesia was independent, there was still political wrangling going on in the elite halls of power. At the same time, the standard of life of the people was far from being equally distributed. The young Asman experienced this. Asman's school was high in the hills, far from his house. He boarded together with six girls and five other boys, which meant he faced constant difficulties. However, this did not make him give up. Rather, he strengthened his resolve to be determined and never give up. He had to become his own leader and determine his own future.

While he was at senior high school, Asman worked at odd jobs. He was living with five other boys and six girls at the house of Aunty Ratu who they called Pue Ratu. Early in the morning they would all be awoken to do their chores. The girls had to make cakes and the boys had to look for firewood. Asman and Sukiman, who were younger than the other boys, were given the job of selling cakes.

Asman and Sukiman had to sell the cakes before they went to school. All the cakes would be put on a big tray. There would be pancakes, Ambon sticky rice-flour cakes, palm sugar biscuits and all kinds of other things. Asman and Sukiman would divide up the route to sell the cakes. 'I used to go towards Jembatan Merah (Red Bridge) and Sukiman towards Jembatan Guntur (Thunder Bridge), lugging this stuff all the way …' Asman said, recalling the hard times in his youth.

Because they had to sell all the cakes before they went to school, they were often late. And so, yet again, he was branded as a naughty kid. 'Once I arrived late, and I was sitting right in the front row, near the window. The window did not have any bars, just shutters that were open. So I jumped in from the side, right on top of my desk.'

'What on earth do you think you are doing, coming in through the window', the teacher asked, angrily.

'The door was locked, but the window was open. So I came in through the window', I replied.

Even though he was branded as a troublemaker, Asman never considered this to be something that would prevent him achieving his ideals. Quite the opposite, he was even more determined to be the best. He wanted people to see him in an unbiased way, not forever looking at his 'bad behaviour' or his rebelliousness, but also to note his actions and achievements. And this came about. Even though Asman was always acting up with the other five members of his gang and being reprimanded by the headmaster, he was the one chosen to be the head of the Union of SGA students (PP SGA, Persatuan Pelajar SGA).

When he was chosen as head of PPSGA, Asman was just starting his second year of senior high school. The PPSGA, like the Inter High School Organisation (Organisasi Siswa Intra Sekolah, OSIS), was responsible for facilities at the school like musical instruments, library books and all school equipment, from desks and cupboards to chairs. Apart from that, and more important, Asman was responsible for the running of all school activities, like inter-school competitions, celebration of national days and even Saturday athletics. On Saturdays, there were no classes. The whole day was spent with arts activities and other relaxed activities like baking cakes, or making corn porridge or green bean porridge to eat together. The girls did the cooking while the boys made crafts and other things. 'The role of the PP was really important, and the teachers did not interfere', Asman pointed out.

Recalling his senior high school days, Asman now feels extremely grateful to the teacher who first punished him. Only later did he realise that the headmaster at SGA had chosen him as head of PPSGA so that he would stop misbehaving, because he would be watched and would become an example to other students. So he thinks that the headmaster and other teachers wanted him to stop his troublemaking. But at the same time, being chosen as head of PPSGA gave Asman a strong foundation for his leadership in times ahead.

No going back

To become a leader is to become someone who has to know their goal, walk towards that goal, and bring it about. This is why only a handful of people are able to assume the authority of leadership. However, leadership is not only about becoming the ruler of a country or being in high levels of power. To be a leader of oneself is no easy task. This is what Asman found. As head of the PPSGA, Asman always demonstrated ideals of leadership in front of his colleagues and teachers. He maintained high levels of discipline in everything he did. Even though there were times when many did not agree with Asman's assertiveness, in the end he could often prove that his 'irritating way' was how a leader should act and maintain his idealism.

Once, something happened. When exams were over, the third year students planned to go on an excursion to Tanung Karang using funds from the Students' Union. When Asman checked with the treasurer, it turned out that the sports teacher, Pak Mudoko, had taken the funds. The next day, with the permission of the headmaster, Asman called Pak Mudoko. He asked for an explanation about the missing funds, because they had been used without notification and without prior agreement, and this was against the rules. When Pak Mudoko was asked to repay the funds, he explained that he could not do so because his salary was only just enough to support his family. In the end, the issue was settled amicably with Pak Mudoko apologising. From then on, Asman was known as someone who was extremely strict on discipline, so his colleagues were in awe of him and the teachers paid him more attention.

Throughout the time of his leadership, Asman truly made the PPSGA productive as a place for creativity and expression, to raise the potential of his colleagues. He asked the students to come after school, every afternoon at four.

> Every afternoon after school I ordered friends to come from four o'clock onwards. There was music, singing, and drama practice, watering the flowers and digging, and they all came, because they also got pressure from home. So you could call our school a model school, because the school yard was good, we had a school garden, a library, and complete

> arts equipment. I took this opportunity, seeing as my idealism was so strong, to make an organisation called IPAS (Ikatan Pelajar Anak Seberang, League of students from over the water).

Asman formed IPAS at a time when his leadership momentum was at its peak. The membership of the league was made up of students who came from 'across the water' in Donggala. Their first agenda was to go on an excursion to Tompe, Asman's home kampung, by motor boat. It turned out that more than one hundred people registered to come, from all over. Asman had not anticipated the students' enthusiasm.

Asman was meticulous in the way he organised this first excursion. He brought along three drama scripts for them to perform, which he had written himself, and also a girl school band. 'I didn't have any idea about music, but I asked someone talented to train them', Asman explained. There was a junior high school teacher who came along from Tambu, from a different school. Once they got to Tompe, the group led by Asman met the district head, the head of police, and the local military head. Then they borrowed the primary school building at Tanjung Padang to perform their drama.

Crowds came to watch. For three nights in a row, the Tanjung Pandang school was completely full, and the tickets were sold out. Not only that, excursion activities got livelier still with competitions like badminton, soccer, volley-ball and table tennis. During the stay at Tompe, the group Asman had brought over not only had fun, they also showed the local people local art forms so that the coming generation and the people of Tompe and its environs would not neglect their cultural heritage.

Asman's leadership skills were truly proven during this excursion. He was the main person responsible for the group and everything went smoothly. He managed to fund the excursion from the ticket sales and also from the sales of flower garlands the girls made, which were put around people's necks in return for a donation. When the motor boat to take them back did not arrive on time, Asman used the time to write yet another drama for them to perform, so that at least the ticket proceeds could cover the cost of their extra stay. He would never give up when confronted with any situation. And it was not just himself he was thinking about. There were many people depending on him and he could not let them down.

Service to the motherland

The Tompe excursion unified the people and school students through the arts. This was the very first time that the *momonte* dance was performed.

Asman studied the dance himself with Hasan Baswan. Back then, the dance was not like it is now, danced only by girls. At that time, boys danced it too. The *momonte* dance made SGA school stand out as innovative and always seeking new developments, compared to other local schools like SMEA, SMI and SGB.

'I had a girlfriend at the time … so I taught her the momonte dance, and then she taught others', Asman said cheerfully. He also recalled that he actually had two girlfriends then, and they both trained other dancers. From then on, the money earned from dancing was put towards the cost of fixing run-down schools, or given to some local officials. So, even though he was known for being firm, Asman also had a soft side. The way he sees it, anything done without a clean heart will end up bad. This was the principle he applied as leader.

Under Asman's leadership, IPAS became the pillar of the school's progress. Asman went on to make the IPAS a co-operative, with himself as head. The first step was to draw up the by-laws and the budget. The co-operative turned out to be a great success. All the students' needs were met and costs were kept down, from writing materials to daily essentials. Asman was a proven hard worker. He performed all his duties with full responsibility. He did this because he did not want the students who would later continue what he had built on such strong foundations, to be unable to continue and develop it further. He wanted to give an example and to pass on to them something they could emulate. This is why he was so diligent about preparing everything well, before he himself would eventually step down and be replaced by new leadership.

However, before this came about, the SGA buildings caught fire, and the school had to move to Palu. Luckily, the co-op that Asman led managed to keep going because the goods sold at the co-op were stored at the shop and collected only when needed. 'It (the cooperative) was okay because the office was me; it went where I went. It was all in my head', Asman explained.

In Palu, Asman's organisational network extended further. He was approached by a board member of IPPI (Ikatan Pemuda Pelajar Indonesia, League of Indonesian Youth).

> I don't know why. Perhaps he had talked to someone outside. He came to school and introduced himself, saying he was a high school student from Menado. We talked at school for a long time. He told me that they wanted to make a branch of IPPI at Donggala. What was IPPI, I asked? He explained. But he wondered how to invite all the schools

> here, and who should be on the board when it was set up – these were the people who should be invited, and this is what should be in the invitation. I helped him make the invitation and I asked friends to help distribute them. So, a few days later there was an IPPI meeting at SGA. I asked the headmaster's permission for us to use the school for the meeting. We then chose the board; I was the chairman and Markus was the secretary.

Asman was very excited when describing his experience. The secretary, Markus, was a young man of mixed Indonesian-German blood who could touch-type.

'You see, when I form an organisation I work non-stop. I do not want anything to fail', said Asman. He began to draw up a work plan for the IPPI. The first program was introducing the IPPI to all schools. And, once again, it was Asman who was responsible for this as the speaker. 'Until I graduated, I always cared for students if I could, because students are the embryo of the nation. These days, they would say they carry the relay baton'. Very soon, IPPI was formed at every school he visited.

However, things did not go exactly according to his hopes. When forming the Donggala branch of IPPI, Asman faced problems with Kisman who planned to form a GSNI branch (a Gerakan Siswa Nasional Indonesia, Indonesian National High school Students Movement branch). This was the Student's movement under the umbrella of the Indonesia National Party (PNI), and Kisman was the local student head of PNI.

In 1964, IPPI had branches everywhere in Central Sulawesi except for Donggala, and at the IPPI conference held in Menado, Asman was chosen as the head of IPPI for Central Sulawesi. This was then ratified in Jakarta. Asman, along with Markus, Maspa, and around ten others from the Donggala regency, went to Jakarta for a conference in 1964. Something happened there that Asman would always remember. At the time, Asman's group was accommodated at the Secretariat office, whereas all the other invitees were put up at a hotel. Needless to say, Asman felt annoyed at this different treatment, especially because it was so noisy at the secretariat that it was impossible to rest. But he remained patient, until one night a dispute broke out between the groups from Toli-toli and Bolaan Mongondo about where the provincial capital should be. 'Ah, this was my chance to be an arbitrator', Asman recounted.

The students from Poso thought that Poso should be the provincial capital, arguing for Poso's long history in Indonesia's struggle for independence.

But the argument put forth by Asman's group who supported Palu as the provincial capital was that the existing relationship of Sulawesi provinces to the national level was geographically determined. Furthermore, large ships could enter the Pantoloan harbour in Palu from the regional governments in both western and eastern Indonesia, and Poso was also accessible from Palu by land.

When he returned from his installation as the head of IPPI for Central Sulawesi, Asman immediately went to see the governor, Datuk Maso Basanankuning. He introduced himself in his new role. Apart from the governor, there was the Youth Front (Front Pemuda) and the National Front (Front Nasional). 'And there was I, representing the Youth Front', Asman said, proudly.

Under Asman's leadership, IPPI's membership in Central Sulawesi rose to around 60,000. Other organisations found it difficult to expand, because IPPI continued to expand at the provincial, regency and national levels. Asman never tired of promoting his organisation.

Asman's ideals of developing education in his town once he graduated turned out to be not as easy to achieve as he had thought. It was impossible to ignore that his competence leading a few organisations and his proven success in promoting them made him sought after as a teacher at many schools. But what could he do? He was too busy with the organisations. This was where his dedication and loyalty lay. On top of this, he still had not found the right person to replace him and continue the organisations he led. This was despite the fact that all the official paperwork for his teaching position was complete, and he had even been asked directly by the head of the Directorate of Education.

Asman was well aware that he could not go on running this organisation forever. On the other hand, he also hoped that whoever replaced him would continue with fervour what he had built. He saw that organisations were also a medium where he could realise his nationalistic concerns, for the country and nation he loved. Therefore, he had to be extremely careful about choosing people whose capability could be relied upon. He preferred to select people directly rather than run conferences. 'Conferences don't necessarily produce anything worthwhile, because there is always jockeying for positions going on, and not a healthy process of selection, so they can end up making bad decisions', Asman argued.

And, sure enough, the people Asman selected did carry out their mandate, just as he had hoped. For example, when one of the treasurers at IPPI contacted Asman to ask about the allocation of IPAS funds collected after

Asman had graduated from school, Asman replied, 'If you agree, I suggest you give the money to those who need it, to an orphanage or an old people's home in Palu.' One month later, the treasurer sent a letter saying that the funds had been distributed as he had suggested. So even when Asman was no longer holding that position of leadership, the people were still loyal to him.

When he finished school, Asman began teaching. As a teacher, he wanted to develop education in Tompe, his birthplace. This meant he had to lead the IPPI long-distance. Even so, the wings of his leadership spread further. Officials in Tompe asked him to form an arts organisation charged with researching Kaili arts and culture.

> The person who asked me to do this was Pak Sompa Yusuf, the deputy *camat* (sub-regent). He later moved to the office of the *bupati* (regent), went back to study, and ended up as head of Bapeda (regional development office) and then to Communications. After he asked me to take charge of developing Kaili culture, we sent out invitations to all teachers, local figureheads, prominent women, youth and traditional leaders. We discussed the aims of the organisation, namely to research Kaili customs. For instance, at that time the Raego dance from Poso was often performed. It resembled the *Dero* dance for harvest celebrations. Then there was *dadendate* and many others still to be researched. In the research program for Kaili culture, we held many discussions with the elders, and would then write up the notes, for instance what the *moraego* meant, the shape of the dance, whether it was dance or song and what its message was.

In this new organisation, named Andolia, Asman concentrated on instilling the principle of working with enthusiasm. He did not want any organisation he led, and which had noble aims for the nation, to be misused for unilateral interests. 'I told them, we must never be ashamed of our organisation, because we are all public figures and teachers', Asman said, recalling his words of advice. He scheduled visits by heads of schools to different villages to promote Kaili culture in all levels of society. After their visits, they would write a report.

Everything went according to plan, until the 1965 incident. Before this, Asman had warned members about the possibility of the Andolia organisation being linked to the political organisations, which that year, were in a frenzy of conflict. But Asman and his colleagues did not hesitate, because from the very beginning when Andolia was formed, they had all agreed on a single purpose, namely to research Kaili culture, and there was no link to any political organisation whatsoever. It was active solely in the arts, and had no leanings at all other than being motivated by the desire to enrich the young generation of the nation with the wealth of the arts and culture of their homeland.

One year later, in 1966, Asman got a visit from Muhsen who brought with him a squad of KAPPI (Kesatuan Aksi Pemuda Pelajar Indonesia, Indonesian Youth and High school Student Action Union) and KAMI (Kesatuan Aksi Mahasiswa Indonesia, Indonesian Student Action Union) members and police, to arrest him.

Shortly after the police took him to Donggala, he was forced to sign a 'confession' that stated he had received weapons for his own use when needed. If he refused to 'confess' he had to be prepared for torture sessions. Asman says that when he was arrested, he was head of IPPI and had no affiliation with in the Indonesian Communist Party (PKI). He knew the Communist Party well, because he was friends with Abdul Rahman Dg Maselo, the Communist Party Number One in Central Sulawesi. Apart from the fact that they came from the same kampung, Asman had family ties to him. Asman explained,

> So how could I not know Abdul Rahman, and how could I not know the Communist Party? The Communist Party was the one that was extremely progressive. Its leadership was impressive, multi-talented, skilled at the arts, Qu'ranic recitation, oration, volleyball, guitar-playing, singing, and they were good looking too.

His relationship with Abdul Rahman Dg Maselo became more intense through their meetings in the Front. Asman was in the Youth Front (Front Pemuda) and Abdul Rahman was the National Front (Front Nasional). However, their meetings were not for Party matters, so Asman was shocked when he was arrested and accused of being involved in an 'outlawed movement'.

From love on location to true love

Asman's days of detention were spent doing forced labour, moving from one place to the next. He and other political detainees were all put to work without pay. Because he was constantly being moved from one work site to another, Asman's family rarely visited him. So he often felt terribly alone. Even so, he regained his spirit to fight and survive when he was together with other detainees who shared the same fate. He seemed to regain his enthusiasm for life. The detainees used to encourage and support one another to keep going so that later they could prove they were not the dangerous enemy or the destroyers of the nation they loved.

On the other hand, as a man, Asman's loneliness often arose because he had no special person near who would give him love and attention. But even in times of loneliness, he did not seek out someone special, but rather gave out love to those who came to him. For he was well aware of the cycle of life he was going through. He was a prisoner, and more than that, a political prisoner, with absolutely no certainty about when he would be released. He would therefore be just a disappointment to anyone who took him on as husband for a shared planned future, and this would go against all the principles of leadership he had held thus far.

Asman told an interesting love story. 'Actually, when I was detained, many women were interested in me. I was surprised, ha ha …' He told of his love for a young Masaingi girl called Lina Momi, a story full of twists and turns. The story began with their decision to run away to Kalimantan together without any money, and went on to the difficulties of maintaining the relationship once Asman was in prison.

> I was not a criminal, I was a political prisoner. I did not know when I would be free, because there was no trial. I also could not forbid her from accepting another proposal, because that was her right.

One year later, his sweetheart Lina married a university lecturer.

No matter where Asman went to do forced labour, he always got involved in some 'love on location', as the young people call it today. For instance, when he was doing forced labour in Donggala at the housing complex for customs officials, he met a young woman of mixed Bugis-Kaili descent, the daughter of a neighbour who used to cook for the workers. Her name was Nur. And there was another woman of mixed Kaili-Bugis descent who was also interested in Asman. When he had to go back into prison, both these girls wanted to go with him. Asman prevented them, of course.

When Asman had to do forced labour at Soulowe, it was a different story again. He had a love affair with a woman called Rusia who, it turned out, was already engaged to an old wealthy widower with five children. This time, their love affair was risky, from secret meetings outside the prison through to being made to recompense the groom's wedding expenses because the girl decided to call off the wedding. Asman was sentenced by the local traditional head to pay damages of one cow, two sacks of rice and some hundreds of thousands of rupiah. The traditional court met three times, and in the end Asman was let off the fine as long as he married the girl. 'I promised the court that I would come back for her two months after I was released, at the very latest', Asman said.

However, as things turned out, Asman did not end up with Rusia. His family married him off to a woman who was connected to the family. Her name was Sena, and she became his life-long love.

Fighting for the spirit to live

In any journey, people will come across steep paths that they must cross to reach their goal. So too with the journey of life. There are many unforeseen circumstances that must be endured to reach the goal of life. They are there as a forge to make you stronger in the fight for a good outcome at every stage of life's journey. In Asman's life, he has had to go through many ups and downs. He has had to accept many life lessons, including when he had to undergo punishment without any due legal process because of the accusation that he was involved with the Communist Party.

'I explained to them. Over and over again when I was interrogated at Laksusda, Terperda and Sapujagad, I told them', Asman said, heatedly.

> I had told them that IPPI was not an organisation linked to any political party or branch or anything, nor did any of its activities give preference to any party. Its activities were aimed solely at high school students. So, if there was anything associated with IPPI, I was involved with it. And I certainly never told them when you are adult you should join the Communist Party. Never!

As leader, Asman's role was overall supervision. He was responsible for everything that emerged from his ideas for the organisation. He refused to become the type of leader who just sat back and enjoyed power but did not have the courage to stand on the front line when his organisation faced problems.

He accepted all torture and punishment with a generous heart. Deep in his heart he believed that through IPPI he was fighting for his ideals to produce students who were not only well educated, but also appreciated the arts and culture of their own country as an asset and force on an international scale. He never for one moment thought there would come a time when he would be turned into a sworn enemy of the nation he had defended and fought for all his life. Even so, he did not want to turn into a citizen who betrayed his commitment to love his country, body and soul.

And so he continued to fight for the truth he held so strongly. This included convincing his family that as an individual he had never been linked to the Communist Party, and, as leader, he testified that the IPPI he had led was solely a social organisation whose mission was to develop the potential of Indonesian youth. 'I did not budge, even when I was being examined by the special interrogators in the office of the Military Police (CPM). I did not budge when Captain Sarwan was yelling at me', Asman recalled, his eyes flaring.

After his arrest, Asman was processed at Donggala. His first interrogation at the hands of Muhsen drew blood. But Asman remained steadfast, and Muhsen couldn't do a thing. Things improved for Asman when the Commander, who had been listening from behind the wall of the interrogation room, came in and ordered Muhsen out. The Commander treated him well. The next day another interrogator from Toraja called Piter Lobo took his turn.

'Sir, if you want to interrogate me, interrogate me. If you want to beat me up, don't interrogate me. If you want interrogation, stop the beatings,' Asman said before the interrogation began.

Asman had to answer some formalities, sign an interrogation report called a BAP (Berkas Acara Pemeriksaan) and was then moved to police headquarters. On the way, Muhsen almost killed him, but once again Asman was lucky to escape.

At the police headquarters, Asman met Lieutenant Semen, head of intelligence (Kasi 1, Kepala Seksi Satu), who he knew well from his IPPI work, because Lt Semen was the person he always had to report to. So Asman's cell was furnished with a mat and pillows at Lt Semen's order. And he said, 'there's no need to lock this cell. I know this guy, he's not going to run away.' Asman was very surprised at this treatment, as most people were terrified to admit to any acquaintance with people said to be connected to the Communist Party, and he was extremely grateful for his kindness.

After a month at police headquarters, Asman was moved to Maesa prison. There it was just one torture session after another from the Eastern Indonesia 'Sapujagad' ('sweep the world') team under the command of Kris Montolalu, and Asman could do nothing about it. However, he was at least able to meet up with his friends. When they were together, for a moment at least, the spiritual and physical pain could be forgotten, through sharing stories of suffering, including their stories of forced labour.

When he was in prison, Asman always wanted to meet Abdul Rahman Dg Maselo, but his request was never granted. He really wanted to know how he was and where he ended up, because there were many wild stories going around about him. He had been renowned as 'lion of the podium'. Some said he had been murdered, some that he had been sent abroad and some that he was in hiding.

Asman and his friends never stayed within the prison for an entire year at a time, except at special times, for instance when there was the national election. Usually, they were in prison for one month, then for the next few months sent out to work without pay building roads, bridges, canals; and to various places, like the police headquarters offices, Manggala Sakti, the aula of the 711 Battalion, and also houses at the police housing complex.

Most of the prisoners' forced labour was for army projects. When they had to carry out government programs, the army had its own 'Construction Company' (Kompi Seni Bangunan) which was a kind of contractor, and it was the political prisoners like Asman and his friends who carried out the construction projects of both the military and the government. 'We were given just two meals a day – no breakfast', Asman said, with a sigh.

'We worked like animals, with no pay. If they said "plough", we ploughed', Asman said. He was disillusioned with a government that could not distinguish between right and wrong. But he never felt ashamed of his own fate. All he thought about was staying alive.

Doing forced labour did not make Asman give in. Together with some other detainees, he found other ways to make some money. For instance, when they were working in coffee plantations, they would go into the forest after a full day's work to find rattan they could use to make carpet beaters, or rope, or anything at all that could be sold. And when they were working in *kampung*s, they would earn a bit of money doing odd jobs like repairing tables, chairs, beds and so on.

Asman struggled not only with the forced labour. There were also the holiday times of Idul Fitri and Christmas. These were times when the prisoners should be together with their families, but they were all cooped up in prison. And in the camps, the prisoners were not even allowed to gather together freely, let alone celebrate their religious holidays.

All the political prisoners, whether members of the Communist Party or not, got the same punishment. This went from electric shocks, being whipped, through to being flogged to death. All were tortured without any process of proof according to the law.

Experiencing all this, Asman surrendered his fate to God, not because he gave up or was guilty of the accusations against him, but because he knew he had to survive in order to prove that all the accusations against him were untrue; that he was a citizen who loved his country and wanted to give it his best by participating in social organisations that developed the potential of youth as the next generation in Indonesia's unfolding history.

Never cease!

After his release in 1979, Asman's struggle did not cease, it became stronger. He felt he had to straighten out his own life and the history of the nation. He has managed to survive to the present just so he can set the record straight.

Obviously, after all the years of detention, Asman lost sources of livelihood that could support him after his release. Asman said with resignation,

> During detention, our strength was sucked dry, and now the only work available is heavy labour. But we are old now, and no longer strong. So all we can do is run little stalls selling things, like this one. Unless you have capital ...

Fortunately, his family always encouraged him to keep on going. After his release, his family never treated him any differently from the others. Moreover, his own children have been able to walk tall without being ashamed of being 'communist kids'.

This is all because both when Asman was free and when he was in detention, he always maintained good relations with people around him and used his leadership talents as much as he could. The reception he received after his release reinvigorated his enthusiasm for leadership and he returned to organisational activities. Asman was often invited as a prominent figure to discussions about social problems. Now no longer involved in prison affairs, he became involved with the management of the elderly in North Palu kecamatan (district), as secretary.

Asman is still a formidable figure. Not because of his former 'communist' affiliations or such, but because of his strictness and high standards of discipline. Even during his ten years in prison, he uncovered many cases of corruption of funds that were supposed to be directed to village development. Asman once questioned a mining project because of the bad effects for society. Representing the people of North Palu, Asman opened the meeting with the members of the regional parliament and the head of the Directorate of Mining. Clearly, the people greatly respected Asman's leadership skills, and there was no reference made to his past.

Asman has never regretted his life experience as a political detainee. To him, a leader has to learn from every tide in life and through this develop skills in strong leadership, which will eventually be of great use in guiding the next generation. The fight to regain self-respect requires firm resolve. Asman reflected,

> The infringement of human rights that was inflicted upon us is now common knowledge in the world. Why don't we take advantage of this? If we fail at first, we must try again. Because we ourselves want to get rid of that stigma that was hung around our necks for so long.

Whenever he recalls how he and other detainees managed to survive loneliness, sickness, disappointment and the crushing of their fundamental rights, Asman remembers how they would pass long nights after an exhausting day's work by telling stories about anything at all; about the families they had left behind, about how they could meet daily needs, and whether they would ever again live as they did before the 1965 incident. And at other times, when they were bored, Asman and the other prisoners would hold a story-telling competition. The one who told the best tale was given a prize by the other inmates. 'There was one person who was a fantastic storyteller, but he has died now. His name was Aminudin Lajamana' Asman reminisced.

They would make up stories about anything. It might be a story from the village, or something made up. The most important thing was that the story had to have an element of struggle in it, so the detainees would keep alive their spirit of struggle. And the story that won, and was the most impressive, was the story about the murrel fish and the rat.

> Once upon a time, in a big river, there was a block of wood that protruded into the river. In that block of wood was a rats nest, with a young female rat who was just coming of age. One day, a murrel fish was playing around in the river and his gaze was struck by this female rat perched on the block of wood. From then on, the murrel fish often went ashore to visit the rat.
>
> And the rat also regularly visited the fish in the water. One day, the rat told her parents that she wanted to marry the fish. Now of course this was impossible. But the rat would not budge, and almost died underwater. When she met the fish, she told him she would revive if

> he found her a chicken egg. The fish had to go on land to look for an egg. When he saw a man drawing water with a bamboo bucket, the fish jumped into it.
>
> Upon arriving at the man's house, the fish seized the moment when the water was being poured from the bucket into a tank, to jump down, take an egg, swallow it and jump back into the bamboo bucket. When the man went back to the river, the fish was reunited with the rat and gave his sweetheart the chicken egg.

On another day, the story had the situation reversed. The fish got extremely ill because he was almost eaten by the man when he went to get the chicken egg. The only thing that would save the fish was crocodile liver. So the rat had to go to the river mouth and climb a coconut tree. The rat gnawed the coconut until it fell into the river and into the crocodile's mouth. The fish was inside the coconut, and from there he was able to take the crocodile's liver and get out of the crocodile when it vomited up the coconut.

The struggle of the fish to save the rat, and the rat's suffering to heal the fish became symbols that nothing is impossible if we work hard to bring it about. With spirit-rousing stories like this, Asman and the other political prisoners found a sense of freedom even though they were confined in a big, damp, dirty shed. They tried hard, using every means they could, including entertaining themselves with storytelling, to relieve the things that gnawed away at their spirits: bitterness, exasperation, sickness and the cruelty they experienced as detainees of New Order politics.

Asman remembers something Gertrude Hartman said in the introduction to her book *Builders of the Old World* (1959), namely that spreading facts and ideas through books, magazines and newspapers is one of the strongest ways to learn the truth of what is going on in the world. We have to know the truth, and the truth will make us free.

Asman personally expresses the misery and incalculable suffering of his friends and all political prisoners; namely that they are free only in the sense of being released from prison yet actually, because of discriminative practices, real liberty and good fortune have never come their way.

From his youth through to his elderly years, Asman has never ceased his fight to realise the potential of the young generation.

> I am old now. It's enough. If there are young people around who don't know anything, well just send them over to me and I will teach them.

> Tawaeli here is one of the areas with the highest number of university graduates, but why aren't they used?

Asman has also spearheaded the supply of free medicines to the aged in North Palu, every Thursday. He concluded the story with his enduring sense of hope:

> It's enough for just my friends and I to feel what we feel. What I hope is that what we went through can motivate us and support us in the fight to reveal the past infringements of human rights.

Interviewer: Nurlaela AK Lamasitudju.
Writer: Fati Soewandi.

Chapter 2

Beny

The search for healing

The two years of bloodshed involving their father Beny, took place before his children were born. Even before Beny married Sara. And the history lessons the children got at school were totally silent about the dark side of this nation's history in which their father had been involved. The film *Pengkhianatan G30S/PKI* ('Treachery of the Communist Party 30th September Movement') which the government required to be shown every year on September 30th and which all primary school children had to watch, certainly did not tell the real facts.

Conversations about these events began only when Beny's oldest daughter asked her father to talk about this part of his life. Unlike her brothers and sisters, Maria had the opportunity to read some books that discussed the 1965 Tragedy from the perspective of the victims. In the beginning, she found it difficult to talk about these things with her father. She wondered whether he would want to talk, and if he did, whether she herself was ready to face his story and his role as a perpetrator.

But Maria grew to understand that it was only through confronting the wounds of the past that someone can be truly healed of their psychological scars. The healing of the nation has to start with the healing of families and society in small groups, which can widen over time. This is difficult to achieve, but if successful, it will contribute to the nation's healing from the wounds of its cruel past. Her father's history is part of the nation's history. And this same history shapes who he is today. Maria felt the need to make peace with this history, no matter how black it is. She was also aware that real peace comes only when the truth is revealed, no matter how bitter it is.

Beny tells his story

Maria made an appointment with her father. On a public holiday, she went to his house. He lived about 200 kilometres from the city of Kupang, the capital of the province of NTT (Nusa Tenggara Timur, Eastern Indonesia), where he lives and works. It took Maria about four hours to get there. She left early in the morning. When she arrived, it was nearly lunch time. Ravenous, she ate the food her father's step children had prepared. Maria's mother had died three years previously.

After lunch, Maria explained to her father why she wanted to talk to him. Initially, she thought that he would object to talking about his involvement as a perpetrator in the violent events of 1965–1966. But he did not refuse to speak about this sensitive issue.

When they started chatting, Beny seemed nervous. Maria was nervous too. They were sitting in the sitting room. To ease the situation, Maria began to ask questions about Beny's childhood. Soon Beny became more relaxed and began to chat casually about his childhood on the island of Alor. He also talked about his schooling before he entered the police force.

Beny was born around 1942 in the interior of Alor Island, Eastern Indonesia, the son of a village head. He himself is not sure that 1942 is the year of his birth.

> Back then, it was not common to write down the year of birth. But I was probably born earlier than this, because when the Japanese invaded Alor (1942) I was already aware of it. I was maybe around seven at the time. I can still remember running to hide because we were afraid of the Japanese planes.

But for some reason, on his birth certificate and official documents, the year is written as 1942.

The island of Alor is known as the 'kenari' (canaga) island, because it has so many kenari nut trees. The nuts are dried and eaten with pounded dried corn that is dry-roasted.

Beny remembers his childhood in the kampung there well. Their life was very simple. He spent his days playing with his siblings and cousins. They would make swings from vines that hung from the banyan trees. Sometimes they made a lot of noise and annoyed the neighbours. One day, the vine holding the swing broke while they were playing. Beny and his cousin Bastian fell. They sobbed loudly. 'It seems that one of my uncles was mad because we used to make a lot of noise near his house. So he deliberately sabotaged the vine so we would fall and stop playing here', Beny said.

Their kampung was up on a hill, about four kilometres from the coast. The entire kampung was enclosed with a cactus fence, to deter enemy attacks.

Before Beny was born there were many fights between tribal groups. This was why the elders planted the cactus fence.

Beny remembers how they used to go looking for *meting* shells on the beach at low tide. Usually they went with their mothers and other women. Work was determined according to gender and the women had to look for small items of food on the beach. Going to the beach was always fun. Beny could run around with his friends to his heart's content.

His father and the men farmed. They planted corn, sweet potatoes and yams. The basic foodstuff was corn. Even though Beny's kampung had rocky soil, there were some places where plants could grow well. Apart from farming, the men also liked to set traps called '*bubuh*' – baskets made of bamboo – at the beach, to trap fish. Many fish could be caught this way and brought home for family meals.

Apart from farming and fishing, the men also liked hunting with bows and arrows. The most common animals they hunted were deer and wild boar. When they went hunting, the men took along their pet dogs. They always divided what they caught on the hunt with everyone in the kampung. 'Whenever the men came back from hunting, it was like a party. Everyone was happy with the meat from the hunt.' The men would talk about their experience hunting. The women would chat away while cooking. The children would enjoy meat they roasted themselves, having rubbed it first with salt.

Apart from cooking and taking care of the home, the women also worked in the gardens, particularly at planting and weeding times for the corn, beans and peanuts. Apart from that, they also did weaving and wickerwork with lontar leaves. Their weaving and wickerwork was mainly for their own use, but they also sold it at the Sunday market, or exchanged it for other daily necessities with people from other kampung who they met at the market.

Back then, polygamy was common in Beny's kampung. His father, who was head of the kampung, had seven wives. Beny's mother had only one child, namely Beny. But from his step-mothers, Beny had many step-brothers and sisters, and in his family upbringing there was no distinction made between them. He considered all of his father's wives his mothers. But sometimes there was jealousy between his father's wives. Beny still remembers his own mother once left the house for months and went to her uncle's place because she felt her husband had unfairly treated her.

In 1947, Beny's mother died of stomach problems. She had difficulties with her digestion and bowel. Beny was about five years old then. He remembers his mother as slim, with clear skin and a mole near her nose. She didn't talk much, but she could certainly complain if something offended her. His mother's name was Makit, which in the local language means bitterness. When she converted to Christianity, her name was changed to Maria. Having two names, a local name and a Christian name, was normal back then. It was like having two identities at once: a cultural identity and a religious one.

Education and work

From the age of six, Beny attended the Sunday school which was run in their village. The children learnt Christian hymns and listened to Bible stories. They were also taught the alphabet. When he was seven, Beny started primary school at the next kampung, which was 12 kilometres away.

> At seven years old I started real school. It was a long way away from my kampung. So I had to board, the Dutch word for that was *internat*. I couldn't stand it. The teacher was nasty. If we were late coming back from our home kampung at the beginning of the week, we were beaten. After just six months boarding, I decided to quit school.

One of his older step-brothers, Christian, was already a teacher in the town of Kalabahi. So he came to pick up Beny and took him to live with him. Beny spent six months there, learning the Indonesian language. In 1950, when he was about eight, his brother took Beny with him when he moved to Kupang. He wanted to give up teaching. He had registered for the air force (AURI) and been accepted.

In Kupang, Beny went to primary school and on to junior high school, graduating in 1958. Then he went to senior high school there. But after only two years in senior high school, a job opportunity opened up in the provincial office of the Directorate of Social Work. Beny decided to stop school and work as a civil servant. After two years in the Kupang office, he was moved to Alor to work in the branch there.

After just one year working back in his birthplace, Beny heard an announcement that there were openings for applications to join the police force.

> I was excited about joining the police, because I really liked their uniform. And what's more, they got the uniform for free. As a civil servant, I had to buy my own uniform.

After taking some tests in Alor and passing, Beny returned to Kupang for six months' training to become a police officer. There were 240 people in the course. The policy was that only the top 100 in the course would be placed in Timor. The rest would get placements outside of Timor (like Alor, Sumba, Flores and so on). Beny passed as number 70, and so got a placement in Timor.

The murdered

When the topic of conversation between Maria and her father turned to the violence of 1965–1966, the mood started to change. There were long periods when Beny remained quiet. In the beginning, Beny remained convinced that the killings of 'members' of the Communist Party was something that had to be done, and was right. But then he grew unsure. Were the killings right?

He spoke as though the events had happened just yesterday. In 1965, he had been in the police force in the small town for only a year. The year before, in 1964, he finished his training at the State Police College (Sekolah Polisi Negara, SPN) in Kupang, and was placed in SoE, a small town 100 kilometres to the east of Kupang. He was still young at the time. Just 22 years old.

Beny was fortunate. His experience as a civil servant in the Directorate of Social Affairs led to him being selected to work as staff in the criminal investigation section. Here was someone who had never completed high school because he couldn't afford it, yet his superiors had entrusted him with this position. In those days, it was not as difficult as it is now to join the police force. You did not have to have finished high school, and you did not have to bribe your way in.

He felt smart in his uniform. Being a policeman was something to be proud of. But the mass murders of people accused of being members of the Communist Party which took place over two years (from January 1966 until the end of 1967) in which he was involved made him ask – are the police really the protectors of the people?

> I wanted to become a policeman first of all because of that smart uniform. But it wasn't just the uniform. The uniform allowed me to protect people who were weak and who stood up for what is right. But experiencing that two years of bloodshed, of people being killed without trial, made me ask – is it true that the police uphold what's right?

In the district (kabupaten) where Beny worked, he calculates that hundreds of people were murdered. He spoke about it hesitatingly.

> Over the whole kabupaten, there were around 700 people killed. During the first phase, when the order came from Jakarta, there were no interrogations at all. People who had been imprisoned for all kinds of reasons like theft, fighting and murder were all 'cleansed'. Anyone held in police jails was killed. And none of them had any connection whatsoever to the Communist Party. The army that had come in from Kupang gave the orders to kill all the prisoners in SoE prisons without exception. When their wives or families came to visit the next day, those people just weren't there anymore. We told them that their husbands had been moved to Sukabumi. When they heard this they passed out, because they knew their husbands had been killed.
>
> It was only in the second and third phases that there were interrogations to find out whether a person was really a member of the Communist Party or affiliated with it or not. Anyone listed as a member of the Indonesian Peasants Front (Barisan Tani Indonesia, BTI) or the Institute for People's Culture (Lembaga Kebudayaan Rakyat, Lekra) was arrested and killed. Most of the victims came from the towns of SoE and Bena in Amanuban Selatan.

Beny still remembers the sites of the executions: Cendana forest near the town of SoE; Nunumeu, which is now the general cemetery of the town; the Nonohonis River on the road leading to Kapan; Nasimetan forest near Oelbubuk; Kobe Haumeni near Niki-niki; and a place on the road leading to the village of Bele near Oinlasi. He also heard that victims who had been arrested and held in Kupang were executed near Camplong, a village around 40 kilometres to the east of Kupang. People still consider these places haunted to this day. Many people do not dare to plant things there. Sometimes people living nearby hear screams in the middle of the night in these places.

That period was utterly terrifying. Everyone was gripped with fear. The army went around fully armed. Army vehicles circled every corner of the town. Almost every night there were gunshots. The murder of seven generals at Lubang Buaya in Jakarta, which was blamed on the Communist Party, became the pretext to arrest anyone considered to be a member of the Communist Party or a member of one of the party's affiliated organisations, and to murder them.

List of aid recipients

One reason why people were attracted to the Communist Party and its umbrella organisations was because of the Party's concern for the people's suffering. At the time, the island of Timor was suffering a terrible drought. For two years there had been minimal rainfall. The farmers were experiencing not only a failed harvest, but a failed planting season as well.

> There was virtually no rain whatsoever. The price of rice and corn skyrocketed. Everywhere, people were hungry. At the time, it was the Communist Party and the Indonesian Peasant's Front (BTI) that were distributing corn, rice, sugar and clothing to the people. They also distributed farming tools like hoes and spades. The women were given thread to weave cloth. As they were hungry, the people gladly accepted this offer without knowing or caring about any party ideology.
>
> Actually the Communist Party was not the only one distributing aid at the time. The churches in Timor were also distributing food that had been donated by fellow churches abroad. The synod leaders of the GMIT (Gereja Masehi Injil Timor, The Evangelical Christian Church in Timor) for instance went around in a truck distributing rice to hungry members of their congregations.
>
> However, for the Communist Party, their officials drew up a list of all those who had received aid. Village officials had those lists too. When the Communist Party was being wiped out, those lists were used to arrest the people who had received aid. Even though not officially registered as Communist Party members, people who had received aid were now considered as being involved in the terrible deeds attributed to the Communist Party. Until today, this is why Timorese are traumatised about being members of cooperatives. That experience was a painful one indeed. Knowing nothing at all, people who had received aid were connected to the Communist Party and lost their lives for it.

The killings were at the order of Soeharto

Beny understood that the killings were at the order of Soeharto to wipe out the Communist Party. People had to be convinced that the Party was dangerous. The period just before the massacres was extremely tense. Communist Party figures had been instigating rebellion against the government and local aristocracy. They criticised the pattern of land ownership that benefitted the *pah tuaf* (Timorese for kampung owners, here meaning landlords) in society, and they campaigned for land reform. It was said that members of the Indonesian Peasants Front (BTI) were instigating rebellion. And the word was that they had already dug mass graves and planned to kill the police, the army, and the *bupati* (mayor).

Beny himself was unsure about the truth of these rumours: How could the Communist Party attack when they had absolutely no weapons? But he remained convinced that the communists were extremely dangerous. The proof was that they managed to murder seven generals in Jakarta.

> Soeharto ordered us to kill those communists. The local police chief passed that order on to us. At the time, no one dared question the truth of the story. Even to utter a word of comfort to the victims was to seen to be sympathising with the communists and you could be killed for it.

Maria and her father spoke for hours through into the night. Maria took her leave. The next day she had things to do. They agreed that Beny would continue with his story when he came to Kupang.

'I almost went crazy'

Their second conversation took place when Beny went to Kupang for a health check-up. Luckily, it was a holiday. Maria had arranged all her appointments to be shifted to other days. She wanted to concentrate on the next installment of her conversation with her father.

They sat in the small room for receiving guests in Maria's home. It was still very early. Rina, Maria's daughter, joined them during the conversation. Maria's husband was out of town on a work assignment. The city of Kupang, known for its heat, was cool that morning. Beny was wearing casual clothes, a sleeveless t-shirt and shorts. He could never stand the heat in Kupang. The small town where he lives now is cool, as it is in the interior of Timor. He prefers to live there. Beny was no longer nervous. But he did stop a few times when he was talking about his extremely intense experiences with violence and killing at that time.

Beny was one of a few executioners who did the shooting. Usually, people suspected of being members of the Communist Party were picked up from their houses and detained. Then the army decided when it was their turn to be killed. The army came from Kupang. Usually they came by truck. There would be about thirty of them, one platoon. They came from all over Indonesia, but the majority of them were Javanese.

The prisoners were ordered to dig their own graves during the day. The shooting usually took place at night. Before they were taken to the execution site, they were beaten black and blue, then their hands were bound and they were ordered onto a truck. When they got to the execution site, they were blindfolded and ordered to stand with their backs to the grave, facing the firing squad. Then they were shot. If some were still alive after being shot, they would be bayoneted. Then they were pushed into the hole. After that, the hole would be covered up and the firing squad would leave the site. The members of the firing squads were given quotas. There was one quota for army, and there was one for the police. 'We were not paid for this. They told us it was part of our duty defending the country.' Most of the people they shot they did not know personally. But Beny wrestled with his inner feelings.

> They told us these people did not know God because of their communist ideology. But the reality was not like this. Some of them were pious. Perhaps it was fear of death that made them pious. This can happen. But in the depths of my heart I knew that most of these people had done no wrong.

According to Beny's calculation, he himself killed 17 people. Just imagine – 17 lives. He tried to tell himself that he was only carrying out orders, but deep inside Beny felt accused. 'I did not feel safe. No matter what, I had killed people', Beny said, his voice cracking. His eyes welled up with tears.

His internal conflict between the requirement to carry out his duty and his doubt that these killings were right later caused Beny mental illness. Following the almost two-year-long series of killings in which he was involved, Beny suffered trauma. It made him 'hot headed'. He was easily angered. He was known among his friends as bad. He would easily flare up in anger and beat his friends black and blue. He was even involved in a shoot-out with one of his friends in the police hostel. But Beny was not the only one to suffer in this way. One of his friends, Bertasar from Flores, ended up with serious mental health problems and had to leave the police force.

Cooling rites

In 1968 Beny was moved to a town 20 kilometers east of SoE. There he worked on getting to know his fiancée, Sara. He had fallen in love with Sara, who was an orphan and, like him, a church activist. Beny was elected to the synod council. Sara was the Sunday school teacher. After a friendship of a few months, they decided to get engaged in 1969. Once they were married, Sara soon saw Beny's hot temper. Small things caused his anger to flare up. And it was not only Sara who was the target. People who went to the police station were also the butt of his anger.

On one occasion, Fia, Beny's sister-in-law, came to visit. She saw Beny hitting Sara. Fila told Sara:

> One of these days he will kill you, Sara, if his temper remains hot like this. Beny needs a cooling rite for his blood and temper which are hot because of the blood of those he has killed.

Fia had a relative in Kupang who was known as a person with 'special powers' and could perform this rite. So Beny agreed to it. Soon after, Beny and Sara went to Kupang.

> They took me to the Liliba River. They had bought a dog. The dog was slaughtered and they ordered me to drink a little of its blood. Then they made the sign of the cross with its blood on my forehead. The purpose was to cool down the hot blood in my body. The rest of the dog's blood was cast into the river. This was to cast off everything hot into the river current. After that, we took the dog meat home, it was cooked and we ate it together.

While they were carrying out this rite, Beny seemed to see the victims' faces. 'I remembered them. After all they were people, not animals. And we had killed them.'

Even though this rite had been performed, Sara was still worried. Beny was not as bad as he had been, but still he could sometimes get extremely angry and attack violently. So when they moved back to SoE in 1969, Sara asked a deacon who was also her friend, Yuli, to pray over Beny. Yuli said that Beny needed the blood of Jesus, not the blood of a dog. So Sara persuaded Beny to agree. Beny was told to sit, and Yuli put her hands holding the Bible on Beny's forehead while praying for him. After that, Beny was at peace with himself.

> After those prayers I felt safer. I offered my wickedness to Jesus. Before Him, I could not hide all the things I had done over those two bloody years. I also could not hide the fear in my heart. It was the forgiveness of Jesus that enabled me to make peace with myself.

'God shut my womb'

Three years after their marriage, Beny and Sara still had not been blessed with a child. Sara had been pregnant three times, but each pregnancy ended in miscarriage. They asked God why this was so. Some deacons, including Sara's friend Yuli, advised them to sincerely ask God's forgiveness for Beny's involvement in the murder of hundreds of people in Timor. 'God has closed your womb because of the killings your husband did', one of the deacons told Sara.

So Sara and Beny decided to ask for God's forgiveness and grace by praying in the church together every night at midnight. They told the pastor and watchman that they needed a key to the building. Late at night, husband and wife would kneel together at the foot of the pulpit and pray for hours asking God's forgiveness for the blood that had flowed at Beny's hands.

They also prayed for Sara's womb to be cooled to receive the life of God through His grace. They even promised God that, like Samuel's wife Hannah in the Bible (1 Samuel 1:9-11), if God blessed them with a child, the firstborn would be offered to serve God in the church as a pastor.

> In 1972, more than three years after our marriage, our first child, a daughter, was born. To me, her birth was the sign that God had forgiven me. She was the child vowed to God. We offered her to God, and I prayed that God would accept our offering. In 1997, when our eldest daughter was ordained as a minister, I knew God had accepted my offering.

Apart from their daughter who became a minister, Beny and Sara were blessed with six other children. All of them, except the youngest, are now working and have families of their own.

Threats from victims' families

In 1990, Beny retired from the police force. He had spent his entire time of service in Timor. So, with his wife and children, he decided to spend his retirement years in an area of Timor where he had spent most of his working life. Using their savings, Sara and Beny built a house for their retirement. A few years earlier, Sara explained, she had taken the initiative to open a small kiosk near their house 'to help out with the costs of educating the children'. At the kiosk they sold daily necessities. After he retired, Beny helped out there. Sara travelled back and forth to SoE and Kupang to buy stock. She even went to Java twice a year to buy things. So Beny took turns minding the kiosk together with their children.

On one occasion, two years after Beny's retirement, when he was in the kiosk with one of his sons, a middle-aged man arrived on horseback wielding a sword. After he got off his horse, he pointed at Beny, angry, and shouted: 'You were the one who killed my relatives.' Beny was scared. Luckily Beny's kiosk was close to the police station. He immediately reported this threat to the police on duty. But before the police got there, the man had gone.

The bloody events of more than 40 years ago traumatised Beny not only because of his inner guilt that he had murdered his fellow men. He was also the target of the anger of the victims' families. Who knows how long the history of this nation will continue to carry this enmity and revenge. The history of this violence has wounded not only individuals and families. The events also fractured social solidarity and cohesion.

Beny's children talk

After her talks with her father, Maria invited her brothers and sisters to discuss their reactions to the fact that their father had been involved in the mass killings on their island in the 1960s, as a perpetrator. She also asked them whether it was important to them to try to make peace with the children of the victims.

Her siblings' reactions were different. Her younger brother Semy answered vehemently.

> The way I see it, Dad did nothing wrong and doesn't feel guilty. He was only carrying out orders. Anyway, do the children of the victims actually feel it important to make peace?

When Maria explained that she had already had long talks with their father and that indeed he felt deep guilt, Semy refused to participate any more in the discussion. But Semy's question was an important one. How would the children of the victims react? Were they prepared to talk? Did they still feel the need for it?

Maria's younger sister Linda, who of all the children was closest to their father, thought much the same as Semy. Their father had indeed been involved, but he was only carrying out orders. 'Father did this not of his own initiative. He was doing what he was told. Back then, if you showed any mercy at all you could be accused of being a sympathiser and you would be killed yourself'. However, Linda did think that mutual forgiveness was important. 'We must forgive one another, just as our Father in Heaven forgives us', she said.

Sadly, Maria's younger brother Eman, a civil servant and graduate in English, refused to say anything at all. 'I have no comment', he said. Maria thought that maybe he needed time to digest the difficult questions she had posed. Or maybe he indeed did not want to talk at all. Maybe her brother represented most Indonesians who think that forgetting is the best way to solve problems

Nia, Maria's younger sister who graduated in law, used the analogy of a judge to explain her father's position.

> A judge who orders the demolition of a house on disputed land has to do that because of her duty. Perhaps deep in her heart she does not agree with it, but because of her role as judge she cannot avoid it. So it was with our father. He was only doing what was his duty at the time.

Even so, Nia added that she and her siblings needed to talk to their father.

> Probably Father still remembers who those victims were. I think he needs to talk face to face with their children. Talk from the heart. To explain what really happened at the time, and that he too was a victim of the situation. Probably their children want to know what happened to their fathers. We must acknowledge, of course, that their loss is not the same as the burden our father experienced. We, as our father's children, can also help to build friendly relations with the victims' families to create opportunities to talk about this nation's wound. I agree with you, Maria. We all need to be healed from this collective trauma of our nation.

After this conversation with her brothers and sisters, Maria was silent for a long time. Their reactions were the same as those of most people in Indonesia towards the human tragedy that involved them and their families as victims or perpetrators. Perhaps Nia, her younger sister, was right in saying that their father was also a victim of Soeharto's crimes.

But no matter how heavy the burden their father and their family bore, this was nowhere near as heavy as that of the victims' families. They had lost husbands, fathers and relatives. They had been banished from social life. Their children had been denounced and taunted. Many had been blocked from becoming civil servants.

Even at church they had been ostracised. Widows had to fight not only to bring up their children to get decent lives, but also to protect them from social abuse and stigmatisation. Maria saw that the suffering of her family was incomparable to the suffering of victims' families. She reflected on all this deep in her heart.

Looking to the future

Forty years ago, Beny was a handsome, fresh olive-skinned young man. He was slim and kept active. His friends remember him as an agile football player. These days, much has changed. His weight makes it difficult for him to walk. In 2012, he will be 70. He has problems with his health these days. Once a month he takes the bus to the provincial capital and back for his health check. Two of his children live and work in the town. The doctor says there are problems with his heart. The size of most peoples' hearts is about one fist, but his is the size of three fists. So he is very dependent on the doctor and medicine. He has to be careful about what he eats.

Sara died three years ago. The family buried her in the yard behind the house. She was a wise woman who helped Beny through his crisis. Now she has returned to her Maker. These days, Beny's children take turns to call on him. Thanks to developments in communications, his children can telephone if they cannot visit.

In the kampung where he lives, Beny is respected as a local figure because he was once police chief there. But more than that, he is respected because he and his wife managed to educate their children, and they are now all working and independent. His life is not wanting, but nor is it extravagant. He knows that this is because God loves him, and has forgiven him for his involvement in the humanitarian tragedy in the history of his nation.

Yes, Beny the father is probably at peace with himself now. He has gone through various traditional and religious rites and feels that God has forgiven him. He also 'offered' his oldest daughter for this peace with God.

But what about the families of the victims? Is there anyone to listen to their stories? Is there any acknowledgement in society of their loss and the pain they suffered? When will society, the nation and the state acknowledge the crimes they carried out on the victims of violence and their families?

Maria has listened to her father's story. Today, she is determined to go and meet the victims' families. Together with some members of a study group formed two years ago, she is now collecting stories from the wives of the victims of the tragedy in various islands in Eastern Indonesia. These old grandmothers talk not only about how they were destroyed. They also talk about the strength that allowed them and their children survive.

Maria sees the next step as collecting stories from the victims' children. The path towards healing herself and the healing of her country is still a long one. Probably there will be those who refuse. Probably the children of victims will be reluctant to talk. Probably the wound is too sensitive to be touched. Probably they too, tend to forget it.

But Maria is convinced that the long path to healing is necessary and one must strive for it. The healed future begins with the courage to examine the wounds of the past and the willingness to strive together for peace between families of perpetrators and victims. The state must be involved and must acknowledge the crimes it carried out on victims and their families. Only in this way will Indonesia's dream of becoming a just and civilised nation be realised.

Now it is the task of Maria, Linda, Semy, Nia, Eman and millions of young people in this country to strive for the healing of this nation from the mental sickness it has suffered for years and years. They cannot just forget this tragedy. Without the courage to confront the painful past and strive for true peace by listening to the stories of the victims and their families, the healing will be superficial at best.

Kupang, early June 2011

Interviewer, transcriber and writer: Mery Kolimon.

Chapter 3

I Ketut Sumarta

Guilty until never proven innocent

Many people say that life is choice. If so, then each of us would of course have the freedom to choose the kind of life we want. However, the reality most of us experience does not resemble our ideal choice.

No one knows what is written on the palm of their hand, other than how to live out the years the Almighty has granted. However, we all believe that what we plant in this world we will reap in the world to come. If the seed is good, then so too the fruit. But if the seed we plant is rotten, then a harvest of good will remain the stuff of dreams. So no one wants to travel the journey of life with bad deeds. Including Ketut Sumarta.

Born in Gianyar, Bali, 68 years ago, Ketut Sumarta lived a simple life. His hopes were merely to become a person who meant something to those around him, and most particularly to God. However, one fragment in his life suddenly made him confront a bitter reality, when his feelings and self-respect were cruelly oppressed.

Sudden target

In November 1965, Ketut Sumarta became a target.

> I was arrested and thrown into prison with no warrant. While in prison, the treatment was also not according to any clear legal process. Instead I was interrogated based on some made up scenario after being asked my name and age. Eventually I was given a letter of release, after more than two years of imprisonment, because there was no clear evidence to prove my involvement.

Ketut Sumarta cannot easily forget those bitter days in the prison cell.

After his release in 1967, Ketut Sumarta returned to his village. He went back to his old life. The difference, though, was that he could no longer be involved in the arts. His movement was restricted. He could not talk freely with people around him.

> Even so, all this did not prevent me from rebuilding the life that had been turned upside down by unjustified accusations. I married a woman I had met at a performance. We married on 7 August 1968.

Ketut vividly remembers what happened next.

One night, on 4 October 1968, the police and the village head came and forcibly arrested him. He was taken off to the regional police headquarters. Together with others who had been forcibly arrested, Ketut was tortured at a motor repair workshop. He does not remember his torturers' names. Ketut Sumarta recalled,

> They were police, but sometimes they were joined by members of the Military Police Corps (CPM). Each one of them would form a group, and each group would investigate one target detainee. I remember that I was in Captain Manubelu's group.

Throughout the interrogation, Ketut Sumarta sensed there was something odd. If a detainee who was the target of group A gave a statement that was not the same as another target in group B, then the target whose statement was different had to revise his statement to fit the prepared scenario for both groups. When the prisoners gave an explanation that did not fit, or refused to agree, or remained silent, the interrogators accused them of being members of so-called 'Formless organisations' (Organisasi Tanpa Bentuk, OTB) or 'Keep Silent Movements' (Gerakan Tutup Mulut, GTM)]. 'Everything had been pre-fabricated. And probably the punishments as well', said Ketut Sumarta, unable to stifle a cynical chuckle.

The detainees had absolutely no idea about their dossiers; how they had come about, why they were made, or what was in them, except for the fact that they had to sign them there and then. If they did not, not only would verbal abuse be hurled at them, but also inevitable physical torture.

> If you refused … well there were consequences … a friend had his foot broken when stomped on with a table leg. Some had their bottom jaws moved around a bit. As for me, one of my vertebrae was broken.

Eventually Ketut Sumarta and the other detainees 'gave in' and agreed to sign the dossiers, but actually this did not mean the torture stopped. There were now fabricated reasons to sentence them with physical punishment. If you defended yourself, or worse, resisted, even a little, then the response was even worse treatment.

Ketut Sumarta was accused of being a night-operating communist. He said with a tone of growing anger,

> So, they made up such and such a group with such and such leadership and so on ... all complete fabrications. With this, I could be 'tried'.

He had no idea about any of it. He was just an ordinary person who wanted to do the best he could for his country and his nation. He had joined an arts group. He and his group often put on small performances of drama and dance. 'Back then I didn't earn anything from the arts, so I reared ducks', he went on. 'Now tell me, how could a duck farmer lead an organisation declared forbidden and endangering the state?' Ketut Sumarta never stops wondering about how to find the answer, which would offer a glimmer of light after the years of oppression he suffered.

While awaiting their sentences, Ketut and the other detainees still had to accept continual torture. For months, even years. There was nothing they could do about it. There were multiple locked doors leading to their cells. Ketut was in one cell together with 14 other prisoners who had been taken in 1965. Every night someone would get 'the bill', as they called it, namely when someone would be taken out of the cells to be finished off or disappeared, no one knew how. And outside of the cells, there were always people being suddenly targeted, as Ketut himself had been.

'When there's no rattan, find roots'

There is a saying 'when there is no rattan, find roots' which refers to a situation when someone has to strive to go on living, however one can, and not give up because of what one does not have. You use what you can. It can also mean that when you are in a tight situation, you have to solve problems in unusual ways. Ketut Sumarta had to face not only such situations, but those that were more tragic. He was powerless to get himself released, or even just to find a moment when he would be treated humanely according to his fundamental rights as a human being.

Blood gushing from gaping wounds, bruises all over his body, intense pain in every joint, and all kinds of unbelievable aches; these were all commonplace to Ketut Sumarta and the other political detainees. Or, to be more precise, the prisoners *made* them normal so they would *become* normal, so they would not be always complaining. To them, complaining was the same as surrendering without a fight. They had to remain determined at least until the day truth would be restored and they would be liberated from injustice.

> Undergoing seemingly endless torture day after day had become a sort of routine to the other detainees and me. I could not get into a sleeping position that was comfortable for even a moment. The other prisoners and I, who had escaped the late night 'call', had to concentrate on getting well. We had to recuperate from the last torture in preparation for the torture bound to come tomorrow. We tended to our own bruises and the pains wracking our bodies with herbal medicine (*beras kencur*) we made ourselves.

These days you can buy boneless chicken. Well, back when Ketut Sumarta was detained the second time, there were detainees' bodies without meat – just skin hanging from bones, the result of vicious treatment by the prison guards. For months, the only food was worm-infested and stinking red cracked wheat (*bulgur*), and many died from malnutrition. *Bulgur* was usually fed to the pigs.

> We would even eat cockroaches. Anything at all, no matter how toxic, we would eat it. Rats, no problem. Basically, anything that entered the cell. Our rations never included any meat.

As he talked, Ketut relived the misery in his face. Diarrhoea and breathing difficulties that lasted days on end were common.

> Like me, for instance. I still have breathing problems today. Finally in 1974 I was treated in hospital because my lungs were spongy. The doctor said this was from the time sleeping in the damp.

However, these dreadful conditions did not suddenly turn the detainees into cannibals. Quite the opposite, the feeling of solidarity between them became even stronger through caring for one another, and because of their shared suffering. If one of the prison guards caught red-handed, a detainee giving some of his food to another, then they would both be punished. It was only after 1974 that detainees were finally allowed to receive food parcels from their visitors. Later, after visits from Red Cross International, the prison relaxed the rules and prisoners were allowed out of their cells into the daylight after being incarcerated so long in such damp spaces.

Things began to improve for the prisoners. They began to learn about planting spinach or Chinese cabbage seeds that their families brought when visiting. Ketut said, laughing,

> We planted spinach and used our own nightsoil for fertilizer. We would carry it in buckets, and then empty the buckets in front of the cell where the spinach was. So the spinach grew beautifully.

At last the prisoners could eat vegetables, and the prison guards also enjoyed their harvest.

> We made a stove out of old light bulbs. We would hollow them out and fill them with ripped up bits of trousers. We would ask for some kerosene. And that's how we did our cooking.

So, these were their happy days, even though they did not last long, and the prisoners were under constant surveillance by their ever-suspicious guards. Prisoners were now allowed to watch television until 8 p.m. Even though they were not permitted to watch the news, at least they could get out of their cells and relieve some of their loneliness. After returning to their cells, all they could do was wait, doing nothing except passing dark times behind bars, until their 'day of justice' would come.

Why would I plot?

Ketut thought that if he could just postpone dying, then he would have the opportunity to fight for his freedom, so that everyone would know what had really happened. He did not want to die as someone accused of an illegal action that he had never done. Even more, he did not want to end his days in prison as a political prisoner powerless to tell people at large, and especially people close to him, that he had done no wrong. He was not an ordinary prisoner, and so the punishment given to him was also no ordinary punishment.

In 1975, Ketut Sumarta was finally tried after being in prison for seven years, and was sentenced to one more year. After eight years of imprisonment, he was still not released, but received a new notice of detention from Kopkamtib (Komando Operasi Pemulihan Keamanan dan Ketertiban, the Command for the Restoration of Security and Public Order). He was now categorised as 'category X', unlike the 'category A' prior to his sentencing.

Finally, on 20 December 1977, Ketut Sumarta was released. The mass release of that time included those who had been tried and those who had not. Only those considered to be leaders and such like were not released.

Ketut Sumarta never stopped asking himself,

> How could I be accused of having been involved in an organisation that was plotting against the state? I was just a singer for *janger* performances. I did once perform a drama about landlords which inserted messages about the Laws for Produce Distribution (Undang-Undang Bagi Hasil, UUBH) and the Agrarian Reform Bill (Undang-undang Pokok Agraria, UUPA). Many people liked our performances, especially farmers and workers. But there were never, ever, any negative reactions that threatened my safety. In the report, it said that I had opposed the government and this was linked to the Communist Party night operations, and that was why I was thrown into prison.

Ketut Sumarta was accused of plotting. Not a single person defended him or even approached him. No one in his family visited him in prison. His voice shaking, Ketut said,

> It wasn't just other people, even my very own father did not dare. My father had a few reasons for not coming to see me. Firstly, no-one told him I was still alive. Secondly, he would be in danger, even though he was just a farmer and knew nothing at all. In the village, anything could be used as a pretext for murder. Even little kids who didn't know anything at all were killed. The murderers were called '*Tameng*' ('Shields'). According to stories from my friends, the killings were going on in many places.

Ketut Sumarta's chances of escaping Tameng scrutiny were small. Especially when everyone in the village was summoned to the *pura* to make an oath in Balinese that meant, 'I curse the deeds of the Communist Party and I no longer want to be a member.' The way Ketut sees it, this oath was very odd. After all, organisations like the Lekra (the Institute for People's Culture) for instance, had been sanctioned by the government, so why did they suddenly have to be cursed, and by their own members? People making this oath were supposed to be spared, to live and be left free. However, in actual fact the oath-making was used to take targeted people away to be 'disappeared'. These 'disappearances' happened from around November to December 1965. 'So now I think back and say, 'you see, because we ourselves did the cursing, we acknowledged having done wrong and so we then could be killed. That's how it went.'

Ketut Sumarta had no impulse whatsoever to be involved in any plots. All he ever did was join an arts organisation for the people, where he could devote himself, as a child of the nation, to furthering the destiny of ordinary people like himself, including via the Indonesian Peasants Front (Barisan Tani Indonesia, BTI).

> Back then, I realised that the laws in operation were not in accordance with the Law for Produce Distribution (Undang-undang Bagi Hasil, UUBH). For instance, sharecroppers were given only one quarter of the crop, yet they had to cover all costs. I thought, just to cover costs two-thirds of the crop is not enough. And what about when there are no crops? Then the entire loss falls on the sharecropper. The UUBH stated it should be 50:50 division and the costs also shared 50:50. So, half for the landlord and half for the sharecropper, both produce and costs. The BTI was fighting for this, and as an artist, I participated too. So, on the one hand we distributed information about these laws to make the farmers aware so they could demand their rights. On the other hand, we also performed *Janger* with stories about this.

However, Ketut had no idea of the reality that would befall him. His involvement in the arts organisation and his fight to wipe out unjust treatment of ordinary people were used against him when he was imprisoned and accused of plotting. 'Why would I plot?' He asked himself this over and over again. Why would he destroy the county he loved, the country he had fought for and served with no care for position, wealth or power?

> I distributed government laws. These were the government's ideas, not mine. So why was I put into prison for them? As for me personally, I thought that apart from loving art, I could promote the government's program.

Ketut shook his head. Until today it makes absolutely no sense to him.

Life is art

The arts have been extremely influential in Ketut Sumarta's life.

> With the arts, we can make an important contribution to the lives of others, for the wellbeing of others. Through the arts, I could inspire the farmers to fight for their rights.

Ketut had always loved singing and playing *angklung*. When he heard someone from Lekra singing a song, he became interested because the song spread information about the government's laws about farmers' rights in produce distribution. The song encouraged people to fight for the farmers' welfare. So Ketut became more active in the Institute for People's Culture (Lekra). Overall, the songs or plays that he and his group performed always referred to some aspect of farmers' issues. They also promoted regulations that dealt with farmers' rights. The idea was to make farmers more aware so they would not be so easily exploited by landlords who exploited the farmers who worked for them, just for their own personal wealth and prosperity.

> It made no sense at all. There they were – they were civil servants now and still owned hundreds of hectares of land. The way we saw it, this was not fair. Distribute the land to the people who work it according to the work they do. And then – it turned out we were the ones sentenced for having committed crimes!

Many policies could be promoted directly through the arts. At the same time, the arts were also the most effective medium to convey ordinary people's complaints to the authorities. Almost every village had a people's arts organisation like the one Ketut Sumarta led. He himself led around thirty members, including children. Together with his group, Ketut put on performances accompanied by Balinese gamelan, moving from one village to another.

Janger was a social dance and had an important role in establishing solidarity and loyalty among the common people. The youth would gather and put all their energy into clarifying social problems and offering solutions through dance and song. Their focus was people around them who seemed to escape attention from the state leadership. The young generation felt keenly that they had taken on a sense of national responsibility. So Ketut Sumarta and his friends found it incomprehensible that because of their efforts to support popular art forms as a means of unifying people, as communication media and as a vessel of creativity, they were later accused of attempting to overturn the state.

His love of the arts makes Ketut Sumarta disgusted when he sees his own nation turning the arts of the people into commodities, with the pretext of cultural preservation. The arts used to be highly respected because they were seen as an extremely effective vehicle for the struggle for national unity.

> For instance, I do not understand why tourists entering a *pura* have to pay to borrow a ceremonial sash. Is this what you call cultural preservation? I do not understand why to keep the arts alive you have to sell them. The way I see it, cultural preservation means education

> and teaching people about that culture without reaping profit from it. Is there no other way? Especially when the Balinese are perceived as unable to compete with foreigners, even though the only thing foreigners do is get highly paid for training.
>
> Once I took a whole Legong group, dancers and musicians, from the village by truck. When we got to the venue, we got rained out on a grassy field, and were paid only Rp 5,000 per person. Now I ask you, is this cultural preservation? Isn't it exploitation? Some say that culture has to be preserved, but then it is exploited like this. How can we preserve culture, but on the other hand not feel like this?

Ketut Sumarta does not accept that the cultural heritage he fought so hard for is now merely used by capitalists any way they like. But despite everything, he still hopes there will be better policies directed at the people.

> People's arts should be revived, if possible. The government can provide opportunities for these art forms. Perhaps even make a government program, so we can promote to the people arts programs that are relevant to them. Not like the situation now, with the leaders just politicising their own positions.

Life inside and out of jail

When Ketut was finally released, it did not mean that his life was free of trials and obstacles. On the contrary, it was then that he discovered new difficulties in re-establishing his life, beginning again from zero. Even so, he was grateful that all the time he had been in jail his wife and son had managed to go about their daily life. But what he was even more grateful for was the help of his friends and neighbours who had looked after his family. Ketut explained,

> It was my neighbours who kept my son alive. One of them used to give meat broth. So when I came back home I felt very indebted to them. Well, at least this gave me the spirit to go on living.

However, as he had thought, there were many more trials to go through in returning to live in society, particularly living with the public opinion that had been formed about people said to have been involved with the 1965 incident.

It was not easy for Ketut Sumarta to even chat freely with a neighbour, or to build a small-scale business just to meet his family needs. He had to go back and forth to the police station dozens of times because people contaminated by New Order propaganda about 1965 victims made reports about him, and they were also easily swayed by others.

> For example, there would be a visit by someone or other, and I would be summoned. "You cannot do this, you cannot do that. It's best you stay indoors. Who knows, you might not be safe, and that would make things difficult for us …" That was the way it went. So the threat was always subtle like that.

Ketut laughed, but it was no ordinary laugh. He did not think of this painful segment of his life as a joke. Not at all. Whenever he recounted this story he felt as though his fellow countrymen had just toyed with his life, or worse, had made him into some helpless target. So his laugh was a laugh of grief. But Ketut refused to sink into depression remembering an earlier episode in his life. Despite all, he had faith in the Almighty. The proof was that God had given him a wonderful woman as his life's companion.

His status as a political prisoner of course greatly affected the people around him, especially his wife. He was not able to fulfil his role as husband and father as in a normal family. It was the same for other families of ex political prisoners. He had to put on a brave front for the sake of his wife and son, to the point where he once said to his wife, 'you are still young. I cannot buy you anything, I cannot support you. If you have an inclination … Who knows, it might help to raise our child, then feel free to marry again.' He said this while he was still in prison. He did not want to be a burden to others. Particularly when he had no idea when he would be released, and had even heard rumours that he might be sent to Buru Island.

To his surprise, Ni Nyoman Sari, Ketut's wife, absolutely refused her husband's suggestion of finding a new father for their son. She was determined to wait for her husband to come out of prison, and they would raise their child together.

And that day finally came. Ketut Sumarta was free. Even though his freedom was not as complete as he had hoped, at least he was no longer continually beaten up, showered with verbal abuse and insults, and humiliated like an animal. His dream of being back with his wife and child had kept him going, and he did not want to waste this 'second chance' to write a new chapter in his life as a citizen of Indonesia.

He returned to his village. As a newly released political prisoner it was extremely difficult to travel beyond the local town without first obtaining a permit from the regional military command. Obtaining this permit was more exhausting, mentally and physically, than he ever imagined. So there was no choice but to stay in his village, even though he had very little experience at digging and planting.

> This is why I worked at whatever I could – from herding pigs, keeping chickens, even doing bicycle repairs, building labour work, carpentry … the important thing was that I could eat. I was determined not to be a burden on anyone.

He was fully aware that life outside prison required further sacrifice and struggle. Everyone around him was still haunted by severe trauma from the massacres of 1965, which they had witnessed happening before their very eyes. They were terrified that another incident like that could happen again. So they were totally bound up in their own private affairs. No one dared help anyone with a 'red' history like Ketut Sumarta, even secretly.

> I'm not kidding. In my village there were guards called '*babinsa*' (*bintara pembina desa*, officers for neighbourhood control) who watched us all the time. Even if we went to take a pee, they would know … let alone anything more than that. We were spied on constantly.

Even though he was under surveillance, just as he had been when still inside prison, Ketut did not see this as an obstacle to getting on with his life. Nothing had changed within himself, even though now he had 'red' status. He was still the father of two children, his son Guntur and daughter Tari, and as their father, he instilled in them values of daily kindness. 'In Hindu teaching, we must always do good. What was done was done, but now we must do good according to our individual beliefs', he said. Ketut has held these religious principles for a long time. He believes that life in this world is like cultivating plants. If the seeds that are sown are seeds of good, then later we will reap good. And if at the time we sow those seeds of good, the season is bad or there are pests, then all we can do is tend those seeds of good so they are not affected by the bad. Because of this, even though Ketut's service via the people's arts was seen as rebellion and resulted in his arrest, he still tries find insight from every obstacle in his life journey. Because in the end, good will win out, even though it goes through one tempest after another. The whole time he was in prison, Ketut never missed the religion sessions.

> It was called Santiaji. The Hindus had their own spiritual leader, but he was from the military. We had this once a week. Islam was Friday, Hinduism Tuesday, and Christianity on Sunday.

Once outside of prison, Ketut Sumarta never wavered in his beliefs. He taught his wife and children to always do good, and to ignore it when people sneered and looked sideways at them because of their past.

> What is important is not other people, but answering to God for what we do in this world, for it is only God who has the right to give us what we deserve for our deeds throughout our lives.

Holding these principles, Ketut was never despondent when he had to face social challenges, for instance, when his children were singled out by their teacher because they did not have the Balinese names Wayan, Made, Komang or Nyoman in front of their names.

Ketut took this in his stride. 'I told my children, "you tell your teacher to ask me directly if she really wants to know". But of course no teacher ever came.' Ketut also did not get too upset when his children were not treated fairly in their formal education.

> According to the rules, my children should have got scholarship support from primary through to junior high school. My children were clever, but their economic status was low, and this is what the scholarships were for. But it didn't happen, because they were the children of an ex- … well, it doesn't matter. They got no scholarship, but then they also were not indebted to anyone.

The fact that he had once been inside jail did not make Ketut Sumarta disheartened. By not being disheartened, he managed to prevent people from ostracising him. He managed to prove to them that he could still live a reasonable life without burdening anyone.

Ketut Sumarta today

Experience is the most valuable teacher in life. Ketut Sumarta has proved the truth of this. His bitter experiences proved to be the effective trigger to revive his spirit and resolve. And it was his bitter experiences that enabled him to find relief by accepting his past as salve for his inner pain. He became increasingly aware that holding resentment for a long time would only prevent him from being grateful to God for what God had given him. This would mean that the seeds of good he had sown would easily be destroyed by the pest locked within his heart. Ketut acknowledges that he did once have a period of religious doubt, brought about when he was forced to make an oath in the name of religion to satisfy the New Order regime's accusations of him. 'I had no respect for those people, because they used religion in that way', he said with a heavy tone of disappointment.

He does feel ashamed and angry. Ashamed, not because he was once imprisoned as a political detainee. Angry, not because as an ex-political prisoner he will forever suffer discrimination. He is not ashamed or angry because of all this, because he must keep positive about everything he went through in the past.

> I must keep moving forward and live for the future of those I love. What I do feel ashamed and angry about is those provocateurs who stamped Bali as the nest of the 'forbidden party'. People outside of Bali praise it as beautiful, friendly, generous. But back in 1965, people in Bali showed absolutely no mercy to one another. Not even towards their own families.

Ketut spoke angrily now, with his disappointment flaring in his aging eyes.

As a Hindu, he is ashamed to have witnessed his fellow men fighting, even though Hindu teachings strictly uphold harmony and peace. He is angry as a Balinese to know that his fellow men were provoked and encouraged by the interests of certain groups, so that their sense of solidarity was weakened. 'Where was their sense of religious solidarity and their ideal of friendship?' Ketut Sumarta challenges. As time has gone on, little by little the dark curtain has opened and Ketut Sumarta has begun to reap kindness from the seeds of kindness he sowed when fortune was not on his side. He is compassionate, as when he says,

> I never show hatred. Now I realise that they did not know that what they were doing was not right, because they had been enticed, or coaxed. They themselves did not really know what they were doing. So I think that is not a problem for me.

This sense of compassion has also made Ketut Sumarta a positive force in his society. He never misses a village meeting. He comes up with ideas and contributes whenever there are ceremonies. 'As for me', he says 'I like to deal with real issues. Like the *pura*, for instance. I see, "oh, this needs to be done", and I am happy to contribute something.' He has even been made a member of the Village Committee. His opinions and ideas are never rejected. Ketut says enthusiastically,

> I fit in. When there is something needed, if I can propose it, I do so. If most people find it good, then my idea is accepted. I myself don't have ideas for my own interests or for my group. So if it is for the majority and I can do it, I will volunteer.

He is never half-hearted in giving what is best for the community. When he first returned to his village, there were bad reports about him almost daily, so that he kept having to report to the authorities. And every time he was 'accused', he would always answer calmly,

> I have never, ever committed crimes. I have never stolen, never committed fraud. I don't think I've done things that are not right. But the landlords might have found them not right for them.

Ketut laughed and went on.

> All I did was perform *janger*, make *anglung* instruments, and distribute information about land reform. So – please judge. That was the government's program, not mine. I was only conveying what the government wanted to be conveyed. So I think that was good. I was helping a lot of people, wasn't I?
>
> I still like to meet my old friends. We might meet at cremation ceremonies and such, and this helps because we miss each another, but we never talk about the problems of the past. We might just say, "how are you now? How are your wife and children?" And as for the arts in my village here, most of my friends are no longer alive, they were murdered back in 1965. But there are the children who don't know anything. They don't know anything, because indeed there was nothing. There was only art, and us loving art. That's all there ever was!

Now, as before, Ketut Sumarta never differentiates in his socialising. The strong family atmosphere in his village has also helped him carry on his daily life after the 1965 incident. He says, with relief,

> It seems that now people can still look at me. Because I never offend them. I never talk about sensitive things. If I talk, I talk about general things, things that can be spoken about, and things that I know.

These days, he has no great hopes in the government. 'I have no illusions and no great hopes that the government will do anything concrete to address this past history', he says. Even so, he is happy when he can talk about the 1965 incident to the younger generation. Because in this way, the muzzling of witnesses to history will not last forever.

> I value deeply any victory, however small. When I can talk to someone and someone writes down my story, this is a victory for me. A victory that I am no longer silenced and can speak about things as they really were.

As for the situation now, he senses that there is more openness about the 1965 events in Bali. The 1965 victims can share their stories with others, so that there is hope for a time when the 1965 events will no longer be deliberately buried or false stories perpetuated.

Ketut Sumarta hopes that the government will at least begin to take concrete steps in dealing with the victims of 1965.

> The government must have the courage to state whether, according to law, the victims committed any crimes. If they did wrong, then how was that so, and if not, this must be clearly stated. So that the wider society can know that those victims were also their own friends. They were their fellow countrymen. They cannot be slandered forever!

Nothing would please Ketut Sumarta more than if he and the victims of the 1965 events in Bali were to have their good names restored, and for there to be no more slander and suspicion. 'We too are citizens, we have a nation, we have relatives. We have never had evil thoughts about anyone.' Ketut Sumarta closed his story, his eyes bright. There were feelings he could not express in words when discussing the bitter experiences of his past. His generosity in sharing his story is the same generosity that healed him.

Interviewers and Transcribers: Team from ISSI (Institut Sejarah Sosial Indonesia, Indonesian Institute of Social History).

Writer: Fati Soewandi.

Chapter 4

Lambatu bin Lanasi

Demanding rehabilitation of his reputation

Kapontori is a sub-regency (*kecamatan*) to the east of Bau-bau, about 50 kilometers from Buton, the capital of Southwest Sulawesi. The population is mainly Muslim. Kapontri is a famous market centre. Traders gather here from all around, selling basic necessities like rice, sugar and flour and there are also people selling fish and all kinds of root vegetables.

Lambatu was born in Kapontori on 14 November 1935. He was the son of Lanasi and Waambe and had seven brothers and sisters. His father was a prayer leader in the mosque, and every night he taught his children their prayers.

In the 1950s, Kapontori was still a backwater. It had only recently got its first primary school. The children all walked to school, most of them barefoot. Only one or two of them wore sandals. When they finished primary school, if students wanted to continue to junior high school, they had to move to Buton. To get to Buton you had to go by boat, and it took a full day. That was if the weather was good. If the weather was bad, it could take much longer.

Most of the people in Kapontori were small-scale farmers. They worked their fields in rotation. Their fields were not very large and they produced just enough for their own needs. Part of this produce had to be given as tribute or a kind of tax to the king of Buton. At the appointed time, this portion was gathered at the village hall to be taken to the regency and then on to the king. It is not surprising that once they finished primary school, few of the children were able to continue their schooling. They had to help their parents with the farming.

The people of Kapontori remained trapped in poverty. There were many causes. For instance there were 'unofficial' demands made on parents who sent their children to school. Apart from paying fees, they had to deposit a substantial 'tax' per child to the regency government in Bau-bau. Then there was the feudal system still operating in the circles of the Buton palace. Even though Indonesia was now independent, the influence of the royal family remained strong. The last king to govern was La Ode Palihi and his heir was La Ode Mukti. The royal circle still felt free to make regulations that frequently burdened the people.

Attracted to socialism

As a teenager, Lambatu began to think about finding a way out of these traps. This is what drove him to continue his schooling at the junior high school in Buton. His parents worked as hard as they could to find the money, so that that Lambatu's ideals could be realised. In 1953 he moved to Buton. His hard work bore fruit and in 1956 he graduated from junior high school.

After junior high school, he went on to senior high school in Makassar. He chose a vocational high school specialising in law (Sekolah Menegah Kehakiman Atas) because it gave a kind of guarantee of work after graduation. The work would be well paid and he would have a comfortable life. While studying, he began to earn some extra money by working at the Makassar state library. 'There I read books about socialism, nationalism, and religion. But I was most attracted to the books on socialism. One of them had the title, "Ways Society Can Develop (*Bagaimana Masyarakat Berkembang*)."' Lambatu was able to earn 250 rupiah a month at the library, which was enough to cover his daily costs like food and the hostel where he stayed. So he no longer had to ask his parents for money.

When he graduated from senior high school in 1963, he returned to his village. This is the way he talked about the struggle he then had to face:

> I returned to my village holding ideals about changing oppression, using the knowledge I now had. In the beginning, the people supported my ideas about changing certain primitive social patterns, for instance, changing swidden agriculture to settled agriculture. People should till the same fields. I showed them by turning one hectare into wet rice fields. I also pioneered the building of a private junior high school in Kapontori. And I taught. And from all this, I earned the people's appreciation and won their support.

There were a relatively large number of students at the junior high school, about 35 in all. The school developed into the pilot for a junior high school specialising in agriculture (Sekolah Pertanian Menengah, SPM). This kind of high school was much more appropriate for people in agrarian situations.

Today, the school he founded still exists, and is run by the state (SPM Negeri 2, Kapontori).

With this strategy, Lambatu did not have to wait long before the people showed their support. One by one, the people followed his example and began to till settled fields, and they got larger harvests.

Apart from his teaching activities, Lambatu was also active in organisations together with his friend Ahyani, who was head of the district (*kabupaten*) level Communist Party committee in Kapontori. In 1964, he was invited to join the committee of the Communist Party in Kapontori. He found communist teachings, with the principle 'work according to your expertise, be paid according to your needs', very attractive. He thought that by applying communism, man's oppression of his fellow men would disappear. People's welfare would be more equal.

In 1965 Lambatu replaced Ahyani as head of the Kapontori committee of the Communist Party. Ahyani had been promoted to a higher position in the Party. Soon after, the 30th September Movement in Jakarta happened. It rocked the entire nation, including Buton. With the assumption spread by Lieutenant General Soeharto that the Communist Party was behind the Movement, all Communist Party officials were arrested and imprisoned without any due process of the law.

Held at Bau-bau jail

Lambatu told his story, his voice slow and bitter.

> In November 1965, two members of the Kapontori military police came to get me at my house. They arrived without any arrest warrant. Without much thought, I went along. I was taken to the Bau-bau prison. When we got there, we – a group of around 20 people including committee members of the Communist Party in Sapolawa, Kapontori – were all put into one cell three metres square. It turned out that the cell was already home to detainees from Buton. I got very scared when I saw what had happened to them. They were covered with wounds, and had bandages on their heads.

His family had been calm at first, because they believed that Lambatu really had been taken away to keep him safe. They thought he would just be kept for a short time while the police asked for information. But it turned out that he was taken to the Bau-bau prison.

The cell had concrete walls. The height from floor to ceiling was only around 2 metres. For the detainees who were tall, this was already torture. Even those who were not so tall were uncomfortable. But it was not the discomfort that he was afraid of, it was the state of the bodies of his friends who had been arrested before him. Some detainees had to be dragged into the cell because they couldn't walk after being beaten up by the guards.

All this made Lambatu's hair stand on end. His heart was thumping. He was extremely worried that he was going to suffer the same fate. But there was absolutely nothing he could do about it. All he could do was pray and ask for God's protection. And what he most feared came about. After a few days it was his turn for interrogation. During the interrogation the officers asked fabricated questions that made no sense at all.

There were three things they kept asking about:

a. Documents relating to the 30th September Movement which had reputedly been distributed to districts, including Buton.

b. Holes that the Communist Party had dug to bury their victims. The interrogator showed a photograph of a sanitary hole that he said was a hole the Communist Party in Buton had dug. This suspicion was linked to the discovery of the seven dead army officers in an old well at Lubang Buaya in East Jakarta.

c. The visit of an Indonesian navy vessel to Sampolawa harbour in August 1965. This ship, which was sailing to West Irian, had to berth in Sampolawa after an engine failure. But the authorities were making the accusation that it was actually dropping 500 guns to arm the Communist Party which was going to carry out a *coup d'etat* in the Buton area.

Lambatu and the other detainees denied these accusations. They felt they knew absolutely nothing about them. Because he remained firm in his denial, Lambatu had to suffer the consequences. An officer in army boots stamped on his foot, or his foot was crushed with a table leg, or he was kicked. Often in these interrogation sessions, the interrogators (made up of police, the military police corps, and a local interrogation team called Teperda, *Tim pemeriksa daerah*) would hit his face. Sometimes they would hit with cane. If they thought the answer he gave was too complicated, then the interrogation would proceed with electric shocks to various parts of the body; the cheeks, the ears, the stomach and the genitals. Once they attached an empty condensed milk tin filled with sand to Lambatu's penis. Then they ordered him to jump up and down. He passed out. They poured water over him to revive him. When he came to, they interrogated him again while giving electric shocks. Usually the interrogations ran from seven at night until four in the morning. The officers stopped only when they thought they had enough for the dossier.

Lambatu also talked about the food conditions in jail.

> The torture we suffered was not only physical and mental, but on top of this, we had minimal food. For instance, we had 50 boiled corn kernels once a day for two months. Then we had 3 pieces of boiled yam twice a day for a month. One spoon of sago, which was like glue for one month. Many friends died because of that.

It was not only the detainees who were tortured. Their families were also terrorised, as happened to Lambatu's wife, Waode Zatina. Zatina and Lambatu had married in January 1964. She was the daughter of an aristocratic family in Desa Watabo, about four kilometres from Kapontori. One year after their marriage, they were blessed with a son. Sadly, the baby was born premature and lived for only three months. Waode was still coping with the death of her son when she had to face another extremely difficult time, namely separation from her husband who she loved dearly.

Misfortune seemed to plague Waode. Two years after her husband was arrested, in 1967, two men from the Military Police office in Kapontori came to her, namely Second Lieutenant Azis Dahlan and Second Lieutenant Ramli. They wanted to search for documents in Lambatu's cupboards. According to them, Lambatu had confessed that these documents were there. The search was carried out at 9 o'clock at night, witnessed by the village head, La Dinu. The two officials left at 10:30 without having found anything, and threatening to return.

A few days later, the two officials ordered the village head to summon Waode for questioning. They were waiting at a place about 60 metres from the entrance gate to the village. Although terrified, Waode had to go alone. It turned out that as soon as she got to the gate, Lt Aziz grabbed her and held a knife to her throat. Waode passed out. Then she was raped. The next morning, La Dinu, the village head, found her on the side of the road on the outskirts of the village. He took her home.

From then on, Waode was traumatised and even went a bit mad. She would often faint, and kept to herself, not wanting to communicate with others. Her family tried to give her advice and to motivate her so that she would forget this dreadful experience. But it seemed that she had been so deeply traumatised that she was unable to get over it. She lost her appetite, and her health was affected. This went on for a long time. Even after Lambatu was released and things returned to normal, whenever she saw a soldier, she would pass out. In 1977 when she went to vote at the local polling booth, she fainted when she saw the soldiers there. After that she became ill, and she died that same year.

Lambatu only knew about the tragic experience his wife had gone through two years after it happened. In 1969 the prison supervisor gave him permission to go home to Desa Watambo to visit his wife who was seriously ill. Lambatu was accompanied by two prison guards. He felt this visit to be a wonderful opportunity. All the way there he felt overjoyed at being able to meet his family. But what he found wounded him deeply.

The suffering of the children of political prisoners was just as bad. They were stigmatised as 'communist kids'. Even though they knew nothing at all. And with this label they had to take teasing, abuse and humiliation, along with discrimination from friends, teachers and society. As a result, many children were forced to stop going to school because they were ashamed and ostracised. There were some who were fortunate and found adoptive parents, so they could continue school.

The most sadistic prison

The interrogations at Bau-bau prison were renowned as the most sadistic in Southeast Sulawesi. Fifteen detainees are recorded as having died here. They were: Basyarif, who was shot dead by a guard before he arrived at the prison; Drs. M. Kasim, the Bupati (Mayor) of Buton who lived in Bau-bau, who was found hanging in his cell; Ahyani and La Rompu, who died a few hours after interrogation; Halili, who died three days after interrogation; and La Idi, La Ratiu, La Pei, La Jiu, La Guntu, La Naunu, La Raahu, La Kanini, La Sarapu, and La Enso, who subsequently died. The bodies of the dead were all returned to their families except for that of the Bupati of Buton, who was buried immediately.

Even though food rations were minimal, the detainees were forbidden from receiving any food from their families when they visited. And while interrogations were underway, the families were forbidden from visiting. Idul Fitri holiday was the only exception when the detainees were given a special treat of an egg and a sliver of beef.

Lambatu and his friends continued to deny the three accusations. The interrogators now focused on the accusation that some government officials in Buton had been involved in the coup d'etat plan. According to the interrogator, they had already received hundreds of guns. However, throughout the whole interrogation time, it was never proven that any guns were hidden by the accused. And we are not talking about 500 guns here – not a single one was ever found.

The interrogation now focused on the subdistrict head (*camat*) of Sampolawa, La Musa, who was accused of receiving guns. He was interrogated with severe torture. He was hit with rifle butts and given electric shocks (using a kind of generator with knobs for the power and the duration). Because he could not stand the torture, he finally confessed that he had received 500 guns from the Communist Party officials, La Ode Mausuda and Masihu Nuin, and he had passed them on to his supervisor, the Bupati Drs. M. Kasim.

This 'confession' was the pretext for the arrest of the Bupati, Kasim. After pressure and incredibly inhumane torture, Bupati Kasim was forced to confess that he was a member of the Communist Party and in April 1964 had been sworn in by M. Jafar, the Party provincial secretary at his home in Buton, and witnessed by A. Rahim, the Party provincial secretary for Southeast Sulawesi. He also 'confessed' to having received 500 guns from the District Head, La Musa. As a result of this confession, Buton was designated a communist hub. The Bupati M. Kasim was imprisoned together with 40 government civil servants from Buton. The sudden vacuum of government positions was then filled by the army. Kasim was replaced as Bupati by Lieutenant Colonel Sugianto.

Bupati Kasim was found hanging in his cell in Bau-bau prison in the early hours of the morning. At that time the light was poor, because to save electricity all lights were turned off at 4 o'clock in the morning. Because of this, when the detainees had to lay out his body it was not clear whether he had hanged himself or had been hanged. According to Dinu who was given the job of washing the body, the body was wounded, and had swollen as a result of torture. The family was given no opportunity to see the body because he was immediately buried in a public cemetery.

Based on the findings of the Head of the Investigatory Team for Buton dated 10 September 1969 from the statements given by the Bupati and the Camat of Sampolawa, the police and the army were ordered to search the houses of all communists suspected of hiding weapons. Not a single weapon was found at the house of Bupati Kasim. And the accusation that he had been sworn in as a member of the Communist Party was also false. The witnesses, like M. Jafar and A. Rahim had already left Buton in 1963. In February 1964 they were in Jakarta before an overseas trip. As for the late Bupati Kasim, in April 1964 was still working as expert staff in the government administration in the South Sulawesi office in Makassar. It was only in November 1964 that he was promoted to Bupati of Buton replacing Abdul Halim.

So the truth is that the cruel and sadistic investigations of the late Bupati carried out by the interrogation team made a good man do something wrong and caused his death.

Move to Camp Ameroro

In December 1969, the government moved political prisoners based on their grouping. The detainees in group A were moved to Mocong Loe in Makassar, South Sulawesi. There were a few prison camps in Eastern Indonesia. Apart from Mocong Loe, there was Ameroro in the subdistrict of Lambuya, Kendari. Ameroro was the place of exile for Communist Party members and members of mass organisations all grouped as category B who came from Buton, Muna and Kendari. Those who were in group C were released but they were still required to report once a week at their nearest Military Police office.

Lambatu explained,

> The Ameroro camp was a project of the Huluoleo Military Command 143 in the district of Lambuya, Kendari. Lambatu was moved to Ameroro. The camp was situated between two villages, Ameroro and Uwepai, about 300 metres from the main road between Kendari and Kolaka. It was about three kilometres from the army home base of Company 723, Huluolelo Military Command 143. Army residences were built in every district, to monitor the prisoners.
>
> Ameroro Camp was not ready for people to move in. There was only a guard post and a house for those in charge. So Lieutenant Nursin was appointed head of the construction project of the camp assisted by three members of the Military Police Corps. The first thing the prisoners had to do was build barracks measuring 6 x 6 metres. Ten barracks had to be built for ten groups of prisoners. Each barrack was to house ten prisoners. When the barracks were ready, each group was allotted 2.5 hectares of land to plant rice. Because we were then considered to be self-sustaining, we were no longer given any quota of rice from the military.

> Apart from planting rice, we were also ordered to plant root vegetables like cassava and sweet potato. After we succeeded with our farming, the people around the camp began to fraternise with us. They came with the camp supervisors to help at harvest time. We also opened a sports field which then became a place for sports matches between villages in Lambuya.

In 1972, the running and supervision of the Ameroro Camp was handed to a military body. Around the same time, there was a fire in the central market in the town of Roha. Yet again, this was blamed on the communists, and with this pretext, the government rounded up more people. The number of inmates in the Ameroro camp rose to 161. They came from three regencies: Kendari 37; Muna 61; and Buton 63.

To satisfy their curiosity about what was going outside, especially the political situation in Jakarta, the inmates secretly bought transistor radios. They would turn them on late at night when they were outside guarding the fields. Those on watch in the fields would tune in to overseas broadcasts like BBC London or Radio Australia. And the next morning, using signs, they would communicate to the others what was happening in Jakarta.

The farming venture ran for two years from 1970–1972. Then work activities were transferred to projects run by Military Command 143 Haluoleo. These projects employed a lot of prison labour, so the only people left inside the camp were prisoners who were old and sick, and the women.

Forced labour

The work projects were quite simply, forced labour. These projects, run by a work platoon of Military Command 143 Haluoleo, included roadwork and building bridges on the main road between Kendari and Lainea, and sawing timber, building roads and the Wua-wua Poasia bridge. This bridge is situated four kilometres from the mayor's office in Kendari, to the east of the roundabout at Pasar Baru, in Lapuko (the district of Poasia) and in Pudaria (the district of Moramo). Projects also included the opening up of land for temporary houses for transmigrants from Andonohu in the district of Poasia. Then there was the building of the Lapuko wharf in the district of Moramo and the Andonohu wharf in Poasia; the settlement for transmigrants in the district of Moramo, and the construction of low-cost housing for military personnel in Benua-benua, Kendari.

For their work on these projects, the prisoners were given only one litre of rice per day and 300 rupiah a month. Only when the project was completed were the workers given clothes.

After existing for seven years, the Ameroro camp was renamed a 'rehabilitation post' (*instalasi rehabilitasi*, known by the acronym *inrehab*). Four inmates had died while carrying out forced labour, vomiting blood. Their poor nutrition was not equivalent to the energy demanded of them.

This forced labour finally ended on 22 December 1977. The inmates were then taken from the Ameroro camp to Nanga-nanga which was far from any town. It was situated about four kilometres from the Kendari main road towards the jungle, near protected forest. Because of its location, there were no health or educational facilities there, and nothing to support a developing community, like a market, a place for entertainment, and sources of information. By being located there, it was difficult for the political prisoners to interact with society.

In the beginning, people were terrified of coming anywhere near the camp, let alone coming in. They had been told that Nanga-nanga was a den of violence and there were many criminals there. The prisoners, whose earlier professions had been schoolmasters, teachers and civil servants, had to accommodate themselves to this situation. There was nothing to do but work hard and live from the forest to stay alive. Some of them did odd jobs outside Nanga-nanga to support their families. They still had a long struggle ahead of them, even if they were no longer behind bars.

Their suffering was even worse because their children, who knew nothing at all, had to experience being stigmatised as 'communist kids'. And with this label, they were taunted, teased, abused and discriminated against by friends, teachers and society. As a result, many children left school because they were ashamed and ostracised. But some were fortunate in getting adoptive parents so they could continue their schooling.

The children had to attend school outside the village. Their parents were most worried during the rainy season. There were often floods that subsided only after three or four days. And if someone was severely ill, it was also extremely difficult because the nearest health clinic was seven kilometres away. It took about two hours to walk there. A woman once died in childbirth because there was no one to help when she haemorrhaged. Another woman gave birth on her way to the clinic. And there were many premature births because the mothers did not go for checks during their pregnancy.

The Nanga-nanga settlement was in Kendari. Today it is zoned in the district of Baruga, on the south of the main road between Kendari and

Lainea. The first inhabitants of Nanga-nanga were 56 people from the Ameroro and Mocong Loe camps. But 14 of them left. In 1977, there were 65 people there, and many among them still had the status of prisoner so they could not move. One year later, when they were officially released, many of them chose to return to their original villages. But 42 people chose to stay in Nanga-nanga. However, this was a very isolated place. And those who chose to stay there still had to 'report' to the regional government authorities. In Nanga-nanga, each person was given two hectares of arable land to plant crops, as outlined in the government regulation of 1 September 1978.

The Military Command 143 Haluoleo then issued papers declaring rights to land titles to those who had worked the land, an income of 900 rupiah per month for a period of two years, and agricultural tools. From 1977 to 1982, the supervision of 1000 hectares of land was under the Military Police, but was then transferred to the provincial government of Southeast Sulawesi.

* * * *

The Reformation era finally dawned in 1998. This time of change brought great joy to the former political prisoners. At last they got full land ownership papers for the fields they had worked for 20 years. They had been asking the government for this since 1996 but were never granted the papers, with all kinds of excuses. It was only in January 2008 that their demands were finally met after they went out on the streets to demonstrate, accompanied by their NGO friends.

Since 'Reformasi', their lives have become almost equal to those of other people. Discrimination has lessened. Apart from getting land ownership papers, they also have the right to vote in elections, to receive the quota of rice given in government programs for the poor, health assistance, and to participate in community discussions at village and district levels about planning and development, as well as the farmers' assistance programs. In Nanga-nanga there is now a health clinic, a school and the road is being repaired.

Lambatu's house is about 20 kilometres from Haluoleo airport in Kendari. It measures 6 metres square, like the houses for transmigrants, and is built from wood. The house has aged along with its occupant and now is in poor condition. The boards are eaten away, and some can no longer support the roof. Lambatu has not renovated his house since it was built in 1968. To him, this original house has great historic value.

Lambatu's hair is white now, and he works every day getting wood and bamboo in the forest. His life is totally dependent on the forest. Because of this, he does not have enough money to fix his leaking house. In 2008, he and 19 other ex-political prisoners living there sent a request to the mayor for repairs. But until now there has been no response.

Lambatu concludes by firmly conveying his wishes:

> What I continue to hope for as an ex-political prisoner, as we were never sentenced in any court for having committed any crime, is that we ask the government to restore our full rights of citizenship, our dignity and prestige, and our good names and respect according to the 1945 Constitution of the Republic of Indonesia. We demand this right in the name of historical truth, upholding of the law, and the correction of history for his nation's future generations.

Interviewer and transcriber: Resma.

Writer: Ika Mustika.

Chapter 5

Leo

Surviving New Order oppression

Part 1: before 30 September 1965

People call me Leo. I was born on 21 August 1945 in Tawangrejo, Central Java. When I was small something happened that I can never forget, namely when the army came to take away my stepfather. Our house was ransacked. My mother cried, begging for my father and grandfather not to be taken. My father and grandfather were arrested by soldiers from the Siliwangi [Division]. They were tortured together with other people who worked in the village office at Tawangrejo. My father and grandfather were accused of having been involved in the Madiun Rebellion [of 1948], the revolt led by Muso. My grandfather was indeed the village head (*lurah*) of Tawangrejo village in Dutch colonial times. When the Madiun revolt happened, the Dutch army had entered the villages searching for freedom-fighters for the republic. If people heard the Dutch were coming, the whole village would go into hiding.

Then, when I was ten years old, I remember my world as multi-coloured. Everywhere there were posters of the political parties taking part in the general election. There were so many of them: there was the buffalo head in a triangle (PNI, Partai Nasional Indonesia, Indonesia National Party), there was the globe held in a lasso with nine stars and Arabic writing (Nahdlatul Ulama, Revival of Islamic Scholars), there was the crescent moon (MASJUMI, Majelis Sjura Muslimin Indonesia – Consultative Council of Indonesian Muslims), the single large star (PSI, Partai Sosialis Indonesia, Indonesia Socialist Party), and the moon and stars with Arabic writing (Partai Syarekat Islam Indonesia, Indonesian Islamic Union Party). The one I remembered best was the hammer and sickle which was the Indonesian Communist Party (Partai Komunis Indonesia, PKI) because at home there were lots of those posters. My mother and father distributed them to people. Only later did I learn that my parents were on the committee of the Communist Party in Tawangrejo.

When I was in the second year of primary school, I moved to the school in Jepara. There I lived with my grandparents on my mother's side. They were the ones who encouraged me to continue with my schooling. So after I finished junior high school, I was sent to Yogyakarta.

I finished my senior high school in Yogyakarta in 1963. Then I went on to study at the Academy for Fine Arts (Akademi Seni Rupa Indonesia, ASRI). I was accepted into the graphic design department. During orientation, I got to know the arts group Sanggar Bumi Tarung which then shaped the journey of my life. The artists involved with Sanggar Bumi Tarung were progressive-revolutionaries. There I met Amrus Natalsya, N.G. Sembiring, Joko Pekik, D.M. Gultom and Misbah Tamrin. They later became very famous painters and sculptors. The Sanggar (studio) was the place where I was most active, apart from campus.

As a student I really admired Bung Karno. I had often heard his speeches, as I had been listening to them on the radio ever since I was at primary school. Bung Karno always inserted slogans into his speeches, like JAREK (Jalannya Revolusi Kebangsaan, the progress of the national revolution), TAVIP (Tahun Vivere Pericoloso, the year of living dangerously to oppose the colonialists, imperialists and capitalists supported by America and England), GESURI (Genta Suara Republik, the pealing bell of the Indonesian Revolution), BERDIKARI (Berdiri di Kaki Sendiri, standing on one's own two feet, meaning not wanting to be indebted to the capitalist-imperialists). The Great Orator [Sukarno] once said, 'The people of Indonesia must form organisations, right to the level of domestic servants!' This statement encouraged me to join the CGMI (Consentrasi Gerakan Mahasiswa Indonesia, Indonesian Student Movement Concentration) whose slogan was 'study, organisation, revolution'. This CGMI trilogy motivated me to finish my course at ASRI and get a scholarship to go to the People's Republic of China.

At that time, the spirit of struggle instilled by the Government promoting the unity of the whole nation of Indonesia and movement towards social change of a just and prosperous society truly inspired everything the people did. Including me. I wanted to serve my country and my people and be seen fighting alongside Bung Karno's government. To increase my skills, I joined workshops and courses run by the CGMI. To me, these courses gave the direction, attitude and motivation for progressive revolutionary youth. The negative aspects of young people are caused by a lack of judgement and experience because of their age. They need instruction so that their spontaneous and emotional thinking can be directed to the correct path. At CGMI I was forged as an organiser, and at Sanggar Bumi Tarung I honed myself as an artist.

In August 1965, together with friends from Sanggar (studio) Bumi Tarung, I received an invitation from the State Committee for preparations for Independence Day celebrations (17 August). The first thing we did when we got to Jakarta was make some posters at the Kartini group studio and help out with finishing the posters and banners at the Lekra (Lembaga Kebudayaan Rakyat, Institute of People's Culture) offices in Cidurian. This was the first time we met Pramoedya Ananta Toer (writer), Zainal Abidin (film star) and Nyoto (one of the top leadership of the Communist Party Central Committee).

On the night of 28 September 1965, one day before our return to Yogyakarta, we listened to Bung Karno's speech for Farmer's Day at the Istora Gelora (Senayan Sports Stadium). It turned out to be the last time I heard Bung Karno directly.

Part 2: capture and arrest

On 30 September 1965, when I got back from Jakarta, I intended to rest a couple of days before attending lectures again. The next morning, I heard the news on the radio that the situation in Jakarta was confused and in turmoil because there was a movement by the Revolutionary Council (Dewan Revolusi) or the Council of Generals (Dewan Jenderal) or … it was not clear.

I was on my way to Sanggar Bumi Tarung. When I got there, I met two friends who had returned from Jakarta the previous day. Together we kept track of what was happening in Yogyakarta while helping one of the lecturers at ASRI, Pak Soeromo at Tegal Lempuyangan who had a commission from Oemar Dhani to make a bronze Garuda statue three metres high with a wing span of 7 meters for a monument for the Air Force.

Over those days in October, Yogyakarta was full of very crude, disgusting and pornographic graffiti on the palace walls and gates demanding the dissolution of the Communist Party along with what were considered to be its mass organisations, like SOBSI (Serikat Organisai Buruh Seluruh Indonesia, All-Indonesia Trade Union Federation), BTI (Barisan Tani Indonesia, Indonesian Peasants' Front), GERWANI (Gerakan Wanita Indonesia, Indonesia Women's Movement), Lekra (Lembaga Kebudayaan Rakyat), HSI (Himpunan Sarjana Indonesia, Association of Indonesian

Graduates), CGMI (Consentrasi Gerakan Mahasiswa Indonesia), IPPI (Ikatan Pemuda Pelajar Indonesia, League of Indonesian Youth and Students), and PR (Pemuda Rakyat, People's Youth).

Members of mass organisations or people with connections to the messages in the graffiti began to get worried. I myself, along with friends from Sanggar Bumi Tarung, was on the alert from about 15 October 1965 when there was news that in the northern square (Alun-alun utara) in Yogyakarta there was going to be a mass assembly ('*apel akbar*') of commands to crush and dissolve the 'the Communist Party and its mass organisations' all over Yogyakarta. Anticipating this, the Yogyakarta CGMI asked the art school, ASRI, for help by providing safe space for the CGMI office. The head of CGMI then gave me and some friends from Sanggar Bumi Tarung the task of guarding the CGMI branch office which was in Jalan Magelang.

In the morning of 20 October 1965, I was calmly sitting in front of the gate of the branch office in Jalan Magelang drawing sketches for my assignment. I was not long there before I saw a crowd of people heading for the Alun-alun to join the assembly. So some friends and I who were on guard there decided to go along and mix with the crowd while still checking on the security situation in the CGMI branch office.

It turned out that the northern Alun-alun (town square) was packed with people, with the centre of activity on the western side. There was a stage set up for speeches. I myself witnessed the deafening roar of the crowd as it was fired up for its parade around Yogya. The crowd was using loud speakers and yelling, 'Dissolve the Communist Party or there will be a flood of blood!' 'God is great [Allahu Akbar]!' and curses aimed at the Communist Party, 'Hang Aidit, the head of the Central Committee and pulverise his cronies!'

I managed to leave before the crowds started leaving the Alun-alun, and got to the CHTH (Cung Hua Tjung Hwee) building, owned by Universitas Republica (URECA). Friends called me in through a side door. I saw that there were many URECA students inside and students from other universities too. They asked me to help protect CHTH and URECA from the frenzied crowd. We estimated that the crowd numbered in the hundreds, probably thousands. The students guarding the building all wore a symbol of young coconut leaf (*janur kuning*) on their arms. They told me to beware of anyone in the crowd not wearing that symbol.

The only things we had to defend ourselves and the building were building materials that were in front of the CHTH URECA buildings that were currently under renovation. We were unified in our determination and resolve to fight back if there was any kind of violence. We waited quietly for instructions, and were forbidden to taunt the crowd passing by. Then we began to hear the shouts of the mob, their yells and curses. When they got in front of the CHTH building, some of them brandished sharp weapons like swords, machetes, kris, crowbars, hoes or other tools.

My friends and I were getting mad now, because people in the crowd were throwing bricks at the URECA sign. So we retaliated with bricks, yelling, 'Keep away from the building!' Success. The crowd moved back. Then we heard rifle shots outside of the building and the brick throwing stopped. Troops had arrived to secure the location, and were in front of the building facing the crowd. We thought we were safe after the army had arrived. One soldier even came inside, a corporal, who said the building was now under army protection. Speaking with a strong Javanese accent, he said that if anyone from the crowd came inside, 'I'll shoot him in the head'.

Then a police commander came in with some of his subordinates. They ordered all of us in the building to gather in one corner, while shooting their pistols in the air and threatening us with their weapons.

My friends and I who were inside the building were ordered to carry all the tools we had brought. Then we were ordered to come outside of the building one by one and get into trucks that were parked ready in front of the CHTH building. We were searched for hidden weapons. But they didn't find any at all. Then we were taken to the police station at Ngupasan. After being taken into the open space there, we were left to just sit around, and they chatted with us. 'Look, the situation in Yogyakarta is unsafe right now after what happened this afternoon at the CHTH building and the regional offices of the Communist Party, so we want you all to keep calm so everyone will be safe', they said.

They promised us all that we would be returned home as soon as the situation permitted, to the addresses we gave. Then, until nightfall, they took down details of our names, addresses, ages, and the names of our families. We were exhausted and hungry, and many people just made up answers. I was one of those who answered honestly, to lessen risks and also, I hoped, to make things easier.

The police recorded that we numbered 134 in all. According to them, the situation did not yet allow us to go home, so we would be 'temporarily' accommodated in the Wirogunan prison in Yogyakarta. Prison rules forbade us from bringing anything at all. So the prison guards noted down anything we had, and took it from us.

We were all put into Block A which was used for people awaiting legal process. Normally, the capacity of Block A was 40, with 10 people per row.

All of us had to attend roll call morning and evening carried out by the guard commander.

Every person was issued with one plate, one bowl and one mug, all aluminium. Our food rations were the same as the criminals. In the morning we got 100 grams of boiled corn and at midday and in the evening 300 grams of rice. We got tea in the morning. The food to eat with the rice or corn consisted of green cabbage boiled with a little flavouring, together with dried salted fish. On Fridays we got half a boiled salted egg with chilli sauce. On Sundays we got one piece of boiled meat.

Because our treatment was not in accordance with the promise made at the Ngupasan police station, two friends tried to meet the head of the prison to discuss our 'temporary' detention. Our go-between requested that two of us be allowed out, at our guarantee. Our point in allowing two of us out was to help manage the condition of the 134 people whose condition was worsening, and whose spirits were flagging.

We had been in the prison for a week and still found it difficult to get used to the conditions of not enough food, not changing our clothes and bathing without any soap. In these miserable conditions we couldn't sleep because it was so crowded. We would plan to sleep all facing left or all facing right, but it had to be all of us, because there was no space for anyone to lie flat on their back. The head of the prison made the offer for some of us to be moved to another block, but as we had been together from the start we did not want to be split up. It was this togetherness that gave us a sense of family-like solidarity, and we did not want to be separated, through thick or thin.

To keep healthy, every morning before roll call we would do exercises together, which one of us would lead. We would do this by standing where we had slept, moving all together so our arms didn't hit each other. To fill the long, boring hours, we would tell stories about songs that we sang, or about cooking and food.

In November 1965, a new group of detainees was brought in, so now we filled every single block in the prison; we outnumbered the 'real criminals' of Wirogunan prison. We learnt that the URECA-CHTH building, which was beside the prison, and the Vreedenberg Fort, were being used as holding centres for prisoners. We inhabitants of block A now had to move to block L. There were also some SOBSI (Serikat Organisasi Buruh Seluruh Indonesia, All-Indonesia Trade Union Federation) prisoners in block L.

Our hope of being sent back home got no response from the prison guards. We got angry and lost control, and our behaviour turned strange, especially because we did not have enough food. We often destroyed the dishes and would make a huge racket when food time drew near.

From the time of the arrival of the new detainees, food rations had decreased. Whereas before our rations had been the same as the criminals, now they were the same as the new detainees. We no longer got the 'extras'. We were discriminated against: it was as though the political detainees were lower than criminals. To guard against individualism and to foster solidarity, we would always eat in groups of three or four, the groups forming automatically before eating.

On Christmas Eve 1965, when all the detainees were looking forward to visits from their families, what happened instead was a visit from the Military Police (POMAD PARA Polisi Militer Anggota Angkatan Darat) from Jakarta who wanted to interrogate the prisoners at Wirogunan prison. Interrogation meant torture. The interrogations were carried out in each separate block, locked of course. All we could hear was the sound of torture. This happened again a month later, on the eve of Idul Fitri (23 January 1966).

Detainees of Chinese descent always got extra discrimination and intimidation from the Military Police. Apart from all kinds of torture, they were made to fight each other. Other detainees did not escape this interrogation, except for me perhaps. When they accused me of being in the People's Youth (Pemuda Rakyat), I explained that I had been in CGMI, and I escaped it.

We spent our days together keeping our spirits up even though we were undernourished. Then we began to barter with the criminals. We would exchange whatever we still had for their food rations. This bartering was met with pro and contra opinions amongst our group. Detainees in other blocks advised us to stop the barter. They said that the food rations the criminals were bartering were actually rations that had been stolen from them. The situation of hunger and torture inspired one of my friends to compose a song titled 'the bleeding bowl'. This song really affected me and all the detainees in the various blocks. The solidarity between detainees was also evident when someone got a package from their family, and they would divide it up evenly among each group in the room.

And then suddenly I and some others got a summons to be moved. I do not remember exactly when it was, but it was already 1966. It turned out that families had heard the news about the prisoners being moved. In the middle of the night, they were already waiting outside the prison. Sadly, the prisoners and their families could not greet each other because when we emerged out of the prison gates we were immediately ordered to get into the trucks and kneel there with our hands above our heads.

The truck convoy stopped at Lempuyangan station. There were already many soldiers wearing the red berets of the RPKAD (Resimen Para Komando Angkatan Darat, Army Para Command Regiment) there. And we were taken at gunpoint into three connecting train carriages. The red beret soldiers were on guard on top of the carriages and at each side. All the windows were closed and nailed down tight. Before the doors closed, we were given a packet of rice with fried salted soya bean cake.

By morning we had arrived in Cilacap, Central Java. We thought we were going to be killed in some place unknown to us. After getting down from the carriages, we were told to put our hands above our heads, and squat in lines making five columns. And eventually we got to Nusa Kambangan island. Again we were taken by truck, to Kembang Kuning prison.

Together with 40 others, I got room number 14 which was guarded by a trusted prison criminal. When the door was unlocked, we were ordered to clean the prison yard or outside the prison complex. We used this opportunity to look for extra food, like cassava.

Over the next few months, under the guard of the criminal prisoners, we had to get firewood. A friend and I were given the duty of looking for kindling to boil sweet potato. Then my friend got the idea of stealing kindling without our criminal guard knowing, and swapping it for salt with the mothers or wives of the prison officers. At that time, three spoons of salt became capital which could keep one eating group alive for a week. Around July 1966 there was news that there would be conditional release of detainees aged over 50 or under 20. I was in that category.

Together with the others in this category, I was taken to Nirbaya prison, and when we got there we were immediately housed in the blocks prepared in advance. I was in a room in block 3 on the ground level, and the room and the door faced the hall or the arts building on the terrace below.

Those detainees with enough energy were made to clean coconut shells, some of the older ones had to sort and prepare coconut fibre to make doormats. The young detainees who displayed enthusiasm for work were taken to work as domestic servants in the houses of the prison officers.

It was not easy to get chosen to be a servant, it was mainly luck. The situation had forced us to turn into individuals who had lost their tolerance and solidarity. Only a small amount of loyalty and solidarity remained. I was lucky in that I got on well with my workmate in our forced labour lifting stones together. His name was Suroto. He was younger than me, but he was very wise. He once gave me advice, 'the suffering and torture that we are experiencing are intended to slowly kill our generation, so therefore we must make sure that there is no fighting among us.'

In early August 1966, Commander Dalim assigned me to office administration duties. Dalim was the Commander of Security, and he was under the command of the leader of prison I, and the deputy of prison II. He made me administrative assistant.

While working there I got some new experience, namely taking the fingerprints of young prisoners who had died during detention. Their fingerprints were necessary for the death certificates sent to the Regional Military Command (KODAM) in Semarang and then to the families. Now, some of the detainees who had died were still sent food and clothing parcels by their families. So my friends and I thought about how we (detainees) could share them. Eventually, by getting authorisation to go in and out [of administration] without being checked, we were able to pass on the parcels to prisoners who came from the same village or area as the person who had died. Of course we had to do this secretly without being found out by the staff in administration. If the package went through their hands it would disappear, or its contents would diminish, because they stole things.

At the end of 1966, I was still busy working in administration. When my duties there were done, I would do some drawing outside of the prison. This gave me the spirit to endure life at Nusa Kambangan. Apart from that, I was able to use my art to get some more nourishing food. I did everything I could to stay healthy.

At the end of 1967, all detainees older than 50 years or younger than 20 years were summoned. The word was that we were going to be sent back to Java. It turned out I was on that list. Together with hundreds of other prisoners we were taken to Sodong harbour on Nusa Kambangan. The guards officially handed us over to the Central Java Regional Military Command.

We were taken to the train station near Cilacap. We marched in two lines. It was extremely difficult to get into the carriage because everyone was pushing at the door. We passed station after station. At one station somewhere, the train stopped for quite a while because we had to wait for adjustment of the track. Then some food sellers started giving us their food for free. We fought over that food. The soldiers guarding the carriages just let it be.

Our hopes of returning to Yogyakarta were dashed because the train did not stop at Tugu station in Yogya. It turned out that our destination had been Tawang Station in Semarang all along. When we got there, we were ordered to quickly get into trucks and squat neatly. We had no idea where we were being taken to, because in that squatting position we couldn't see the direction we were going, or the road.

Eventually, after a long trip, we were put into an old Dutch fort in the area of Ambarawa, Semarang. We became inhabitants of what was called 'KAMSING' (Kamp Pengasingan, Camp of Exile) IV Ambarawa under the authority of Diponegoro Military Command.

'Ambarawa, town of my memories, is witness to my suffering. I will never forget the cool evening breezes piercing my soul'. These words are from a song a fellow prisoner composed in the Ambarawa camp. This song built a strong emotional connection between the 1965 military detainees accused of involvement with the communist party or the coup who were already in the camp, and the 1965 political prisoners. The sincere solidarity the military detainees showed us when they saw our condition upon arrival from Nusa Kambangan, made us feel as though we had found an important lost treasure.

Among the political prisoners installed in the western block was the oldest, a man aged 66 named Warsiman, who had been moved there from Jakarta. He would enthusiastically give us young ones advice that inspired us, saying, 'You must have strong bones and brilliant minds to survive imprisonment'.

Because of this, we young prisoners did our best to restore our mental and physical health in Ambarawa by getting an increase in the food parcels sent by our families, and by sport. We practiced volley ball and became Ambarawa Camp's undefeated volley ball team.

In the middle of 1968 the political prisoners were photographed and had their fingerprints taken for administration purposes. At the same time, we heard that prisoners aged 50 and over had been released. We had no idea whether it was true that they had been released or just moved to another prison.

Then a further release happened. This time it was the army military police prisoners (POMAD PARA, Polisi Militer Anggota Angkatan Darat) who were released and immediately given new assignments (fully reinstated with uniforms and weapons) as 'platoon guards' (tonwal, Peleton Pengawal) to check the food packages sent by families. In the beginning, we all thought that because the ones doing the checking were our own friends, they would be sure to treat us well. But we were wrong 180 degrees. Before, a package would never be damaged when it was examined, after our friends were made 'guards', the packages were smashed.

At Ambarawa, my work assignments kept changing. In early 1969, the military prisoners and the political prisoners were put to work building an arts centre for performances, administration buildings, and an accommodation block for the families of the prison guards. So I was a builders' labourer.

Then the Camp Commander asked me to become a tailor. I had been recommended for this work because when I had been in Nirbaya prison, I was given that work. I was also asked to be a domestic servant in the house of First Lieutenant Abdul Aziz who was in charge of camp logistics.

On another occasion, I was made to work in a small food kiosk near the Ambarawa Catholic convent. This was when I was able to meet my mother. She told me about the suffering my family had gone through since I left. Our meeting, even though coloured by sadness, was the most significant moment in strengthening my resolve to keep going.

Once more we heard rumours about release and movement of prisoners. But by now we all knew well what New Order laws meant, and that 'release' meant to remain a prisoner, but be moved to a new place of detention. There was also the news that those grouped as category B prisoners were to be sent into exile.

I have no idea how I ended up being put in this category. I was taken by truck back to Nusa Kambangan. Over the following days, while in transit, I and some others were ordered to decorate some of the prison building walls. After we had been together for a few days, it became clear that our classifications were determining where we were going to be sent. We were in the second group to be sent off to Buru Island.

We were given kapok pillows. I was given the task of writing numbers on the pillows with black ink. We were also given uniforms for our departure, namely short-sleeved shirts and long trousers. If the clothes were too big or too small, well too bad, what was important to them was the fact that we all looked the same, wearing brown. We had to carry our things packed tight, as our two hands had to be free. So our pillows and clothing were wrapped up inside our mats and tied however we could, and we carried them on our backs.

At last the awaited day of departure arrived and around the end of December 1969, the 'chosen prisoners' boarded the ship Tobelo which was anchored at sea in Segoro Anakan. But unlike our usual conditions, once on board we were treated in a friendly way by the guards. We got exactly the same food as them, with nutritious dishes.

On the fifth day, with moderate speed, fair weather and relatively calm seas, the Tobelo was sailing freely. Then, in the middle of Kayeli Bay, the ship dropped anchor. We were ordered to disembark. Landing craft had been prepared to take us to Namlea which was the harbour on the northern bay. From the pier to Transito – our transit accommodation while awaiting allocation – we were guarded by a battalion from the Pattimura Military Command, most of whom were Ambonese. After our registration was finally complete, we were divided into three units: Wanapura, Wanareja and Wanayasa. Each unit was to house 1000 prisoners.

The news went around that the New Order was making the island of Buru into a project clearing the jungle and swamps for rice production, with dry fields for other crops. The unit in charge was called Bapreru (Badan Perencanaan dan Rehabilitiasti Pulau Buru, Body for the Administration of Buru Resettlement and Rehabilitation). Bapreru was headquartered in Namlea, headed by Major Rusno who arrived with the first group of political prisoners in July 1969. Bapreru prepared a warehouse for food, tools and equipment. Another semi-platform warehouse was built on the edge of Waiapu swamp.

I was among the 500 or so young prisoners, high school graduates and students from agricultural high schools (SLTA) who were housed at Unit 4, Savana Jaya. At the time, no one wanted to be the commander of this unit, because they doubted that we could meet the targets of the government program, and this would obstruct their promotion to higher rank after their service at Buru Island.

On the first day we were told to go to our barracks, with each barracks housing 50 people. Each barracks had to have a leader who was appointed by the platoon guard (tonwal). The barracks leader was responsible for us all to be present every roll call morning and evening.

There was one kitchen for every five barracks. At that time, the prisoners who worked in the kitchens had to calculate rations enough for 6 months, because the fate of 500 people was in their hands. The government gave us rations for only 6 months. After that we were to be on our own. We had seeds and seedlings for beans, peanuts, vegetables, soya beans, rice, and corn, all sent from Namlea. And so, with limited tools, we had to transform the Buru wasteland.

As a political prisoner during the New Order regime, I felt as though I was experiencing the suffering our forefathers went through before Indonesia's independence. It was like the *romusha* during the Japanese occupation or the forced labour during the colonial period, when people died with no rituals to mark their passing. On the island of Buru, we had to attend roll call morning and evening with no exception if we were sick. Medicines were extremely restricted.

Days and months went by, and unit 4 became the pilot for the planning team to determine where wet rice fields and dry crops would be planted. A team had been formed to survey a planned road from Sanleko to the town of Namlea. This road was to go through mangrove swamps and eucalyptus-covered hills. One of the Bapreru programs was to build a dam on Saibini River. After they surveyed the river to its source, they concluded that there was not enough river flow to irrigate the rice fields planned for unit 4, Savana Jaya.

Baperu's initial target was self-sufficiency in food after the government subsidy ended. However, this target was threatened because the emergency dam that had been built for irrigation was insufficient. There were reports that the dam had collapsed in the middle of the night because of heavy rain. The Commander ordered all prisoners out to work that night to fix it.

The pressure of forced labour was increasingly inappropriate to our nutrition, particularly when we had not had any rice harvest yet. There was one failure after another in the agricultural sector, so in the end we could eat only our cassava crop.

The agricultural failures were caused by changes in policy from the new unit commander coupled with the cruelty of the replacement guards in the units. The situation was terrible. There were negative thoughts, and growing suspicion between the prisoners. This happened because there was a group of prisoners whose ambition it was to develop good relations with the unit command. They wormed their way into getting their forced labour reduced.

Once, unit 4 received a visit from the Swiss humanitarian branch of Red Cross International. We were all called up, and not permitted to meet the Red Cross visitors. We all had to leave the barracks to work in work placements so that Buru would look habitable and not like a place of torture. The sick bay became a particular focus of attention, even decorated inside and out by the Bapreru health officers.

At that time, Units 1 to 3, which housed the first group of prisoners to be brought to Buru, had succeeded in their planting and harvest. However, they did not enjoy the product of their harvest. This was taken for the business interests of the Bapreru officials. If any political prisoner complained, he would be taken into custody beyond the Namlea eucalyptus hills under extremely tight and cruel guard. Some friends and I once managed to steal some of the harvest stored at Bapreru. There had been over-production because of the 'success' of the forced labour program. Luckily, we were never found out.

In 1971, the Commander of Unit 4, Captain Hasan Basri, summoned me. He needed some artists and painters from all the units for the Namlea Fair that Bapreru was putting on. The purpose of the Fair was to promote Buru as an agricultural project and rice warehouse for Eastern Indonesia.

The people in Namlea were enthusiastic about the Fair, especially the outdoor film screenings near the shore at Kayeli Bay. Once the Namlea Fair was over, some of the prisoners and I were asked to make ensigns and posters in Arabic calligraphy with Qu'ranic quotes. We were ordered to draw the Arabic letters by hand, to fill orders from the Bapreru staff.

Because of the strenuous work, I collapsed. I got hepatitis. My friends nursed me, and also force-fed me with healthy food like liver and traditional medicines. After six months, I regained my health.

To help dispel boredom and loneliness, the prisoners developed entertainment like ketoprak (traditional Javanese drama) by former BAKOKSI (Badan Koordinasi Ketoprak Seluruh Indonesia, All Indonesia Ketoprak Association) Mataram members. Others performed *ludruk*, wayang kulit and dramas inserting jail-type humour. This helped to lessen the burden of the daily, weekly and monthly punishments. The Bapreru Commander also allowed us to play volley ball and football.

In Buru, sports competition between units became a source of healthy fun, and meeting each other also gave us some relief from loneliness. But for the unit commanders, our competitions were an opportunity for gambling. The other entertainment was black and white television, but under strict guard. We were only allowed to watch entertainment programs. We could watch world news and other news but only with the sound turned off. So it was like watching old silent movies.

Shortly after, there was a pilot project to build houses at Savana Jaya village for the prisoners' families who were to follow them to Buru. These houses were made of wood with tin roofs. They measured about 7 x 6 metres square with a front yard of 3 metres facing the road. A small column monument was built at the housing complex. The day before it was to be unveiled by Baprepu, my friend Rukmono and I were given the job of working overtime to carve the writing on the column.

On day 'H', we inmates of Unit 4 were sent far from the place of the opening ceremony. We were sent to other units. From that day on, Savana Jaya was to be only for those political prisoners whose families were there. The other inmates were asked to move to village houses in block D before the first families arrived. I got the house number 57 in block D, which housed 5 prisoners. We thought that this was just for prisoners who were unmarried, but it turned out that many others had to stay, especially those with skills to support village development.

At that time, around 1972 or 1973, the families of political prisoners had begun to arrive and were housed in block A Savanajaya. Some of these prisoners whose families arrived were confused, because now they had to part from their friends in the unit who had so far been with them constantly. They were also sad to see that their families were becoming prisoners in Buru from generation to generation.

Rukmono and I helped carry the children and the women from the boat to shore, as there was no pier. The friends whose families had arrived were too busy crying, tears of mixed sadness and joy. We were also asked to carry the government documentation team's cameras. Apart from that, we had to decorate the house number 2 in Block A. This was given to the Seyohadi family. He had been appointed the 'village chief' of Savana Jaya, and this was going to be filmed for government documentation to be broadcast on national television.

The documentation team also documented the political prisoners at work in the rice fields, and at the saw mill in the forest between units 14 and 15. At units 15 and 16 they documented the farming and agriculture. I was given a cameo role in this documentary film; I had to act that I was meeting friends in the saw mill to tell them about the arrival of the first batch of families. I also had some short dialogue when I asked my friends to request the government, via Bapreru, to send their families in the next batch.

Around 1974, there were visitors from Switzerland who wanted to interview the inmates of unit 4 Savana Jaya, but the authorities would not permit it. We prisoners were told to keep well away from the visitors who were taken to the village clinic which had been prepared in advance. Only a few prisoners were ordered to greet and accompany them, and carry their bags to Sanleko.

The day after the visitors left, there was an extraordinary roll call for all inmates. The Commander, shrieking, demanded to know which prisoner had given a letter written in English to the Swiss visitors, when carrying their bags to the boat that took them to Namlea. The letter was unsigned but described the prisoners' real situation, saying it was nothing like what they had seen because everything had been staged.

While waiting for the confession, all the prisoners were left standing in the rain. Because no one confessed, the chief guard threatened to use brand new technology to find the culprit – a lie detector. I got really scared, even though it wasn't me who had written the letter. Over the next few days the search for the culprit went on with prisoners being summoned one by one to the Commander's office and ordered to write, so their handwriting could be checked against the letter.

At the end of 1974, the prisoners were split up and moved to some units on the Waiapu valley, because there were plans for the arrival of the second batch of families. This second batch arrived in 1975. I was moved to Unit 1 Wanapura, which had rice fields, agricultural fields and the largest garden of all the units, because it was the oldest one. There were 1000 inmates in Unit 1, housed in 11 barracks, and the head was Dalimin. We had to learn to fit in with these inmates in Unit 1 who were mostly farmers.

When there was a change of commander, the new commander brought in cars for the transportation of him and his staff, and some prisoners were taken on as drivers. Because of this, the road from Mako to Savana Jaya village, which passed units 14 to 16, was repaired. The new commander also brought in horse carts, horses and buffalo which were prepared as transport between the units and to help with the farming. Not long after that, we got motorised hand ploughs for ploughing.

Unit 1 got 23 horses and 30 buffalo. I agreed to train and watch the horses that were still wild, because no one else wanted to do it. After my experience with the horses, the camp commander and his staff trusted me to take letters to the commanders of units that could not be reached by motor bike. After my work herding horses, I was raised to be head of barracks and I worked at the unit.

In 1978, Colonel Karyono replaced Colonel Sutikno as Camp Commander. At Unit 1 Wanapura there was a photographer called Mulyadi whose job it was to document the activities of the prisoners. The unit commander asked to be photographed together with the inmates when there was a meal in the rice fields, for him to remember his time of duty in Buru. The photos were not to depict any bad situations there, even though they happened. It had to be a beautiful memory of a place with yellow rice ready for harvest, the rice harvest, and the vegetable crops, or something depicting the prosperity of Buru, because the photos would be scrutinised if they were sent or taken to Java.

A few times, rumours were rife that prisoners were about to be released. Prisoners called Dedi, Keddy and Tarvi had been released from Unit 1 Wanapura and Unit 3 Wanayasa. They were released in extraordinary circumstances, because no other prisoners knew. The word was that the three of them had been spies whose job it was to spy on the other inmates.

There was another prisoner called Doctor Merapi who was released but immediately sent to work as a doctor in the clinic at Mako.

The other releases were of prisoners aged over 60. This happened only in unit 5, even though there were many other prisoners over 60 in other units. And actually, the prisoners in unit 5 had been in Buru only since 1976, so only for two years. So the rest of the prisoners called them the 'tourists'.

Something that cheered us up – apart from awaiting news of being sent home – was when a squad of guards came to the barracks. They asked our forgiveness because they had often punished us, explaining they had to do their duty. They asked for our blessing because they were being sent off to East Timor.

1979 was the year of release for all the prisoners on Buru. So the world would know about it, some humanitarian journalists were invited to Buru to meet prisoners and to explain that they had come to release the communist political prisoners. These journalists said they would not leave Indonesia until the communist prisoners were back home or with their families.

Part 3: release

At the end of 1979, all the political prisoners were sent home, in batches. I had already decided that when I was moved or released I would take with me the tools I thought important and my guitar. My friends had made this guitar for me when I was in the Ambarawa camp.

The prisoners from Central and East Java were taken together by boat to the Tanjung Perak harbour in Surabaya. Captain Doctor Merapi was on board too because some of the sick ones did not want to be left behind in the Mako clinic or Namlea hospital. They preferred to die back at their own homes. In the middle of the journey we were all given suitcases with shoes and a shirt which was not a uniform – we all had different ones.

Eventually we arrived at the destination and were immediately taken to Pancasila sports arena in Surabaya. The Commander of Brawijaya Military Command welcomed us. Then, after the welcoming ceremony, we were given some money and a certificate of release which permitted us to travel to our destinations. We were instructed that when we arrived at our homes we had to report to three different regional authorities, the military (Koramil), the police (Komsek) and the sub-district (*kecamatan*) government office. We also had to attend regular '*santiaji*' sessions, which were compulsory reporting plus listening to lectures about loyalty to Pancasila and the state. Actually, having to carry that letter of release which functioned as a permit was not so different from reporting at the camp posts on Buru Island. The only difference was that now we were released and in our places of origin.

We were divided into groups, those going to Semarang and those to Yogyakarta, and taken by bus and army trucks with canopies. We arrived in Yogyakarta at three in the morning, and were immediately greeted and given more advice at the Military Command 72 until 4:30 in the morning.

No one was there to meet me. My friend Wakijo and his parents invited me to stay with them while arranging for papers for a change of address from where I lived before my arrest. The Wirobrajan military office had contacted my last address, but the person who owned the house was terrified and would not admit I had ever lived there. The Military Commander ordered me to stay temporarily at Wirobrajan military command until my papers were sorted out.

In the afternoon I went to the place I used to rent, to meet the owner. She was shocked to see me because she thought I had been dead since 1965. She greeted me warmly and so I ended up not staying at Wakijo's place or at the Wirobrajan military post. It took me two days to organise the signing of all my papers of residence at the various offices (RT, RT, MPP and Koramil). I became a permanent resident in the area of Wirobrajan. I was not allowed to leave Yogyakarta for one month, and I had to attend the 'santiaji' sessions every week at the local police station in Wirobrajan.

Then the *santiaji* courses were reduced to once a month. But we were not allowed to skip class. There were about 40 or 50 of us, all ex political prisoners from Buru whose Identity Cards had stamped on them 'ET' for Ex-Tapol' (ex political prisoner), who had to attend these sessions that ran from seven in the morning until 8:30 at night. And at the end of them we had to read out the Guidelines for Understanding and Implementing Pancasila, which were known as P4 (Pedoman Penghayatan Pengamalan Pancasila).

I stayed for a month at the house of Uncle Jayusman and his wife, who were teachers at junior and senior high school. Uncle Jayusman sent news to my mother in Blora that I had been released and was now staying with him. My mother came immediately. When we met, she asked me to go with her to Blora to attend the wedding of my younger sister. I agreed. I took the risk of leaving Yogyakarta.

When I returned to Yogyakarta, I met Hasyim who had previously also been in prison in Nusa Kambangan and then in the Ambarawa camp. He had been sent home in 1968 and was now a successful businessman. He invited me to start up a business in silver and batik painting, which were trendy at the time. We opened the Hasyim-Leo gallery. In order to learn something about batik, Hasyim sent me to Sutrisno, a batik artist who had become a businessman and the owner of the Galereas De Belas Artes.

Not long after that, the local priest in Wirobrajan, Sugiyarto, introduced me to Oni Ponirah who was also an ex prisoner, from the women's prison in Plantungan. In 1980 we married. Even though we both worked – my wife doing child care – our income still was not enough to live on and we had to ask for help. So we lived at my in-laws' house.

My wife gave birth to our first child on 12 February 1981, a daughter who we named Pipit Ambarmirah. The birth of my daughter spurred me on to get ahead in life. Sutrisno advised me to work more on my creative talents and to add to my income by helping out with poster design at the Sanggar Seni Seniman Merdeka [studio of independent artists]. And sure enough, I began to get swamped with orders for posters whenever there was a state celebration for anniversaries of major cities in Indonesia.

Actually, I was hoping to get invitations for posters outside of Yogyakarta, but as a former political prisoner I had to get permission whenever I left the city. I avoided this whole permit process, because if the studio knew of my identity as a former political prisoner, there would be unwanted consequences.

In mid 1981 my family and I rented a house in Sleman. In this new house, I started to make my own batik paintings and secured a place in the batik painting market in Yogyakarta. My income was enough to cover an extension on the rental of our house. Our second daughter was born in 1982. I named her Nilo Anjarwarih.

For the Independence Day celebrations (17 August) in 1983, a friend invited me to Jakarta to help decorate the floats for the parade. I joined the group of young artists who mounted an exhibition right in front of the dias where the president and vice-president sat. I was terrified that my identity as an ex political prisoner would be found out. My friends, the young artists, often made fun of anything connected to the Communist Party. I kept away from the media so my identity would not be discovered. I just listened and kept my mouth shut.

I also became an art teacher and taught at the Wirobrajan Christian junior high school (SMP BOPKRI, Badan Oesaha Pendidikan Kristen Republik Indonesia). I really valued the profession of teaching, even though the pay was bad. In 1985 I changed my teaching job to work with disabled children at the orphanage on the road to Kaliurang run by the Foundation of Bethesda Hospital.

Once, when my wife was staying with one of our children who was in Bethesda Hospital, she got called to attend one of the *santiaji* sessions. I went myself and asked for her to be excused because she was with our child in hospital. I was rebuked because I was there representing someone else, even though this was my wife. A few days later we got a summons and the family went to the local district office.

Another day, the Commander of the Military Command in Sleman came to our place because he had received a report from Mantrijeron Command that we had moved without getting the required permission. I was ordered to request permission to move, because ex political prisoners were not like ordinary citizens, and these were the rules. As a result, a few days later, the local village head and the local head of security who had known us for more than five years at Nologaten Catur Tunggal in Depok, Sleman, said that reluctantly he had to ask us as a family not to extend our rental on the house once the lease expired, and to move back to Mantrirejon.

This affected my business, because my batik paintings had begun to take off. I also lost the foreign students I had studying batik. Meanwhile, my batik paintings which I signed 'LEO' were already being distributed all over Europe. My paintings depicted Indonesian social life, and they were promoted in Holland, made into a coffee-table book and reviewed by a Dutch magazine. My friend Johan, a Dutchman whose wife was Indonesian, also exhibited my paintings at the Indonesian-French restaurant, in collaboration with Kusni Sulang, an Indonesian exile in Paris.

I then started to help drawing for the serial comics in *SAMIN* magazine by Moh. Farid and Yayak. The stories were about exploitation of child labour. Soon after, the contract finished and I stopped teaching the disabled children. In 1990 when the lease ran out on my house, my wife and four small children and I, were forced to move back to live with my in-laws in Mantrijeron.

The authorities in Yogyakarta continued to discriminate against political prisoners residing there. We had to continue going to the *santiaji* sessions even though in other places this was no longer required. When we asked about this, we were told 'we have not received any instruction from the central government.' The Commander of the Military Command in his briefing to us said that political prisoners were now considered to be good citizens and were given the right to vote in elections. We were required to vote for Golkar because this would continue the progress of development. I no longer went to the local authorities to arrange for travel permits. I thought the only important thing was to attend these *santiaji* sessions.

I did all kinds of work to support my family and get my children through school. I got work making posters and interior decoration at Batam, as part of Minister Habibie and Tutut Soeharto's project. Our group was made up of 20 young artists. I also once worked at Surabaya Fair. Most recently I joined an NGO in Timor Leste. I had to teach art. I worked for 18 months in the town of Same and another six months in Dili. My wife asked me not to go back to Timor Leste, but to work in Yogya and stay with her and the children.

My eldest has graduated from university now, is married, and lives in Kota Gede with her husband. My second and third children have also graduated from university, and the youngest is finishing his study at the Indonesian Institute of the Arts (Institut Seni Indonesia, ISI) in the Interior Design department. Even though my wife and I are former political prisoners who were never tried, and were inhumanely treated by the New Order, we have managed to build our lives like other citizens.

Transcriber and interviewer: Leo and Pipit Ambarmirah.

Writers: Anandito Reza B. and Putu Oka Sukanta.

Chapter 6

Lestari

My ideals for my country

This is the place I was born
Cradled and raised by my mother
The place of sanctuary in my old age
Until I take my final rest

If you want to meet Ibu Lestari in Jakarta, it is very easy. Just go to the Walujo Jati Home in Jalan Kramat V. If you don't find her there, then you might go to the offices of the National Commission for Human Rights (Komnas HAM) or the National Commission for Women's Rights (Komnas Perempuan), or the Indonesian Association of Families of the Disappeared (IKOHI, Ikatan Keluarga Orang Hilang Indonesia) or the Commission for the Disappeared and Victims of Violence (KontraS, Komisi untuk Orang hilang dan Korban Tindak Kekerasan). These institutions will definitely tell you where she is, because she is well known to them all. Ibu Lestari often attends their events in her continuing fight for her civil rights taken by the State.

Ibu Lestari is of small stature, and rather stooped, but when she speaks her voice is clear and her eyes shine bright with fire. When she was asked to talk about her life, she gave a series of interviews, as recorded below.

Village childhood

My name is Lestari and I was born in 1931 in the village of Ngawi which is in the District of Ngawi, in Madiun, East Java. During colonial times, villagers did not usually record the date of their children's births, so I do not know the month or day of my birth. I was one of the lucky ones because I got some schooling. In my village there were only three girls who got the opportunity to go to school back then.

In Dutch times, my father was a construction foreman, so he was well regarded. Because of this, it is not strange that he had two wives and fourteen children. I was the fifth child out of seven from his first wife. I have two siblings still living, the rest have died.

My first schooling was at primary school, from grades 1 to 3, together with the boys. When I started grade 4, I chose to go to the special primary school for girls. At that school, apart from general classes like geography, history, arithmetic and sport, we also got special classes like batik, sewing, weaving, knitting, crochet, cooking and ironing. It was a terrible shame that the classes that I loved had to stop because new rulers arrived, namely the Japanese fascists. The coming of the Japanese was really bad because all the materials we needed for handicraft suddenly vanished from the market after people raided all the shops.

Every morning I went to school, which was not far from my house. I would walk barefoot, because in those days being barefoot was normal. Not like today when you have to wear shoes and neat uniforms. And my school was also very simple. It was a semi-permanent structure which consisted of a few classrooms and a room for the teachers. In the classrooms there were desks and chairs for the students, a blackboard, chalk and a long ruler. There was also a cupboard for books, equipment and the crafts materials for the girls' classes. Even though it was simple, I was happy because I really loved school.

The 'older brother' spirit spread by Japanese propaganda changed the relationship between teachers and students. Whereas formerly it was distant, now it became closer. However, on the other hand the Japanese occupation interrupted the process of teaching and learning at school. Cloth for sewing, and writing materials disappeared from the market. And the time for study became more limited. We were more often herded out of school to look for caterpillars on the castor oil plants beside the road than studying in class. And there was much more physical education like gymnastics and marching.

The Japanese occupying army ordered the formation of some new organisations, one of them being the *Fujinkai* which is like our neighbourhood welfare group today (PKK). The head of the Fujinkai at the village level was usually the wife of the village head (*lurah*), and that is how it was in my village. But the lurah's wife was illiterate, and so I was asked to accompany her in the Fujinkai meetings at district level. This was my first experience of being in an organisation. At that time I had just finished my primary schooling. I had to write down notes from the meetings and also get the girls of the village together for marching lessons.

When I finished primary school for girls, I went on to study at the higher primary school (Sekolah Rakyat Sempurna II) which was an amalgamation of Taman Siswa and Mardi Siswa. [Indonesian education movement. Trs]. Among the teachers there were some who were nationalists (the 'Taman Siswa group) and some who tended more towards the Dutch curriculum. I was one of the active students at school. I was often given leadership tasks. Sadly, when I finished this school I was forced to end my schooling. One of the reasons was that during the Japanese occupation, my family's finances were very difficult. Indeed, at that time, almost everyone in Indonesia experienced shortages of food and clothing. This is why this period is called the time of famine. Every day, my family and other people in the village had to eat *tiwul*, which is dried cassava that is pounded, steamed, and eaten with grated coconut. In the morning, breakfast was the crust left when you cook rice in a pot, again eaten with grated coconut. Because it was difficult to find any cloth, I remember we had to wear clothes made out of old mosquito nets. One of my uncles became a *romusha*, namely a forced labourer. Usually, the romusha were sent to work in the mines, and most of them never returned.

The other reason I had to leave school was because my stepmother wanted me – as a girl – to work in the kitchen. My stepmother, my father's second wife, had become my replacement mother since I was five when my own mother died giving birth to my youngest sister. Sadly, my stepmother could not understand my love of education.

My oldest brother was the first person to instill in me the importance for girls of education and a broad outlook. He was a graduate of Taman Siswa, and in the Dutch times he began teaching reading and writing to young people in our village. Every week he would give me one cent to take out books from a library run by a clerk in the information office. I would always take out books of folk stories. The library was at his house. It was very simple. There were not many books. Even though it was simple, it was tremendously useful for the children, including me, and I went there regularly to borrow books.

My oldest brother was also the first person to introduce me to the idea of nationalism. Back then, the only history lessons we got at primary school taught us about ancient Javanese kings. But my brother taught me other, more inspiring history. He taught me the nationalist anthem *Indonesia Raya*. He also introduced me to the pioneer of education and equality for women, Ibu Kartini, and it was he who encouraged me and my older sister to commemorate Kartini's birthday. He gave us five cents to make a yellow rice cone with an omelette. Then we gathered the village girls together. My brother then talked and told them all who Kartini was and what she had done.

It was only later, when I became active in Gerwani (Gerakan Wanita Indonesia, the Indonesian Women's Movement) in 1951 that I really understood my brother's words and his purpose. I respected Ibu Kartini even more. The more I became involved in organisations, the more I got to know other nationalist figures, like Ki Hadjar Dewantara, the founder of Taman Siswa and a major figure in the nationalist education movement.

When I finished upper primary school, my time was completely taken up with domestic chores and helping in the garden, and I got no further opportunity to advance my knowledge. I began to get bored. I wanted some other experience. I also wanted to be independent, particularly because my relationship with my stepmother was not good. So I decided to look for work in Surabaya, East Java, following the advice of a friend who had already gone there and found work. In 1950, after convincing my older brother and getting a small sum of money, I set off for Surabaya. I went by bus, carrying just a few basic things. I decided to leave home and look for work, so I could be independent and not have to answer to anyone.

Away from home and joining organisations

A friend of mine helped me get work as a child minder for a family in Bojonegoro, East Java. It was through this job that I got to know members of the Communist Party, and through them I got to know organisations. The house where I worked was also the office of the Bojonegoro branch of the Communist Party. My job was to serve coffee and cakes at every party meeting. Because of this, I used to hear snippets of their conversation. Over time, I became more curious. Every time I took in the coffee, I would try to sit outside the room where they were meeting so I could listen to the discussions. I was really impressed with a woman teacher who was very clever at making speeches. Her name was Bu Warmi. I thought to myself, I want to be like her.

One day in 1951, Bu Warmi invited me to take part in a congress. Because of my curiosity and because I was so impressed with her, I went along. I was so happy and proud to be able to take part in that congress. It turned out that it was a congress of a women's organisation called Gerwis, (Gerakan Wanita Sedar. Movement of Alert Women). This was the beginning of the establishment of what was later called Gerwani, (Gerakan Wanita Indonesia, the Indonesian Women's Movement). I had gone knowing absolutely nothing at all about what was going to be discussed at the congress. I was probably the youngest member in the Bojonegoro group. Apart from our group there were also groups from other places like Tuban and Lamongan. We all stayed at the Penilih hotel in Surabaya. While we attended the congress we went everywhere by becak (pedicab).

The congress was led by Ibu S.K Trimurti (who was a Minister of Labour during the Soekarno era), Bu Wati, Bu Sri from Solo, Ibu Darini, and others. My youthful spirit of nationalism was really fired up. I could take part in a congress that I saw as incredibly important for my gender. One item on the agenda at the congress that really interested me was polygamy. I knew from personal experience just how awful it was to be a child whose father was polygamous, and who was forced to be brought up by a stepmother. Polygamy affected the children badly. And when I was older, I also often heard stories about how my mother had suffered when my father took his second wife.

But it was only at the congress that I better understood that polygamy was an unjust practice for women. And women had to be brave enough to fight for it to be wiped out. Another agenda item that impressed me was something that had long bothered me, namely women's poverty. At the place where I stayed, every morning very early I often saw market women bent double with loads of charcoal and firewood walking to the market.

This sight always made me feel sorry for them, and also ask what, exactly, were the root causes of their poverty and oppression. When I went home after the congress I was given many books to read, and I realised that the root of the Indonesian people's poverty was colonisation. Poverty had to be broken with education. After taking part in the Gerwis congress I was more convinced that this organisation was right for me. I wanted to fight to improve the destiny of Indonesian people who were still oppressed, particularly women, through Gerwis. And in Gerwis I also found a strong sense of solidarity. This sense of solidarity never wavered, even when later we were all imprisoned. And it was also my Gerwis friends who cared for me after I was released from prison.

When I got home from the congress, Bu Warmi started encouraging me to learn about organisational matters. I studied the Gerwis statutes and bylaws. I helped to distribute the decisions of the congress, and to recruit new members. The Gerwis recruiting was done by a kind of roadshow from village to village. In this way, the support of village women for Gerwis kept increasing, compared to other women's organisations. When we went into an entirely new village, we would work together with another existing organisation there like BTI (Barisan Tani Indonesia, the Indonesian Peasants Front) or Sarbuksi (Serikat Buruh Kehutanan Seluruh Indonesia, the All Indonesia Union of Plantation Workers). Sometimes we would begin the familiarisation process with a talk for women in the village hall. Two topics that always attracted the interest of village women were campaigns against polygamy and child marriage. After the talk, we would follow up with door-to-door visits to everyone who had attended. That way we could meet the village women directly and exchange ideas with them.

Once people were interested, usually the women themselves would spread news to others. When there was a group of ten, we would form a branch and then immediately hold some activity we thought was right for that area. Apart from Gerwis's campaigning against polygamy and child marriage, there was also a literacy campaign, fairs to sell things made by women, and *arisan*, which are traditional gatherings of women where all participants contribute an amount of money and the winner of a lottery gets all the money. All events were shared and voluntary. For instance, a family with a larger house might provide the place, and the others would bring chairs, tables, people to help and so on. After Gerwis became Gerwani, it managed to have a representative in the Religious Affairs Office (Kantor Usuran Agama) as an advisor alongside representatives from other women's organisations.

We also held talks in the villages to explain to members the reason that certain organisations were opposing the Round Table Conference which was disadvantaging Indonesia. We also explained to them about the National Front and the Crush Malaysia campaign. We made a curriculum to fight illiteracy. In drawing up this curriculum, we used words that women are familiar with in their everyday lives and which had become part of the organisation's programs, for instance anti-polygamy, distribution of produce and so forth. To further develop their capacity to think, every member of Gerwani was required to read the organisation's bulletin. We would include news about the development of the organisation in various areas which could be used as models for other areas.

In 1952 I was chosen as the head of Gerwani for Bojonegoro. I was just 22 years old, more or less. After working for seven years, I was taken to join Gerwani's Regional Leadership Committee (DPD, Dewan Pimpinan Daerah) for East Java, headquartered in Surabaya. As board member, I was increasingly busy, and often had to visit other areas in East Java and Madura on a program called *turba* (*turun ke bawah*, going to the grassroots). All DPD members were required to '*turba*' and follow the principle called 'the three togethers' (*tiga bersama*): work together, eat together, and sleep together with the peasants. Many of the Gerwani members were peasants. So, when the Indonesian Peasants Front (BTI) launched its action demanding a fairer distribution of produce, Gerwani joined. Gerwani also worked together with SOBSI (Serikat Organisasi Buruh Seluruh Indonesia, All-Indonesia Trade Union Federation) in demanding a reduction of the price of basic daily necessities.

In Surabaya I met a widower called Suradi. He was a Communist Party functionary. We got to know each other. There was a twelve year difference in our ages. We got to know each other slowly, and fell in love. In 1962 we married. I was already 30 or so by then, but I had been totally occupied in activities for the people. At the time we married, we were considered to have married very late. I indeed had been too busy and too much enamoured with my work to think there was any rush to marry. In our marriage, although we both were working, our life remained simple.

Once I bought a blouse on credit and wore it to a function at the Governor's offices to celebrate Independence Day. My husband asked, 'how much did you pay for that blouse?' I said 'I got it on credit'. He wasn't angry, but the next day he gave me some money to go and pay off the blouse and advised me never to have debts because this was a bad habit and would later be a burden to the family. My husband was not the type who liked to get angry just because I did something he didn't like. He would give me his views and advise me what I should do. We lived together as husband and wife very happily, giving each other mutual support in our organisational work and at home.

We were blessed with four children: Hernowo, Dani, Indah and Nani. One day my husband came home bringing a lighter from a friend who had just returned from the People's Republic of China. I thought the lighter was great, and my husband was very pleased with it because it was a gift from his friend. The next day the lighter was nowhere to be found and I asked the eldest, Hernowo, half accusingly, 'where is your father's lighter?' He was silent. That night, after the children were asleep, I wondered how I should have acted. The next morning my son Hernowo came and gave me back the lighter which he had taken to bits. Seeing this, my husband was not angry with Hernowo, but instead he was pleased to see his curiosity, and said this was the sign of a clever child.

We shared the housework. My husband would draw the household water from the well every day, and I would cook and bathe the children. It was very important to us that we divided the domestic chores, not only between the two of us but also with the children. Dani, the second son, was in charge of the garden. Every morning my husband and I would leave for the office together, because it saved money for me to get a ride on my husband's bicycle, and we would come back home together in the evening. If my husband still had work to do, I would get a ride with other friends heading in my direction, or occasionally take a *becak* (pedicab). But I couldn't ride a *becak* every day because I didn't earn enough for that. What I found so pleasing about having married an activist was that we would exchange ideas about our respective organisations. I learnt a lot from my husband about the Marxist concept of dialectic materialism which helped sharpen my understanding and analysis of people's problems.

Torn apart and living hand-to-mouth

I heard on the radio about the military take-over; what came to be known as G30S. As the day went on, the situation became more tense. My husband was out of town at the time, he had been away on work matters for two days. Because the situation was becoming more tense by the moment and things were getting out of control, everywhere the news discredited the Communist Party. My husband went into hiding some time in 1966 in a village in south Blitar in East Java. At that time, the only way my husband and I could be in contact was via a courier. In the city, members of Gerwani, the Communist Party or organisations now considered illegal had no space to move. Every single day the Brawijaya Division Military Region Commander (Pangdam) would give speeches urging the arrest of 'communist' and 'leftist' activists. Members of Gerwani were in total disarray. Many activists in the outlying regions were arrested, disappeared and murdered. The rivers near Kediri were full of corpses. But for the time being the atmosphere in the city did not change. Only in certain places you could see the military always on guard. Those of us being hunted down could really sense the increasing power of the military.

One of my husband's friends warned me to be careful and to leave the house as soon as possible. My feelings at the time were a mixture of sadness, fear, and anxiety. I had four young children then, and my husband was not with us. Hernowo was in the fifth class of primary school, Dani in the second class, our third child Indah was just five years old, and the youngest Nani was only 18 months. I left my three oldest children, Hernowo, Dani and Indah with the elderly woman who helped in the house. I left home taking the baby, and went to the house of my cousin who worked as a civil servant in the army, to ask for advice. He advised me to stay and hide in his house. Meanwhile, my housekeeper took the other three children to her own house. And my husband's friend's warning was right, because just three days after my children and I left, an army truck ambushed my house.

From then on I lived on the run, moving around Surabaya from one friend's house to another. Once, my baby and I had to overnight in a storage shed for chicken feed and kerosene. Wherever we hid, we never stayed for more than two days. During the day we would have to hide indoors. At night, usually around 8, we would move to the next hiding place, taken by a courier. My family who sheltered me covered my living costs while I was in hiding. I tried to help as best as I could by doing work around the house to repay their kindness.

During this time, I had no contact with my three older children. Every now and then my housekeeper would come and bring me some news. Hernowo had to help her picking swamp spinach to sell in the market to earn some money. Because my housekeeper was finding the financial burden increasingly difficult, she decided to take Hernowo and Indah to their grandmother's place, my mother-in-law that is. My housekeeper took Dani with her to her home kampung in Malang. So my family was split up; I was moving from one place to another, my son Hernowo and daughter Indah were with their grandmother, my daughter Dani was with my housekeeper in Malang, and I had no idea where my husband was. As a result of this, my son Hernowo did not get a proper schooling. He had to quit school. And the same thing happened to my second child. I was very sad about this because my hopes were to give my children the highest education possible. My third child, though, was able to graduate from junior technical high school.

One day in late 1966 I got a message from my husband telling me to move to a village in south Blitar. I went by bus with the person sent to bring me from Surabaya to Blitar. I had no idea that the remnants of the Communist Party in Blitar were forming a rebel movement. I had no opportunity to ask my courier any questions. The most important thing to me was to save myself because it was becoming increasingly dangerous to stay in the city. The south of Blitar was still a very isolated, poor area. It had once been the base of the people's army (Barisan Tentara Rakyat) during the Indonesian revolution for independence.

The village house where I stayed was actually the home of relatively well-off people. Well off meant having a house with a tiled roof and wooden walls, and owning many coconut palms. Even so, life there was still backward. There were no such things as stoves for cooking, and they ate only dried cassava, not rice. I had to adapt to this life in a very short time. I had to walk barefoot everywhere, including moving to a hiding place that was two days' walk away. But with all this hardship, together with some friends hiding out in the same village, we managed to form a play group for the village children. Even though we were on the run, I gathered the children from the houses around to play and to learn. I taught them children's songs, how to count up to ten, and gave them lessons in good manners.

In South Blitar I managed to meet my husband a few times. I ended up pregnant with our fifth child. Because it would be impossible for me to look after a baby, I decided to give the baby, a daughter, to a childless couple. They changed her name. It turned out that this couple then got frightened because of the military propaganda about arresting anyone harbouring Gerwani activists. So they just left my baby in a graveyard. Fortunately, she survived. A soldier found her at the gates of the cemetery, and rescued her. The soldier was also frightened, and gave the baby to the local headmaster. The headmaster, also frightened, gave the baby to a family that sold fruit in the market. It was these fruit sellers who brought up my daughter. Later, when I was released, I managed to go and see her. This was a deeply moving reunion. We embraced and cried together.

It turned out it was not this child that I lost, but my daughter Nani who had been with me on the run. Just before I was arrested, I left Nani with a friend who was hiding me. I later heard that the army set fire to her house and everything in it, and from that moment on I lost every trace of my daughter Nani. To this day I still live in hope that we might meet again.

In August 1968, I was arrested along with some colleagues. This was when the army was closing in on South Blitar. They set up guard posts all over the place, especially at village entrances and exits. They would often ransack the villagers' houses. Every few days, the people would have to gather in the middle of the village for lectures on how evil and bad the Communist Party was. There was a military operation to hunt down and round up anyone on the run. The army had about 10,000 civilian paramilitary assisting them. Two of my friends and I made plans to escape. A young man from the village who acted as our courier was helping us. Very early in the morning he took us to a cave on the sea shore, which I had never known about. The cave was called a *ruba*. But unfortunately one of the women could not walk fast enough, and so it was already daybreak before we got there. We had not realised that a squad from the 527 Battalion together with some paramilitary were standing on the edge of the cliff, and had been observing us. They had deliberately not interfered because they wanted to know our hiding place.

When they thought they knew enough, they started firing at us. My friend's husband died instantly. So we finally decided to come out of the cave and surrender. We were dragged to the top of the cliff, pulled up using women's wrap-around waist bands (*setagen*). When we got to the top, they tied our two thumbs together using a very strong type of thread. That was to make it difficult for us to run away.

We were taken to the village guardpost and the army commander told us to eat. We slept there one night, and then were taken to the larger district guardpost. There I met seven other women who had been arrested before us. After staying there for one week, we were taken with armoured car escort to the headquarters of the Military Police (CPM, Corps Polisi Militer) in Malang. This is where our interrogation started. In short, we were ordered to confess that we were members of the Communist Party and were involved in the murders of the generals at Lubang Buaya in Jakarta. And I had never been to Jakarta in my life. I was, though, a member of both the Communist Party and Gerwani. After my friends and I had been interrogated, we were sent to the women's prison in Malang. As a result of the interrogation, I was classified as Group B, which had no meaning to me. All I knew was that Group A was considered to be the most dangerous, Group B the relatively dangerous, and group C the less dangerous.

My prison cell measured about 5 x 5 meters and had eight inmates. The walls were thick, as it was a building from colonial times. To look out of the cell, there was just one window which was high up above the door. In front of our cell there was a dedicated guard. For the first three years I slept on a mat. Each of us got one mat. We were not given any blankets, so to keep out of the Malang cold we had to cuddle up together. This was the only way to keep warm. It was only close to our release, following a visit from the International Red Cross, that we were issued with mattresses, pillows and blankets.

Our breakfast every day was ground corn. Each person got four spoons, placed on an orange plate. If we got boiled corn, usually one serving was 16 or 17 kernels. This was served with grated coconut. We got rice only at lunchtime. Sometimes we got four spoons, at other times eight spoons of rice per person. This was served with boiled marrow with carrots or water spinach. Sometimes we were given vegetables cooked with a bit of coconut milk. To stave off hunger, we would look for our own food, especially sugar and palm sugar for energy, by selling our knitting and crochet to the prison guards.

We were treated differently to other prisoners – the eight of us housed together and isolated because we were considered to be dangerous to others.

We were given only 15 minutes out of our cell to bathe and move around. Apart from that, we were given one hour outside every day, when the other prisoners were at work outside the prison, and we used this time to play badminton, and plant spinach and tomatoes as extra food supply. The whole time in detention we were not allowed to read. This felt like real oppression because we had no idea of what was going on outside the prison walls. So we worked out a way to collaborate with the mainstream prisoners. They would bring in bits of the newspaper and hide them in the back bathroom. We prisoners in the isolation cell were not allowed any communication with other political prisoners. The only thing we could do was call out their names when we walked past.

To pass the long hours in the cell, we would knit or crochet, and anyone who knew a foreign language would teach it to the others. Or we would just joke: we would imagine the beams in the ceiling turning into chocolate and us feasting on it to our heart's content. Sometimes we would talk, trying to understand why we had been treated this way. But we could never find the answers, and that is what tortured us the most, apart from being separated from our families.

All in all, the prison wardens treated us well enough. There was only one incident when they pulled out the spinach we had planted, so we had to protest by singing the 'Internationale' to get the attention of the prison director. Twice while I was in prison I was permitted to meet my husband who was being held in Sampang. His condition was dreadful, as a result of torture. He had a heart condition, and he eventually died while performing his morning prayers during fasting month.

My husband was arrested, tried, sentenced to death and imprisoned at Sampang, Madura. But before the execution was carried out, he died of a heart condition. One day the prison wardens forced me to choose a religion. Before this, my husband and I had never given religion much thought. But because of the situation, I decided to become Christian (Protestant). I saw that it was mainly the Christians who sent us things in prison. My friends and I ended up spending 11 years in that prison isolation cell. I was released on 31 December, 1979.

Even after my release I still had to report regularly to the authorities. These 'reporting in' sessions consisted of us having to listen to lectures called '*santiaji*'. This went on for a few years. After that, I went to Surabaya looking for work so I could support myself. I worked as a child-carer. I changed employment quite a few times, usually working for Chinese families over a period of ten years as a child carer. I eventually stopped this work because I l did not have the strength for it. You have to be strong to look after children, and then there are times they are sick and you have to stay up with them all night. My employers did not know my background, even though my identity card was stamped with ET (Ex-Tapol, ex political prisoner). I was deliberately vague, because I was always afraid they would sack me. Luckily, none of my employers ever looked closely at my identity card.

Because I had not lived together with my own children, my relationship with them was cool. Their spouses, too, were uncomfortable if I stayed in their homes for too long, because of my status as an ex political prisoner. To me, this was the most painful thing of all. Even so, I did not want to be a burden to my children. I wanted them to have a calm life, and because of this I decided to live together with my old friends. It is they who truly understand me and with whom I have a strong sense of solidarity. Now I live in an old people's home in Jakarta. I heard through an old friend I met back in Malang that there was an old people's home in Jakarta that had opened for former political prisoners. Because I lived alone, I thought this would be a good idea for me. I decided to contact my old friend who runs this home. In the end, I moved and now I live in this home with other ex detainees.

These days I devote my life to work for the expression of truth. I love my motherland and my people. As long as I am in good health, I never turn down invitations to attend discussions or seminars organised by the various institutes for human rights. I was invited to Japan in 2004 along with other victims of state violence from South Africa and Chile. I am also willing to help out victims of human rights abuse, and this is why I do not want to stop the fight. I enjoy telling my story and struggle to anyone who comes and requests an interview at the old people's home or at other places. I am happy that there is a young generation that cares about their nation's history. My duties are not over yet!

Interviewers and transcribers: Team from ISSI (Institut Sejarah Sosial Indonesia, Indonesian Institute of Social History).
Writer: Rini P.

Chapter 7

Luh Sutari

Plaiting stories

Ni Luh Sutari is around 60. Her wrinkled fingers skillfully plait young coconut palms. She makes squares that will be used for religious offerings called *canang* that hold flowers, incense and other things. At a glance you would not think her any different from other Balinese women her age. She makes dozens, even hundreds of *canang* for family offerings and ceremonies; cooks, tidies the house and looks after her grandchild. The activities of her husband, Wayan Partha, might be considered a little more unusual. He makes herbal potions for his alternative medicine and acupuncture practice. Something you would never guess from a brief meeting with Ni Luh Sutari is the memories she keeps of a series of tragic events she experienced more than fifty years ago. Hers is just one of thousands of heartbreaking stories from the time when Bali was in the grip of the darkness of the political turbulence of 1965. This was when there were massacres of tens of thousands of people considered to be sympathisers or supporters of the Indonesian Communist Party, including her oldest brother and other relatives.

Sutari managed to survive. But her life subsequent to the six years that immediately followed the terrifying event is like the second act in a tragedy which remains close to her and has left a lasting impression. It is like an ongoing nightmare, but one that really happened.

While plaiting the offerings, Sutari tells her story, every now and then massaging her leg which hurts because she fell near the house altar. She tells her story of the past, but every now and then jumps to the present. Her voice is quiet, almost a whisper, but full of emotion, and every now and then she chuckles. Her fingers continue to plait the young bamboo leaves, and it is as though she is plaiting her memories of the past, one by one.

Ni Luh Sutari was born to a farming family in Blahbatuh, Giyanar. She was the seventh of eleven children. Two older siblings died as babies. Back then, her parents were relatively progressive in their ways, and sent their children to school. Her oldest brother, who was later murdered in 1965, even became a primary school teacher. Sutari herself, or Tari as she was known, did not manage to finish junior high school. 'I was at junior high school but could not continue because I was afraid with all the taunting ...' To Sutari and others labelled 'red', this was more than just teasing. The verbal attack was a kind of terror that resulted in a profound psychological trauma for those who survived. Sometimes the taunts would be accompanied by physical violence, like being chased, tortured or killed.

Sutari was indeed raised in a 'red' family, a label used at the time for people with 'leftist' leanings. The dichotomy of 'right' and 'left' ideologies was not something that young Sutari understood. What she, and the majority of Balinese understood at the time was that 'red' meant you were a Communist Party (PKI) sympathiser and 'black' meant you sympathised with the Indonesian National Party (PNI). These were the two largest political parties in Bali in the early 1960s. Her oldest brother, who was a teacher, was one of the Communist Party figures in their village. Her older sister was a member of Gerwani [Indonesian Women's Movement] and her husband was a leader in the Barisan Tani Indonesia [Indonesian Peasants Front].

The political climate at the time encouraged everyone to choose a political party and affiliation. 'If you didn't choose one, you were considered wishy-washy', she said, chuckling. Even in the first year of junior high school, almost all the students would join a student organisation that was associated with a political party. And Sutari did too. But she did something unusual. She wanted to be different to her older brothers and sisters who were all 'red', and so she decided to join the student organisation that leaned towards the National Party, namely the GSNI (Gerakan Siswa Nasional Indonesia, Indonesian National High School Students Movement). 'I joined the GSNI because I wanted to be different. My sister Runi was already in Gerwani, she was even a leader ...' Sutari said, referring to her elder sister Wayan Mandra. It turned out that her father and her siblings respected her choice. The choice of different political affiliations never caused any problems in the family. The house was always busy with meetings and choirs, and even though Sutari did not join in, she enjoyed the sense of community and family.

After the events of 30 September 1965, the current of political turbulence spread like a huge wave that engulfed every corner, including the island of Bali. To Balinese who had some political awareness, the tensions and competition between political parties could not be avoided, it was absolutely everywhere. This time, the turbulence was like lighting the fuse of a huge bomb that exploded in the middle of society and totally destroyed the existing order, right to the villages. Victims fell who had no connection at all to that political conflict.

So it was in Sutari's normally quiet neighbourhood. Around mid-December 1965, people started pelting with stones the houses in the village of people considered to be 'red', or setting them on fire. Like the mass extermination of rats in the rice fields, people began to hunt, beat and kill those people considered to be Communist Party members or sympathisers. Some people were dragged from their homes, paraded around and then taken to the village graveyard. Before their death, they had a chance to see the hole dug for their mass grave. About 14 people died in her neighbourhood (*banjar*). Among them were two of Sutari's cousins who were murdered at the onset of the chaos.

Sutari never knew who the people doing the burning, hunting and torture that happened almost every night, were. Some of them were a gang, dressed all in black and carrying short swords. They were called *tameng*. Sometimes, they were neighbours, friends, even close relatives, or people no one knew and no one knew where they came from. 'The ones who came to my house were wearing army camouflage, and they carried guns', Sutari recalled.

While this tragedy was going on in her village, Sutari was facing terror and pressure at school. She was tagged 'red' like her older brother and sister, and taunted by friends and even people in the street she did not know. They did not care that Sutari was a member of GSNI. Although she had been a member of this organisation for three months, she had not yet been recorded in the files, but had been an extremely active and enthusiastic participant in their activities and meetings. Sutari guessed that someone had told people that her brother was the Communist Party leader in Blahbatuh. Luckily for Sutari, a geometry teacher at the school defended her. 'Leave her alone, she is one of us, she is a member of GSNI', she said. 'I was afraid to go home to Tojan', Sutari explained. 'I did not want to continue school, and that is why I never finished junior high school'. She left the home of her relative where she was boarding while attending school in Denpasar and went back to the village, a 30 kilometre journey, getting a ride on a truck that stopped on the street.

Sutari arrived back home in her village. The situation was still chaotic. Her father, Ketut Liku, was afraid that his house would be torched. So he put a bed at his neighbour's place so there would be a place for Sutari and the other children to sleep if their house was set on fire. He did not realise that this move would have unfortunate consequences.

> A relative told one of those guys wearing army camouflage that father had stored a bed. They came and questioned Father as to why he had done that, and he said it was so his children would have somewhere to sleep if the house was set on fire.

This answer infuriated the guy in army drills, and Father was beaten unconscious. Sutari clearly remembers how her father was prodded with a rifle butt and made to get up, staggering. It was the children's innocence that saved the day. Seeing the four children cowering with fear on the bed, they did not set fire to Ketut Liku's house.

However, Sutari's older brother and sister were not so lucky. Her sister, Made Seruni, escaped murder because she was pregnant with her first child. But her husband, Komang Sarjana, was arrested and taken away by closed truck. According to stories in the village, he was taken to the area of Masceti beach and murdered there. As for Wayan Mandra, Sutari's oldest brother, he was killed at Padang Bai.

> Even after things started going crazy at home, my brother managed to come home from Padang Bai where he was teaching. When I asked him, he said he was safe because his friend had given him the buffalo symbol [of the PNI. Trs]. Wayan Mandra had requested some kind of travel document to return to Padang Bai, from a friend of his, Tama, who was village head at the time. Tama said to him 'I haven't got a travel permit, but I have a death permit'.

Without paying much attention to this, Wayan Mandra left the village and returned to Padang Bai.

Ketut Liku got the story of what happened next to his son from a young girl who said she witnessed what happened to Mandra. A few days after Wayan Mandra arrived at Padang Bai, Tama and another man came to pick him up saying that they had to take him back to the village for his safety. Without being in the least suspicious, Wayan Mandra went along. It was on that journey that he was murdered.

In less than four months, Sutari had lost two members of her family and four relatives in the tragedy that took place from late 1965. But it was her father who felt the greatest loss in the death of Wayan Mandra, his eldest son in whom he had such pride, a clever young man who was such an example to his younger siblings, to his father and to those around him. He was the hope of the family. To make it worse, the death of his oldest son was the result of the treachery of one of his own friends.

Ketut Liku's sadness led to deep depression. When Sutari told of her father's pain at the death of his son, she was moved with emotion.

> Father would often lose his senses, and ask himself why wasn't it him who died, why was it Wayan Mandra who was still young and clever … and he would go on and on like this …

Sutari said, her eyes welling with tears. It is not clear whether Ketut Liku even realised that after the death of his oldest child and after the terrifying chaos subsided, his daughter Ni Luh Sutari still had to live under the dark shadow of the 1965 tragedy. Her subsequent suffering took the form of her marriage to one of the paramilitary *tameng*. The tragedy was nowhere near over for Sutari.

Less than six years after the events of December 1965, a relative introduced her to Darmawan who came from Blangsinga. From the outset, Sutari knew that Darmawan was a *tameng*. But he was the one she ended up marrying in 1971 when she was just 18. Her father never agreed to the marriage. Ketut Liku reminded his daughter about her brother's murder. 'If you want to marry, then marry someone following the same path of struggle as us, not a *tameng*. Remember, your brother followed this path until his death.' But Sutari was stubborn and remained firm in her decision. Apart from thinking that if she married Darmawan she would be safe and life would be calm, she had also fallen in love with him.

So she married without her father's blessing. It was an older brother – the third child in the family – who represented his father at the wedding. Darmawan then immediately took Sutari with him to Lombok. Over the next three years, Sutari's life with Darmawan made her realise that her father's fear and worry were right. Her husband liked gambling and womanising. He was once surrounded by an army platoon because he had been having an affair with the one of the soldier's wives. When he lost at gambling, it was always Sutari who was the target of his anger. He would beat her and drag her around. Once he threw a machete at her, but luckily Sutari ducked and the machete hit a cupboard.

But what hurt Sutari the most was her husband's verbal abuse. 'You're just Gerwani, and I could kill you right now …!' This is one threat of his she remembers. Darmawan would always bring up the fact that Sutari could not have children, even though she had been pregnant a few times and suffered miscarriages. She wasn't sure whether it was the way her husband treated her that caused the miscarriages. She asked her husband for a divorce many times, but could never understand and still can't, why he threatened to kill himself if Sutari left him. Her haunting thoughts about this bloodthirsty former *tameng* who had killed many people and could at any time even kill his own wife, made her determined to find a way to leave Lombok as soon as she could.

Eventually, after three years suffering her husband's abuse, Sutari got the courage to ask Darmawan's permission for her to go home to Bali, saying she had to attend the commemorative cremation ceremony of her brother, Wayan Mandra. He refused at first, but finally allowed her to go. When Ketut Liku saw his daughter return home, he was both moved and anxious. He felt that Sutari was still too young to understand what she was going through. His greatest worry was that his daughter would agree to go back if Darmawan came to Bali to get her.

As it turned out Ketut Liku did not have to worry. Sutari never returned to Lombok. She decided to sell tomatoes and eggs and to take a sewing course in Denpasar. Darmawan never came to look for her. Sutari's courage grew as time went on. In July 1975, she decided to divorce Darmawan. This was a brave decision, and also ended her nightmare of being trapped in the dark shadows of a political tragedy, years after that tragedy had occurred. Actually she had been very young at the time and did not ever really understand what was going on, and was certainly not involved in any political conflict. To her, the cruelty was not directed to affiliation with any political parties or ideology. She was not 'red', yet could not free herself of the tragedy.

Meeting Wayan Partha, her current husband, is the part of the story that makes Sutari smile. At the time, her father was suffering back pain, was stooped over and could not walk. Wayan Susila, a relative from the village who had been a political prisoner in 1968 in Pekambingan prison, introduced Wayan Partha to Sutari's family as an expert in acupuncture, and also as a friend he got to know in prison. He was imprisoned because in his youth he had been a member of IPPI (Ikatan Pemuda dan Pelajar Indonesia, League of Indonesian Youth and Students). He acquired his skill in acupuncture while he was in prison. Many people testified to the results of his treatment, especially his fellow inmates, and he was often asked to treat family members of the military or prison guards, without any payment of course.

When he got out of prison in 1978, he worked for a while at a travel agency. When he met Sutari, he was already 30. 'I thought he must have a wife, and at least two children. I blushed when he said he was still a bachelor', Sutari recounted, with a chuckle and a blush in her cheeks.

Ketut Liku's back pain vanished after a few treatments. Wayan Partha and Sutari became friends, and they ended up getting married in 1978. This time, Ketut Liku gave his blessing and was happy to have a son-in-law who he saw as being on the same path of struggle as himself. 'Partha knew everything about my past and even when I said I probably could not have children, he did not mind', Sutari said.

Sutari finds it hard not to be impressed by Wayan Partha. He is very artistic, and made an embossed painting of the island of Bali which still hangs in a prominent travel agency office in Bali. His revolutionary spirit has never flagged, even though he spent time behind bars. In the 1990s, he was a member of the personnel staff of a five star hotel in Bali. He managed to get the hotel staff to form a union. Now, in his retirement he has decided to devote himself to acupuncture. This gives him many opportunities to help people in need.

Wayang Partha and Ni Luh Sutari are two people drawn together by similar history. This is not a past anyone wants to remember, but it makes them able to accept one another as they are. Wayan Partha has also been able to slowly heal Sutari's past trauma, which still at times plagues her physically and psychologically. Her father's deep sorrow at the death of his son and her own bitter past with her first husband, still often give her nightmares.

These days, Ni Luh Sutari and her husband live right beside his family in Denpasar. They live in a typical Balinese compound with various buildings for different households. They adopted one of Wayan Partha's nephews, and from him they have a grand-daughter who they are extremely fond of. Whereas many former political prisoners later had to cope with discrimination from their families, Wayang Partha and Ni Luh Sutari are probably among the lucky ones in that many of their family were also 'red'.

> No one in the family or among our neighbours ever directly drags up our past, but many people know about it, because every time there was an election, we had to attend a 'Santiaji' or propaganda course, and we were ordered to join Golkar … I don't know what they say behind our backs …

There are many things Sutari wants to talk about. She meets some friends now and then who have gone through similar things, or her husband's friends from prison, and these are times when she can talk about her difficult memories. But there are some memories that she stores tightly, that appear now and then in her dreams about her father, or in her tearless sobs.

As Sutari finished telling her story, she looked out of the large window in the sitting room and saw her husband Wayan Partha moving from the pavilion used for family ceremonies, in the part of the compound planted with shrubs and flowers. He was coming over to do some acupuncture on Sutari's leg. Smiling and moving her painful leg, Sutari whispered, 'since I married Partha, I have stayed right here, and never wanted to go anywhere else'.

Now in her sixties, Luh Sutari continues to plait young coconut leaves. When she tells the chapters of her story it is as though she is weaving together the fronds of memory. She is weaving a tray, a place where she arranges her prayers for old age and her hopes for the future generation; including her hope that what she experienced in the past will never happen again, to anyone.

Interviewer and transcriber: Roro Sawita.

Writer: Roro Sawita.

Chapter 8

Nadue

Always loyal to my country

The events of 30 September 1965 completely destroyed Nadue's future as a teacher of young girls.

On the 24th November 2010, a small group of us studying Women and Culture, made up of Ina, Pulu and Papa Pius, rode motorbikes to Kampung Keka. We went through guava plantations along the Para River and eventually came to a beautiful platform house. We asked the woman there for directions to the house of Mama Nadue, and as luck would have it, this woman was Mama Nadue's daughter. Her name was Edo. It turned out that Edo had been Ina's friend when they were both at junior high school. Edo was extremely surprised to see us, and immediately went to call her mother who was taking a bath in the river in front of the house. We were invited to sit on the back verandah. About fifteen minutes later, Nadue arrived wearing a casual dress with red flower patterns and her hair still wet. We greeted each other in the Sabu way, touching noses. Ina looked at Nadue, her body and face thin, but her eyes alert and sharp, even though it seemed she bore a heavy burden. She seemed fit. Ina said that she remembered that in her childhood Mama Nadue was known as an excellent teacher of algebra and English. The gathering was a reunion between Nadue, Ina and Papa Pius, especially between Ina and Edo who had not met since they finished junior high school in 1980. Papa Pius, our translator, introduced himself and explained to Nadue the purpose of our visit. When Ina introduced herself, Nadue immediately asked after Ina's mother-in-law.

Nadue eagerly talked about her childhood from the time she was adopted by the Soleman family – moving between Rote, Baun and Kupang and attending primary school at Airnona and Bonipoi. She then went on to vocational high school for teachers (Sekolah Guru Atas, SGA) in Kupang. She spoke about the physical abuse she suffered from her aunt, Martha Soleman, but her determination never to give up on her ideals. She continued her schooling through to graduation. Then she asked to return to Sabu to work as a teacher there. Here she interrupted her story to again ask after Ina's mother-in-law, Mama Sia. Ina explained that her mother-in-law was fine, but had been in a wheelchair since October 2007.

When the family stories came to an end, Papa Pius returned to the purpose of our visit, and gave her a letter from the Women's Network of East Indonesia (JPIT, Jaringan Perempuan Indonesia Timur). Nadue read the letter carefully, paying attention to the letterhead, and finally took out her thick reading glasses. Papa Pius then asked Mama Nadue if she would agree to be interviewed, and for us to record the interview. He then let Ina take over the interview, as Mama Nadue did not need to be interviewed in the Sabu language. Mama Nadue agreed, and Papa Pius sat with us during the interview.

Nadue had never imagined that she could give important information to others. She was extremely honest and open in explaining who she was. Because of this, when she spoke about herself she began to sob. She talked with us about her painful experiences as a result of being labelled 'communist' and a Gerwani activist. Her sacking that meant she could never again be a school teacher. More than this, because her husband was murdered, she became a single parent having to support the family and do all the work in the house. Her children and family were stigmatised. 'We were consumed with emotion at the time' she said, her voice shaking. As we listened, we were unable to stop the flow of our own tears and cried along with her.

She initially became a member of Gerwani because she was approached by the local head of the Communist Party in Sabu, Uncle Kore, whose wife lived in Nadue's neighbourhood. Nadue said straightforwardly that the programs of the Communist Party and Gerwani were excellent, and they answered people's needs. Uncle Kore saw that she would be a good recruit because of her potential as a teacher of mathematics and geography, and her mastering of foreign languages (English and German). Over and again during the interview, Nadue said, 'that was my sin, leading to my condition now'. She was speaking through her tears. Ina interrupted, 'None of this is because of anything you did wrong, but because you were a victim of events.'

Throughout the interview, Nadue's daughter Edo also talked about her suffering through discrimination as a 'communist kid' and 'Gerwani daughter', at church, school and in society. Her younger brother who became a civil servant was also marginalised in the same way.

We ended the interview by praying together. Ina embraced Nadue while praying. It was already six in the evening when we took our leave. Before leaving the house, Ina remembered something she wanted to ask. She went back and embraced Nadue and asked her whether, as a Gerwani leader she had a tattoo on her thigh. Nadue said she did not. We then again took our leave. We are using our interviewee's familiar name, Nadue, with her permission.

This is the way she told us about her life.

Childhood

When I was born, I was called Ati, which was a common name for Sabu girls. But my everyday name was Nadue. When I was baptised, I was given the name Maria. I was born in the kampung of Para on Saturday, 20 December 1934, the child of my father Daud and my mother Linje. I was the second of six children. My father had completed primary school in Kupang, yet he decided to become a farmer because he felt freer running his own life. My uncle and aunt on my father's side had attended school in Makassar and Batavia [now Jakarta. Trs.].

I lived with my grandmother when I was small. I was a tomboy and liked to do things that were not normal for girls, like swimming in the river when it was in flood, or fighting with my friends, and I loved climbing trees. My grandmother (on my father's side) decided to tell my father about these hobbies of mine, and I got a few beatings from him.

I was born and raised during the Dutch, Japanese and revolutionary times. When I was about six I started primary school in Nahagadai-Seda-Sabu. I was in the fourth class when the Japanese arrived. If the Japanese saw a pretty young girl, they would try to get her as a 'comfort woman'. They also kicked people out of their houses so they could live there. My father was summoned by the Japanese army because he dared to scold Japanese soldiers on horseback for ruining his rice fields. All we could do was pray, not knowing if father would return home or not, because we all knew about the cruelty of the Japanese.

We really felt World War II in Sabu. We could hear the allied bombs falling on Seba harbour in 1942. When there were Japanese ships in the harbour, the local houses were all on fire. The people living near Seba harbour ran to find shelter in the school or other places. Some of them dug shelters. I had to stop school because of the war.

Education

A year later, my father's sister, Mama Soleman, came to Sabu and asked my father if I could go to Kupang with her. My aunt had graduated from school in Makassar. Her husband, Soleman, who was from Rote, was a policeman. They took me to Rote, and I went to primary school there. The school in Ba'a was a long way from the village of Oemau where we lived, but I walked there and back, by myself, every day. The path was hilly. The school was near the hospital and the prison. The headmaster was Pak Bartels. I was the only one from Oemau to go to school in Ba'a. I was afraid walking that distance by myself because I had to pass groups of drunken men on the way. I used to always pray that I would be safe. And, luckily, I was. One day one of the drunks set fire to a beehive just when I was going past. I was stung by the bees, and swelled up. But nothing could stop me wanting to go to school.

In 1947 my adoptive parents moved to Baun-Amarasi because my adoptive father had been fired from his job as police chief in Rote. He applied to work in the government office of the Amarasi sub-regency in Timor, and was accepted. So we moved to Kupang, and lived in the kampung of Fontain, one kilometre from the town centre.

In Kupang, I entered junior high school in Airnona, four kilometres from home. My life in Kupang changed radically. My aunt started getting lazy and kept giving me more and more heavy work to do. I had to do all the housework, including fetching water from the river for the house. The path from the river to our house was very steep. I also had to cook, clean the yard and throw out the rubbish. I had to fill the bathing tub with water, do the washing, and then water the plants – all with water I carried from the river. I had to do this work before I left for school and after I got home.

My aunt would hit me, and once hit me on the nose. I have the scar to this day. But my adoptive father treated me well. And even though I had all that housework to do, and had to walk a long way to school, nothing diminished my desire for schooling.

In 1952 I graduated from junior high school. I registered for senior high school in Kupang, at the state school (SMA Negeri). The headmaster was Simon Kitu Tibu Luji who also came from Sabu. He was also headmaster of the vocational school for teachers (SGA, Sekolah Guru A). When this school was opened in Kupang, I was already in the second class of senior high, but I took the entry test for SGA and passed. So I changed schools, and because of the different curriculum, I had to start again at first year and graduated in 1957.

When I graduated, my adoptive parents' married daughter asked me to work for them in their home. I asked myself, 'What's the point of studying so hard at school just to be a servant?' So I looked for information about work opportunities, and found that a junior high school had opened in my own village in Sabu in 1955.

I went to meet a prominent Sabu person living in Kupang, Pak E.R. Here Willa, and told him about my longing to become a teacher. I said, 'Sir, I have graduated from SGA but still found no job. I would love to teach in Sabu and become a civil servant.' He said, 'well, that's great, because as it turns out we still need teachers.' He gave me a letter of introduction. Happy, I returned home and took my leave of my adoptive parents. They were not at all pleased about this, and regarded me as ungrateful, saying, 'even a dog knows how to wag its tail to show thanks, but not you. Now you think you're somebody you just sweet-talk your parents so you can go back home to Sabu'. But nothing could stop me. I wanted to work as a teacher.

Teaching

I left Kupang for Sabu by boat in 1957. Bearing my letter of introduction, I reported to the headmaster of the state junior high school (SMP Nasional), Leopol Lay. I was taken on as a teacher in an honorary capacity. I was the first female to teach arithmetic, algebra and history. I also mastered English. Later there was another female teacher, so there were two of us. Her name was Naema, and she is still alive today. The SMP shared the same location as the vocational school for teachers, about 300 metres from Seba harbour.

The desire of young people for schooling at that time was very strong, and was the same for boys and girls. In the first intake of the junior high school there were 12 boys and 12 girls. Some of the village children had to walk a total of about 30 kilometres to school and back, but they never gave up and were hungry for schooling. The long distance was no obstacle to them. There were more girls than boys in the vocational school for teachers (Sekolah Guru B) because on graduation you could immediately work as a teacher. My fellow teachers came from Sabu, Java and Bali. Their dedication was extraordinary. In Sabu, they built the future world of education for the people and for the nation.

Marriage

In 1960 I married a fellow teacher, because we had fallen in love. The man I chose as my husband was called Rohi, and he was one of the first intake of students in the vocational high school for teachers in Sabu. He was teaching in a primary school run by the Evangelical Christian Church in Timor in Lobodei, East Sabu. In those days, it was common for teachers to wed because we often met, and teachers were highly revered as sources of knowledge. My husband was younger than me, but he was a good man, always with a smile on his face. We were posted in different places. I was in the west of Sabu and my husband was in the east. But this was not a problem in our marriage. However, not long after we married my husband moved from Lobodei to the Evangelical church primary school in Ei Wou which was near our home in Keka.

We were blessed with three children: Rihi, born on 3 August 1961; Edo born on 8 February 1964 and Idje in January 1966. The year Rihi was born, 1961, was a year of good fortune for me, because that was also when I got the official notification from Jakarta of my appointment as a teacher and a raise.

Introduction to the Communist Party and Gerwani

My husband and I were first introduced to the Communist Party and Gerwani through our teaching friends. In the 1960s, all the national political parties were in Sabu. Most of the party organisers were teachers and civil servants. One of the central figures in the Communist Party, perhaps even the leader, was Uncle Kore. He often came to our house and talked about the Communist Party programs. To be frank, my husband sympathised with their cause because their programs answered the people's needs: like land issues, education, and assistance in bad times through agricultural assistance and food. Uncle Kore would come to our house for discussions after school, and this was one way he would share Party information with us. After my husband declared his support, Uncle Kore talked to me about programs for the advancement of women. I accepted information about the organisational structure of Gerwani (Indonesian Women's Movement) and it looked good and interesting to me. Uncle Kore also said that all the wives of Communist Party members joined Gerwani.

Another person who promoted Gerwani's theme of women's advancement was Uncle Welem, who fired me up with visions of a better future apart from being just a female teacher. Seeing the reality of women who were illiterate and backward and with the information about women's advancement from Gerwani, I was drawn, consciously or not, to accept Uncle Kore's invitation to become the leader of Gerwani for Sabu. Uncle Kore himself chose me.

The deputy head was Susi Med'o, and I forget who the others were when we first formed the Gerwani branch there.

Sabu society has both matrilineal descent lines called *hubi* (the name of the female palm blossom) and patrilineal descent lines called *udu*. So women and their eldest male relatives have an important role in organising social groups. Female organisations are called the house of *tegid'a* (*ammu tegid'a*). They meet annually to renew relations; renew information about weaving, descendants and hierarchy within the descent group; food, birth, and group ethics. For instance, sons may marry only descendants of their mother's descent group. The organisation is led by a woman whom the group considers capable. The involvement of Sabu women in social organisations is culturally long-established, and nothing strange or new.

Probably this was why my husband had no objections to me becoming the local Gerwani leader even though our children were still small. Moreover, he witnessed Om (Uncle) Kore's dedication in furthering Gerwani's programs for women's development.

One day Uncle Kore asked me to give a public outdoor speech for Independence Day and the anniversary of the Communist Party. I forget which year it was. I left my children Rohi and Edo with a neighbour so that I could attend.

I still remember some of my speech, for instance: 'Indonesian women should not be content with just the three basic things: giving birth, caring for children, and cooking in the kitchen. They must fight alongside their husbands for the development of the women of Indonesia. In the past, our primary duties were to marry, look after the children and the kitchen, but no more!' Independence Day celebrations used to be really festive, with all kinds of dance performances, cock-fighting and a fair. All schools, civil servants and political party officials came along.

I imagined all those eyes looking at me, confused by my speech, surprised, or angry … I didn't know. But anyway, I did my duty and talked about the important ideas of women progressing beyond their biological function. Probably my speech was the topic of people's conversation, at schools, at church. But my presence there that day later brought disaster to my life.

When I finished giving my speech, I went home to enjoy my own routine duties as mother and teacher. I never sought out new members [for Gerwani] or held meetings in houses as people later accused me.

In 1964–1965 Sabu suffered a drought, and there was famine. I was fortunate as a civil servant and our family was better off than most. People were looking for anything at all to eat, like palm leaves, tamarind seeds and other plants.

A dark time that buried dreams

In late 1965, I went to Kupang to visit family. I was pregnant at the time with my youngest child, Imanda. In Kupang, I heard on the radio that there had been a coup. A few days later I got news from my family in Sabu telling me not to come home because the situation there was chaotic. My family said that there was a story going around that I had carried a bomb in my trousers. And I never even wore trousers! This made me sad and anxious, but there was nothing else for me to do but go back to Sabu and my family. Heavily pregnant, in December 1965 I took a boat to Sabu with other passengers. Arriving in Sabu, I got off the boat together with the other passengers. I could see a crowd waiting on the wharf, and they attacked, chased and terrorised a man, Tol Tari. I have no idea where they took that man. Luckily I myself did not suffer any physical violence. I was also not detained like my other relatives, or like my husband, so some people were jealous and said 'it's okay for her, she can just sit around at home!'

The reason why I was not put in detention is that when the authorities came to take me, I asked permission to see the District Head to discuss my pregnancy. I asked him 'What happens if I give birth in detention?' And he said, 'You can stay at home for the present, but after you have given birth you will be put in detention.'

And sure enough, after I had given birth to my youngest child, at around five in the evening the authorities came, with the mob, to my house and took me to the hospital complex and the prison. I was arrested with no warrant or explanation. I just went along. I took my baby with me, and my family came too, because I really felt that this was the day of my death. I asked for my family to come so that if I was killed, I could give them my baby to take home. On the way, under heavy guard, I passed Pastor Kana Lomi who had been accused of being a communist. He gave me a sign, his hand slicing against his throat, that my husband had been killed. We used signs because we had all been told to keep quiet. This sign made me completely mute, and we could only look at each other. It felt as though my heart was sliced to little pieces while trying to stifle a scream of pain at the news of the death of my husband and the father of my children. My life went black with sadness. And meanwhile I was being rounded up like a criminal without knowing what I was supposed to have done.

At the hospital I was subjected to incredible treatment – my long hair was cut. In those days, women's long hair was their crowning glory. Without any reason, an army person cut my hair short in a rough way. I still feel the stigma of that hair-cutting incident to this very day, when women with short hair are nicknamed 'Gerwani'.

After the haircut, as a punishment for some crime I did not know, I was told I had to report to the authorities. There I was asked strange things, like: 'Did you hear about the blood-thirsty incident? You must have heard about it from your husband. If you were a man, I would beat you!' and he swung a long sharp-toothed blade called a 'sting ray tail' (*ekor pari*) by my face. To every question, I answered that I didn't know, because indeed that was a fact.

Apart from being terrorised, I was also made to clean the toilets and bathrooms at the police station, the district offices, the church, and the houses of officials. One day, when I was cleaning the complex of the Seba town church, an old Dutch building, one of my former students who was then the district head (camat) was in charge of our punishment. She said, haughtily, 'How come these women are allowed to go home?'

She acted as though she knew all the ins and outs of what had befallen me. Not long after that, the head of the State secondary school (SLTP) sacked me from my teaching position. I did not accept that, so I went to Kupang to the regional office of the Education Department to inquire about my status. I met Pak Adjip. He called me over:

'Hey … where are you teaching now?

'I'm not teaching any more, Uncle.'

'Whaaaat? … Why is that? Now let me see … tomorrow you just come to the office and pick up a formal letter and then go back to Sabu.'

Then I visited Pak Dan, also on the staff at the regional education office, at his home, and he greeted me warmly and said, 'Come to the office tomorrow, okay?'

So I returned to Sabu and presented my letter to the District office of education. But the answer I got was the same as before: rejection. I wanted to scream at the difference of information between the offices in Kupang and in Sabu.

In 1972, I tried once again in Kupang, asking about my status at the Provincial office of Education there. I met my old high school friends, including Pak Piga Rade. This is what he told me. 'I am terribly sorry, but there is nothing we can do. You must know yourself the current political situation. You are already in your 40s now, so you should give up trying to get these papers through.'

When I heard his reply, I gave up all hope. There was nothing more I could do. My only thought was my children. I was a single parent but I had no income to support them.

My futile experience of seeking justice made me despair. And in this state of deep depression, I burnt all my documents that had any connection with my work as a teacher.

I had no skills in agriculture or weaving like most Sabu women. I had to move and make a living from farming. The fluctuating economy and my meagre finances meant my family covered the costs of my children's education, and brought them up. I felt like a worthless parasite, a burden on others, while also blaming myself, seeing this as my sin. Even though I did not understand why I felt I had sinned. Perhaps my family and even my children did what I did: they secretly blamed me as the instigator of this disaster. It affected not only me, but the lives of my children and my extended family. To all the members of my family, I beg forgiveness. This was not my wrongdoing, this was something I could never understand, why I experienced all this bitter pain. And I am thankful for their support for the children.

One day Rohi was teased by a policeman when he went for a test to enter the police force. The policeman said 'Your father was Communist, wasn't he? You'll see soon enough ...' Rohi went home and cried. He said. 'Why did our father have to be a Communist? We are all victims.'

And whenever something happened at Church or in the community, people would always say, 'This is because they are communists!' My children would hear this and feel stigmatised.

Self confidence

For 45 years now I have kept quiet about the wickedness of the State towards me and my family. And then, suddenly people came and wanted to listen to me. This was impossible. When on 24 November 2010 I heard that there were people doing research, I was suspicious about their purpose in coming to visit me in my home. They brought a letter, which I scrutinised carefully. There were friends of my teacher Pa Pius; Ina, my daughter Edo's friend from junior high school days, and Pulu, a Sabu girl. I willingly poured out my tragic story, which filled my heart to the brim because it had been stored there for such a long time.

Then I had the chance to go to Kupang. Full of trepidation, like someone sick with old age, I finally steeled myself to go to Kupang. My children and my grandchild who is studying theology at a university in Jakarta encouraged me to go. So with my daughter Edo accompanying me, we flew to Kupang and at the airport we were met by the team, Pak Putu Oka, and my son Rohi.

This first friendly meeting in late March 2011 in Kupang began to heal the wounds in my heart and Edo's, through the stories we shared, crying together, gasping for breath and embracing in prayer, and then agreeing with Putu Oka and his team to expose the story of my life.

It turns out that I am still someone, that there are still people who want to listen to this bitter history, who believe in me. And what is most heartening is to meet with friends from Alor, Kupang, Soe, Sumba and Jakarta. It turns out that I was not the only one to suffer this State crime, but there were so many people. So now I have found my self-respect as a human being. My dream is to return to Sabu and help friends and relatives with the information I got in Kupang that we are victims of State crime. I feel the voice in my heart saying over and again, 'I never did anything disloyal to my country or to my people.'

Now I live in peace, after that meeting in Kupang enlightened me. I am a new person with a sense of calm, enjoying my children who have their own families; some work for government, some in the private sphere. Edo and her family agreed to return to Sabu and we have become close, they look after me in my old age; this is a great joy to enjoy old age, thanks be to God.

> *I pray that I have the strength to go on until God calls me to His bosom; that I can accept all that passes with self-control, because I am emotional; that I can accept this reality patiently. Whatever happens, I hope Ina will pray for me. Please Lord, forgive the sins of my children and my family. Let us live in harmony.*

Interviewers and transcribers: Pius, Ina dan Pulu.

Writers: Ina and Pulu.

Chapter 9

Niko

Clarity at last

The sadistic tragedy that happened in Indonesia is now in the past. For decades, the stories of those who were imprisoned and murdered have always been told as though they deserved to be killed because they betrayed their country. The events themselves have begun to disappear from memory, or are made to disappear, including by those who experienced them first hand. They, or their families, want to forget the savage massacres.

But one afternoon in November 2010, three people could be seen walking in the public cemetery in Oesao, a village in the Babau district, about 30 kilometres from the provincial capital of Kupang, [West Timor. Trs.]. They seemed to be searching for something. One of them approached a house close by. Soon after, she emerged with Rina, a woman of about 60. Rina was wearing a casual blue day dress and her teeth were red from the betel nut she was chewing. The other two people came up and chatted with her. The three were members of the Women's Network of East Indonesia (JPIT, Jaringan Perempuan Indonesia Timur) who were seeking stories about victims of the 1965 incident and burial sites. Rina pointed out a place near the graveyard. This plot projected outwards, and was planted with *bidara* trees. One of the JPAI team took a photograph. Rina also gave information about the names of people killed and buried in that hole. But during the conversation she became uncertain, and asked them to check with her husband because he had been present as a prisoner at that very incident. As her husband was working at the market, they decided to wait for him. Rina asked a friend to fetch her husband from the market.

A while later, Rina's husband, Niko, arrived. He looked old, with greying hair, a lined face, and many teeth missing. He pointed out a different burial hole to the one his wife had shown. He gave extremely detailed information about the number of victims, their names, and the time of the massacre.

Hearing his story, the team wanted to talk with him further, and Niko invited them to his house.

Niko's house was small, simple, but comfortable. He had a flower garden in front, and a grassy yard. In front of his house was a kiosk where he sold snacks, shampoo, flour, bottled water and other things. This kiosk belonged to Niko. Rina worked there every day while her husband traded in the Oesao market. The visitors were invited inside the house. They introduced themselves and explained that the purpose of their visit was to seek out the sites of mass slaughter in 1965. Because it was now dusk, they decided to meet again the next day as the team had to return to Kupang.

The next day, the team rose early for their journey to Oesao. They went by motor bike. They had to drive through the Oesao market on the way. The market was busy with all kinds of activity. There were people trying to sell their wares to passers-by. Children were running around with plastic bags and offering their services to carry things. In the middle of all this cacophony sat Niko. He was bent over a trolley full of cakes. Every now and then he would get up from his plastic chair to serve a customer. He looked friendly and happy and joked with his customers. Although now 72 years old, he seemed energetic, although his body was no longer as fit as his younger days.

When the team came to the market, Niko's attention was devoted to his cake stall. But at three in the afternoon when the market began to close, Niko was nowhere to be seen. The JPIT team asked a young woman looking after the cake stall where Niko was, and she said he had gone home to rest. Her name was Lina. She was Niko's daughter, and she always minded the stall when her father rested.

One morning the team went to the market again to see Niko and buy some cakes. The cakes were truly delicious, and filling, which was just as well as the team had had no breakfast. While munching on cakes, they chatted with Niko. When they shook his hand, they noticed his rough skin, a sign that he did hard work. Time passed quickly and it was suddenly time for Niko to go home and take his rest. The team offered to walk back home with him under the hot sun. Even at his age he easily walked nearly a kilometre from the market to his house. He did this every day.

When they arrived, Rina was minding the kiosk. She greeted everyone warmly and invited them inside. After sitting for a while, she went outside and brought them all some cold bottled water. While drinking, they chatted for a while, and then took their leave as Niko had to rest.

A few days later, the team returned to Niko's house and discovered that he was sick. His legs were troubling him and he could not walk to the market. He greeted the team, even so, and invited them to chat. Niko was happy to talk about many things, including his past. While he was talking, his son Kris came in. Kris had just returned from working as a motor-bike taxi driver. The team members introduced themselves to Kris and explained the purpose of their visit. Kris sat and joined them, listening to his father's stories. He was happy because he could hear his father's life story which he had never before known clearly.

Niko was extremely loving towards his son. According to his wife, Niko spoiled his children, especially his daughters. Niko chose to work himself rather than bother his daughters, and he preferred to walk to market and back rather than ask his children to take him there on the motor bike. But that was how he was. He did not want his children to spend all their time working and forget to enjoy themselves. He wanted his children to grow up carefree and happy, and to have no regrets in the future about their childhood. After remaining quiet for a while, Niko told his story, loudly and full of emotion.

Childhood and marriage

Niko was born to a farming family in Oesao. They lived hand-to-mouth. Because of this, when he married Rina in 1963, Niko thought long and hard about how to support his family. As a man, Niko had the responsibility to provide for his wife and family. So he worked hard on other people's rice fields. But he never earned enough, because he had to divide the crop with the landowner. This is why the ambition of Niko and other farmers was to own their own rice fields. This dream seemed possible when the government announced it would give out land to those in need. So Niko and other farmers like him registered their names at the local Village Headquarters, and paid the required sum of 45 rupiah.

Not long after their marriage, Niko and Rina were blessed with a cute, chubby son. Their family life was complete with the birth of a son and heir. In 1965 they had a second son, which made them happier still. But this happiness lasted only a few weeks because of the 30th September affair. This affair was a black page in Niko's life. It stole his happiness. He had to part with his wife and children. Niko was accused of being an accomplice of the Communist Party that was stealing people's land. His desire to get his own rice fields was what led him to disaster.

Niko's arrest: dark times 1965–1966

One day in December 1965, Niko was passing his time as usual, with no sense of foreboding. Suddenly he was jolted by the news that he was going to be arrested for interrogation because of his participation in the 30th September incident. Niko was confused and anxious, and could not think clearly. Together with some neighbours he was taken along to the village headquarters for interrogation. Their arrest was clearly improper, because no one carried a formal warrant. Also, they were given no opportunity to question the reason for their arrest. During the march to the village headquarters Niko didn't ask the people who had arrested them anything. He remained silent, marching along with many questions running around in his head: 'What have I done wrong; what could I have done to make them arrest me?' He could find no answers.

At the village headquarters, (the home of the village head was being used for this, as the building for the village headquarters was not yet built), the people arrested were interrogated by some police they did not know, but who probably came from Kupang. They had questions fired at them, like, 'Are you a member of the Communist Party? How does the Communist Party operate?' Pak Niko answered 'No!' to the first question, but this did not change anything. The questions were mere formalities because even though he answered no, Niko was not released. He ended up with more interrogation and was then imprisoned.

Our self-respect taken away

Niko and his friends were held at the village headquarters at night, but during the day they were taken back to their homes. At the village headquarters they had to work. They did whatever they were told without question.

> They suspected us of being Communists, so they ordered us to do anything they wanted. If they ordered us to pick up shit we would do it. Anyone who opposed them was beaten up. Those who did what they were told were okay.

Not only did they have no right to speak, the only thing they could do was follow orders. Their freedom of speech was taken from them, and space to move limited. Not only that, Niko and his friends had to walk around the village wearing billboards. Villagers came out to look. Many of them jeered, but a few were sympathetic. Niko and his friends were ashamed, because it was as though they were criminals who had to parade their crimes, and because of the severity of those crimes there was no forgiveness for them. The people regarded them as no more than trash, completely worthless and deserving of no respect at all. 'They saw us as not even human. They would talk to us as though they were talking to some filthy rag.'

The rough treatment dealt to them came not only from the government, but also from the local people. People would beat the prisoners when they came home. Because of this, Niko did not dare to go back home when he was permitted to do so, 'The people were so arrogant that I preferred to sleep in the cold of the village headquarters rather than go home and get punished by the mob.'

Trucks and the rumble of death

Rrrrem, rreeem, reeeem. The sound of the trucks was like the sound of death to the prisoners. Anyone loaded on to the trucks and taken away would never return. The prisoners heard stories that those taken away were murdered. They were taken blindfolded to Babau, the district centre, then again by truck to the place of slaughter which was already prepared.

> When the trucks stopped it was a terrible sound. The horns were the sound of death. When the trucks stopped it was like the instruments of death you hear on the radio. Even the geckos were quiet. The birds went still. The roosters stopped crowing. In 1965 the world was still. The world was still!

Around eight at night, the sound of the trucks, the rumble of death, could be heard, as though summoning them to their death.

> When we heard that sound our hair would stand on end and we would experience the most terrible fear. Some of the prisoners would be loaded on to the trucks. We would wait for them to come back, but none of them ever did, to this very day.
>
> Anyone whose name was called quickly climbed up on the high tray of the truck. If they were not quick about it, they would be pushed up from behind. At eight at night, after we had eaten, the trucks would arrive with the army. When someone was called they had to go, and if they went it meant they would be murdered and never come back.

Around mid-December 1965, it was Niko's turn to be picked up by the truck. Niko was terrified and sad, terrified of death and sad because he had to leave his family – his wife and his baby. He was given the opportunity to go home and say farewell to his family. 'My heart was in pain to see my family sad. They wept openly before me at my fate. I could not bring myself to wipe away their tears, all I could do was accept the situation.' Death was now right before his eyes and Niko had to accept it. His family could not accept it, but they could do nothing. They were only poor farmers with no influence. Rina was desperately sad, could not speak, and only prayed. Before Niko returned to the village headquarters, Rina gave him her sleeping coverlet, and Niko gave her his. His heart was heavy taking that piece of cloth, but he took it with him and returned to the village headquarters. The piece of cloth helped him to feel close to his wife and children.

The day felt short, and suddenly it was dusk, and darkness fell. Darkness that filled Niko with dread. Niko did not want the day to become night. He wanted his death delayed. He was in a state of confusion facing his own death. His ears were sharply focused on the sounds around him, dreading the rumble of approaching death. Time moved on, but the rumble of the truck did not come. Niko stayed wide awake all night long, until the dawn light. The dawn turned into day. Niko was still at the village headquarters. In his heart he gave thanks to Jesus and asked himself, 'why didn't they come to get me?'

And that was how Niko and his friends spent almost every night through the month of December. They never slept soundly. 'We were always on full alert, our ears listening out for the rumble of the truck. We were terrified to sleep in case we never woke up again.'

Rina accused

In a state of exhaustion while being detained, Niko had to witness his wife herded into the village headquarters for interrogation. She was interrogated even though she was nursing her baby who was just a few weeks old. While being questioned, she was permitted to go home to feed her baby who was crying with hunger.

> It wasn't even 40 days since the birth. My milk was flowing everywhere. They ordered me to go home to feed my baby. I was very afraid returning home. Because I was terrified, I went straight back as soon as I had fed my baby. I was always scared of them kicking me if they thought I was taking my time.

Niko and his family were powerless to refuse or oppose their treatment by the local authorities. At the time, everyone was terrified. They could only 'surrender' to God. 'Times were harsh. Terrifying! I surrendered my fate. Only God knows. If I have truly done wrong, then kill me.'

When Rina was interrogated about her involvement with the Communist Party or Gerwani (Indonesian Women's Movement), the questioning went like this:

Q: 'You know something – your face is pale.'

A: 'No, sir, I don't know anything. I don't know anybody. I have just given birth. I am pale because I have recently given birth.'

Q: 'You wrote down your name so you could get some land, and now that you are questioned, you go pale.'

A: 'No sir. I don't know anything, I have just given birth.'

That's the way they were treated. Rina was also taken for questioning without any official warrant. Apart from being accused of being involved with the Communist Party and Gerwani, she had to suffer the accusations from Niko's family. According to her mother-in-law and sister-in-law, Rina was pleased that her husband had been arrested because now she could remarry.

> My mother-in-law said that I would be pleased if my husband died so I could marry again. My sister-in-law did not like me, and they were angry because they thought I was just enjoying myself, even though they had no idea of what was going on in my heart.

A bright dawn of freedom

Niko was summoned one morning by the police guarding the village headquarters. They told him that he was free because there was no proof that he was a member of the Communist Party. Niko was taken home. He felt happy and relieved, all his fears of the rumble of trucks disappeared. Now he had to build a new life with his family even though when he was released the authorities said that former detainees were people ostracised by the community. They were returned to the community so they could be reaccepted.

Niko's family was waiting for him at home, and greeted him with tears of joy. A relative, child, father and husband had returned home. These were the cries of victory of poor people. Rina hugged her husband and cried her heart out. She had thought that they would never meet again. But now her husband was home and they were going to have a happy life.

Niko thought that his release meant that his rights would be truly restored to him. But this was not so. He and others who were released had to report to authorities from 1966 through to 1977. They had to report in that they were still alive, and that they were not doing anything detrimental to the State. Apart from that, every Independence Day, on the 17 August, they had to take part in the official ceremony at the office of the District Head. Niko and his friends had to stand apart in a special line, as former Communist Party members. This was particularly difficult to bear, because their own children also had to take part in the ceremony.

> They had released us, it was their decision, not ours. We were nobody. We had to report. On the 17 August we had to join the ceremony. My wife had to do this too, until 1976 or 1977.

Eventually they realised that their freedom was a sham.

'Communist remnants'

People started calling Niko, Rina and their children 'Communist remnants'. After he got out of prison, Niko and his family were ostracised. They were considered to be trash, useless people. They were not fit to be anyone's friend. People were afraid to get close to them. They were just dirty rags to be trampled on. Their self-dignity was belittled. Niko was stigmatised as a 'Communist remnant'. Rina explained:

> They thought we were a nuisance. If they quarrelled with us, they would call us "communist remnants". My sister-in-law even yelled at me in that way. If we did anything wrong, out would come the "Communist remnant" accusation. My children get called that even now.

These words were often used to abuse Niko's children at school. Their friends and even their teachers would use this phrase to taunt them. In the end, Niko and Rina's oldest son, Son, stopped going to school. He could not bear the bullying. Their second son Paul suffered the same treatment from his schoolmates and his own teacher. But because he didn't really have much idea what 'Communist' meant, he didn't take much notice. Only when he was in his teens and knew what it meant, did he discover the truth. He was resentful of the people who had called them 'communist remnants'.

'If it is true that you were a Communist, Dad, why didn't they murder you back then? Why do they call you that now?' Paul asked his father. He went to his uncle and asked what really happened. He also found old people who knew exactly what happened and from them he got a different story from the one going around that accused his father. Armed with this information, Paul would challenge anyone who called them 'remnant communists', including the District Head when he slapped his father in the market because he had not paid his taxes. To Paul, the matter of taxes had nothing to do with 'remnant communists'. So why did the District Head link them? Paul took a different stance to that of his brothers and sisters. He worked for a private business in Kupang.

Melki, another of Niko's children, had another story. When he wanted to enter the police academy, snide comments about him being the son of a former communist stopped him pursuing that career. Melki now lives and works in Bali.

Niko's son Kris, listening to Niko's story, interrupted to say, 'At last I have heard Dad's story.' Lina remained silent. Son and another of Niko's daughters were not present. None of Niko's children was able to work as a civil servant. They became traders, motor bike taxi drivers, and worked in the private sector.

Rina cried and said that only God knows all. They just had to accept the jeering and abuse. This continues right to the present, for every time Niko stands up for his rights and his property, these acts are always accused as being a rebellion by 'communist remnants'.

> Our movement has always been limited in every way. There are things we cannot do. Like when someone's cows eat our plants, we can't get angry or talk about it. If we speak up, they'll say we are 'communist remnants.

The events of 1965 have also affected the relationship between Niko and his sister. Their relationship had never been good, but the 1965 events made things much worse. Even when one of their relatives died, Niko's sister did not come to the funeral because Niko and his family were there. It is still difficult for them just to greet each other.

The Church stayed silent

In the terrible time just after his release, Niko had to face the hatred of society. He was seen as an evil criminal that should be killed, as someone useless, a traitor to the country, trash, and all kinds of other abuse. Faced with this situation, Niko and his family had to find some motivation. They longed for people to drop by and visit, and give them support. But words like support and good cheer were a rarity.

From day to day, month to month, not a single person came to knock on their door to chat or share experiences, including the Church. The Church never visited or checked up on Niko and his family. Even though Niko was registered as a member of the congregation, offering support and showing readiness to listen to his stories would have helped him keep up his spirits and sense of self confidence. The Church was silent.

The Church did absolutely nothing to handle the problem. The Church was afraid to speak up. This was also because the situation forced it to take a stance of silence. If the Church had acted to defend the victims, the Church itself would have been accused of being Communist.

God is our Saviour

Now, 45 years after the events of 30 September 1965, Niko and his family live contentedly. Their children all have work, and some of them have married. Niko is now a grandfather and he adores his grandchildren.

While talking about his past, Niko reflected about how his wife and he remained strong because their God gave them strength when they were weak. God always protects those in the darkness and in terrifying situations.

> Because of God, the whole family is as it is now. Mama is now a leader of the congregation at Church. Our children are also active in the church, in various types of service. We always find time to go to Church on Sundays. We do this as a way of saying thanks to God. Thank you Lord Jesus.

The meeting ends

The meeting of the JPIT team with Niko had gone well. Niko and his family were happy because there were still people who wanted to hear their story, and who did not look down on them as former prisoners. The team was also happy to hear this valuable story of their nation, a story almost lost. The young generation has a lot to learn, including the story of Niko and his family who continue to live their lives, even though life has not been good to them. With a happy expression, Niko said that he would be pleased to meet anyone who wants information from him. At the end of the conversation, the team asked Niko: 'Are those old trucks still around? And how do you feel when you see them now?' Niko answered, 'Yes, the trucks are still around. When I am at the market and they go past, it reminds me of 1965. But now God helps me, and I am safe.'

Eventually, Niko managed to overcome his fear of the rumbling sound of trucks, and he is still living today.

Interviewers: Tatiana, Alice and Nancy.

Writers: Alice and Nancy.

Chapter 10

Permadi

Life in painting

The young man called his painting 'The Ship of Indonesia's Armed Struggle'. He executed it with pen strokes, inspired by German painting. He wanted to give it to the Republic of Indonesia's leader who was coming to Takengon, Aceh. He had heard that some Indonesian leaders were going to deliver speeches in the square, so he found time to do the painting.

It was 1948, and Indonesia, including East Sumatra except Aceh, had been retaken after World War II by the Dutch and the Allies. The Dutch had arrested the Indonesian leaders. President Soekarno, Sutan Sjahrir and Haji Agus Salim had been exiled to Brastagi. The Vice President, Mohammad Hatta, together with Mohammad Roem, Ali Sastroamidjojo, AG Pringgodigdo, Assaat, Air Commodore Suryadarma and other senior officials had been exiled to Bangka Island. To safeguard against a vacuum of power, Soekarno had appointed Sjafruddin Prawiranegara as acting president and a few ministers to establish the Emergency Government of the Republic of Indonesia (PDRI, Pemerintahan Darurat Republik Indonesia) with its capital in Bukit Tinggi.

The Dutch spread propaganda that the leaders of the Republic had been arrested and therefore the State of the Republic of Indonesia was null and void and the entire region of the Republic was now under Dutch control. In the areas not under Dutch control, Indonesian leaders made counter propaganda that the Republic of Indonesia had not been defeated. Meanwhile in Takengon in central Aceh, a radio station for the armed struggle called 'Rimba Raya' (Glorious Jungle) was established to keep the spirit of nationalism alive in Aceh. Through this radio station, and their outdoor speeches, the Indonesian leaders wanted to spread the word that the Republic of Indonesia was still standing, that Indonesian independence had to be upheld, and that maintaining independence was something that not only the leaders had to strive for, but the people too.

He rolled up the painting neatly and managed to give it to Ir. A Kapau Gani, one of the ministers, while travelling with the group from Takengon to Bukit Tinggi. The artist was Permadi Liosta. He believed that a person could demonstrate his sense and spirit of nationalism not only by taking up arms to drive out the colonisers, but also through art. Permadi Liosta's love of art later became brushes and paint that created shape, colour and paintings on the canvas of his life. Despite all that was painted on that canvas, he remains steadfast in his belief that art is beautiful.

* * * *

Permadi Liosta was born in Takengon, Aceh on 25 November 1930, the third of five children. He was raised in a Gayo farming family. His family owned some rice fields and other dry fields, typical of small-scale farmers who Soekarno called Marhaen, after a farmer with that name he met in West Java.

Permadi is an unpretentious person and likes to joke. His memory is extremely sharp for someone 80 years of age. He told his life story with a calm expression and intonation, never with outbursts of revenge, never appearing as someone who was in Salemba prison and experienced the wild jungle of Buru Island for eleven years. He is someone the Javanese would call *legawa*, or sincere. Seeing him reminded me of something I once heard an artist say, 'art refines behaviour, refines sensitivity, refines thought, and refines reason.' Maybe it is indeed art that has made him make peace with his past. He chose art as his life path, and he has never regretted that choice. He can say wisely, 'I consider all that happened as the history of my life.'

* * * *

Permadi Liosta's life story begins with his love of art. It was because of art that he decided to travel to Java and study visual art, was entrusted with helping with the establishment of Lekra, (the Institute of People's Culture) in Bali, and represented Indonesia at exhibitions in Europe, until eventually the New Order regime suppressed his creativity in Salemba prison and in the prison camp on Buru Island. Permadi Liosta's interest in painting began at primary school. His talent was honed further when he continued his education at high school (Perguruan Pusat Murid, PPM) at Takengon. This was when he made the painting 'The Ship of Indonesia's Armed Struggle'.

His passion for study led to his decision to go to the People's University of North Sumatra (Universitas Rakyat Sumatera Utara) at Tapanuli.

Together with six friends, each bearing one kerosene tin full of rice, he trekked through the jungle for one month. They often had to shelter from the rain under makeshift tents made with banana leaves, and hide whenever there was a Dutch army patrol. When they arrived in Tapanuli, the situation was not promising. The college had been burnt down by the Dutch. Another college had been built in the Aceh jungle, but this suffered the same fate as the Tapanuli one. It was bombed by the Dutch, and all that remained were blackboards and the flag. The college then had to move to the banks of the Alas River in Gayo territory, Aceh. When Permadi completed his studies at university, he returned to Takengon and joined the revolutionary army. He was given duties on the front in the Pangkalan Berandan area to chase out the Dutch who were trying to control Aceh. Permadi became war correspondent sending news of the fighting to Langsa to be forwarded to newspapers in Banda Aceh.

When his soldier days ended, Permadi wanted to go to Java for further study. His high school teachers had instilled in him the need to 'be independent'. So he and a friend started to save money by planting crops and doing odd jobs to get the money to go to Java. But it turned out they had only enough to get as far as Medan. When they got there, they had to work again to save some more. Permadi worked at a printing house, on construction sites, and made posters. Then one day he read a magazine. He saw a picture of Hendra Gunawan from the Pelukis Rakyat (Artists of the People) group in Yogyakarta painting a huge work, so large that Hendra himself was dwarfed by it. Permadi was seized with fervour, and could no longer rein in his desire to become an artist. So he wrote to Hendra Gunawan,

> Pak Hendra, I want to be a painter. I want to join Pelukis Rakyat and come to Yogya. But I have nothing other than my fierce desire to become an artist.

Hendra wrote in reply, 'Come to Pelukis Rakyat right away.'

So after he got his pay and sold his bicycle, Permadi and his friends went to Jakarta on their way to Yogyakarta. But they ran out of money. They did not have enough to get to Yogyakarta. Luckily, they could stay in Jakarta at the house of Hasan Gayo, a former freedom fighter who was also from Gayo. It seemed as though their meeting with Hendra was just awaiting the right moment. They had not realised that Hendra was a friend of Hasan Gayo, until one day Hendra arrived at Hasan Gayo's house.

'Here they are, these village kids who want to go to Yogya. They want to study,' Hasan Gayo told Hendra.

Permadi fronted up to Hendra. 'We've got no money. We can't get to Yogya. We're flat broke.' And they did not want to ask Hasan Gayo for money because this went against their principle of being 'independent'.

But sure enough, the next day someone came to take Permadi and his friends to Yogya. Permadi was impatient to join the Pelukis Rakyat group and study with them. Until now, he had felt confident enough to call himself an artist, but when he saw how amazing the artists at Pelukis Rakyat were, he realised that becoming an artist is a long process and hard work.

The Pelukis Rakyat studio was a place where painters and sculptors gathered. They came from various backgrounds, ethnicities, religions, affiliations and ideologies. The studio was established in 1947 by the artists Affandi and Hendra Gunawan who had for many years been involved with arts organisations like SIM (Seniman Indonesia Muda, Young Indonesian Artists) in Yogyakarta. At Pelukis Rakyat, everyone studied together and many artists lived at the studio. There was a large hall and two big bedrooms. Hendra Gunawan and his family occupied one of the bedrooms. During the day, the hall was used as a workshop where the artists created and studied painting or sculpture. At night, mattresses would be arranged in rows in the hall and the spare bedroom, for the artists staying there to sleep. It was at the Pelukis Rakyat studio that Permadi met the top painters and visual artists of the time, like Affandi, Hendra Gunawan, Edi Sunarso and Trubus. And this was also where he learnt the philosophy, 'Art for the People'.

'Art for the People' was people-focused art. It was a philosophy that developed alongside the political ideology of the time that tended to be socialist and realist, so Pelukis Rakyat artists adopted themes of the people as objects of their work. By familiarising himself with 'Art for the People', Permadi was introduced to the true experience of painting. He went to the sites of his paintings. He carried his canvas and brushes on the roadside, to the market, to the rice fields, to the mountains; he painted the farmers harvesting rice, and various expressions of ordinary people. His painting skills were sharpened, and he learned sculpture too.

In the early 1950s, President Soekarno asked for statues to be made for commemorative monuments in Indonesia's large towns. Some of these statues and monuments were made by sculptors at Pelukis Rakyat. Permadi himself got a commission through Pelukis Rakyat to make a carved panel for the Military Corps Police (CPM, Corps Polisi Militer) in Jakarta. By this time, Permadi's paintings were in demand and sold at exhibitions.

His achievements and hard work were recognised when in 1954 he was commissioned to make the statue with the symbol of Airlangga University.

Initially, Hendra Gunawan was going to make the statue, but Hendra gave the project to Permadi. The statue, which became the symbol of Airlangga University, was a replica of the statue of Airlangga, the King of Kahuripan, depicted as the figure of Visnu mounted on the Garuda bird, with a dragon snake grasping the Garuda's claw. In the same year, on 10 November 1954, Hero's Day, Permadi attended the official opening of Airlangga University, opened by President Soekarno. The huge four metre high statue was covered with a yellow and blue cloth. The cloth was then drawn aside to symbolise the official opening, and the statue has remained there to this day, in the grounds in front of the Faculty of Medicine at Airlangga University.

After the Airlangga statue project, Permadi got more commissions, including a carved pane, for the Madiun Council offices. This project went well, but Permadi's health declined. He went to the Bethesda Hospital in Yogyakarta for a check-up and a black shadow was diagnosed on his lungs. After a week in hospital, he went to the sanatorium in Pakem, near Kaliurang. There he befriended a Dutch doctor. With the help of this doctor and the International Union of Students (IUS), he was recommended for treatment in Beijing. Permadi went to China together with four other Indonesian students. After six months of treatment there, he returned to Yogya, and went back to Pelukis Rakyat. Soon after, he decided to move to Bali. And it was in Bali that he got to know Balinese artists and went on to establish Lekra (The Institute of People's Culture) in Bali.

Permadi arrived in Denpasar, Bali, together with Fajar Sidik, a lecturer from the Indonesian Arts Academy in Yogyakarta (ASRI, Akademi Seni Rupa Indonesia) who was also active in Pelukis Rakyat in the late 1950s. At that time, Lekra was still just an embryo in Bali, but its rival organisation, the Institute of National Culture (LKN, Lembaga Kebudayaan Nasional) had already been established with Raka Sandtri as its head.

Balinese artists who knew that Permadi was from Pelukis Rakyat in Yogya, asked him to establish and lead Lekra in Bali. Permadi rejected the idea of being its head, but he agreed to help establish Lekra in Bali. He asked for a Balinese to be chosen at its head. So Rika, a Balinese from Singaraja who had just finished his studies at the Arts Academy in Yogya was made head. Permadi himself became head of the visual arts section.

Lekra developed quickly in Bali. Many Balinese artists joined. There was competition in the arts world between Lekra and LKN as the two major forces in the arts in Bali at the time. Permadi says that Lekra was more active in the arts world there, one reason being that the Governor of Bali at the time, Suteja, prioritised Lekra. As Governor, he commissioned many arts performances by Lekra artists. On the other hand, LKN did not have close relations with the Governor of Bali. The Lekra artists were also often invited to formal state occasions and to greet visiting international guests, at the invitation of President Soekarno and the Minister of Culture at the time.

In early 1960, President Soekarno invited Lekra to mount an exhibition of paintings in East Germany, Hungary and Bulgaria. Permadi was called to Jakarta to accept the mission of curating the exhibition. He set about the task of gathering paintings to be taken. He asked the advice of Affandi, his senior at Pelukis Rakyat.

'Pak Affandi, the central Lekra committee has appointed me to take an exhibition to Europe. I am terrified. What should I do?'

Affandi, who had a lot of experience mounting exhibitions abroad, understood Permadi's anxiety. 'I am sure you are quite capable of doing this, Permadi', he said.

Then he gave some advice.

> One thing I would say is that over there do not link art and politics. Keep them separate. If it is paintings, keep it at that, if it is art, keep it at that, there's no need to muddle them with politics. But if you feel capable of linking art and politics, then that's okay too.

Permadi left for Europe with Rustamaji, a Lekra artist from Surabaya. They went to East Berlin. The exhibition at the national gallery in a baroque architecture building in the east of the city was opened by the Vice Prime Minister of East Germany, who gave a speech. As leader of the Indonesian exhibition, Permadi gave a speech in reply. Permadi remembers this moment as one that stirred his sense of nationalism. His friend Rustamaji was also moved to see Permadi on the podium, under spotlights, the bulbs of the journalists' cameras flashing, and the event broadcast on German television. After Permadi's speech, even before he got off the podium, Rustamaji came up to hug him, his face beaming.

During the exhibition, Permadi had many discussions with the German curator. Many German artists came along, especially painters and academics.

'Where is the Indonesian element here?' a German artist asked indignantly.

Permadi replied, 'well, what about these German paintings here, where is the German element? This is European. French and Italian paintings are like this too.'

Permadi showed the artists a book with reproductions of Balinese paintings. He had brought copies of the book to give out to artists in Europe.

'This is like Rousseau's paintings!' one of the German artists said. Permadi pointed to a picture of a very traditional Balinese painting from Klungkung.

> Now how can this be like Rousseau? Tell me, when was Rousseau born? Just look at the colours of the Balinese painting – it is clearly very old. In Indonesia, we have many styles of painting. Java, Batak, Irian, Bali – every area has its painting. What we have brought here for this exhibition are paintings that depict contemporary national life. Right now, this depicts what it is like in Indonesia. Just like in Germany, people are demanding their rights ...

Permadi was proud of himself for giving such a diplomatic answer.

Apart from the exhibition, Permadi was also invited to participate in discussions and to give a painting demonstration at the arts academy in [East] Berlin. He gave the demonstration together with a lecturer, and there was a model for life painting. This is where he discovered a difference between German and Indonesian painting of the time. The German teacher painted extremely carefully and in great detail, so that his painting was like a life portrait. 'What is art?' Permadi then asked the academics and students. Permadi's painting was praised as a work of high art. Unlike European paintings that were executed with a brush, Indonesian painters like Affandi, Hendra Gunawan and Permadi often used their palette knives. The unique impression this produced, combined with the realism that Indonesian artists pursued, made Indonesian paintings much appreciated in Europe.

The exhibition that Permadi organised in Europe went off well. Many artists, critics and ordinary people came to see the Indonesian paintings. Soon after Permadi returned to Indonesia, he joined the committee organising the Asia Africa Film Festival in Jakarta for the 10th anniversary of the [1955] Asia Africa Conference.

The Governor of Bali put Permadi in charge of the performances during the Asia Africa Film Festival. Many Balinese artists were on the organising committee, but it seemed that artists from LKN (Lembaga Kebudayaan Nasional, the Institute of National Culture) did not want to participate. So the Lekra artists were very much involved in the activities taking place during the film festival.

When the film festival was over, Permadi and Bachtiar Siagian, an artist from the central Lekra branch, went to Klungkung together to take photographs and make a film about the lives of Klungkung fishermen.

They had to spend a night in Klungkung. Rumours circulated about an underground political movement. It was said that Permadi and Bachtiar were in Klungkung waiting for a ship from China which was coming with guns. Permadi and Bachtiar heard about the rumour from a friend. The friend told them to return to Denpasar as soon as possible because the situation in Bali was heating up.

When they got back to Denpasar, Bachtiar said he wanted to return to Jakarta immediately. He planned to give his rolls of documentary film together with the films he had shown at the Asia Africa Film Festival to a Japanese friend for safekeeping. Permadi and Bachtiar parted ways in Denpasar.

On 1 October 1965 at seven in the morning, Permadi was at home in Denpasar and had just woken up. Still sleepy, he was lying in bed and used his toe to turn the radio on. The news he then heard was that the Revolutionary Council led by Lieutenant Colonel Untung controlled Jakarta, and had rescued President Soekarno from an attempted coup d'etat by the Council of Generals. Hearing this news, Permadi rushed to the home of the Governor Suteja. The Governor said, 'ahh, let's just wait for the command from President Soekarno.' The critical situation in Jakarta had not yet spread to Bali.

By around the beginning of the next month, November, there were stories about killings going on in Banyuwangi. And then the slaughter came to Bali, first of all in Negara, then Buleleng. The people of Denpasar still had a period of calm, until there was an announcement saying that everyone had to remain in their own place of residence, and it was forbidden to sleep anywhere other than your own house, or to receive any guests to stay overnight. It was unclear where this announcement came from. The situation in Denpasar began to be chaotic and the only thing people could do was believe they had to obey this announcement.

Walls of houses were painted with signs of political parties. If the people living there were members of the National Party, then 'PNI' was scrawled, and if they were members of the Communist Party, then it was 'PKI'. In early December 1965, the army para command regiment (RPKAD: Resimen Para-Komando Angkatan Darat) arrived in Denpasar. Arrests started. Some people were thrown into prison, others were taken out of prison to be executed somewhere else, and many others were just killed in front of their houses, or on the side of the road.

What happened to one of Permadi's friends, Gde Mangku, a Lekra poet from Bali, is a distressing story. Permadi's house in Denpasar was often a gathering place for Lekra artists. The day the announcement appeared, Gde Mangku was at Permadi's place. Gde Mangku quickly returned to the place he rented, because he remembered that his mother was alone at home. That very night, not long after he got home, a gang came to get him. Gde Mangku was taken to the area of Kapal and executed. Permadi asked many of his friends about Gde Mangku until he finally got an explanation about what had happened. The son of the landlord was at the place the incident took place, acting as secretary to an officer who had forced him to come to the execution site. He saw Gde Mangku ordered to stand facing the grave which the military had ordered the locals to dig. Before he was shot, Gde Mangku made his last request. Then he sat in prayer position and prayed to God for the safety of his mother. Gde Mangku was then shot and his body fell into the hole. His fate was so sad. One by one, Lekra artists were hunted down and murdered. Permadi was sure that he would be targeted soon enough. His position as one of the high Lekra officials in Bali meant it was impossible for him not to be known to the mob and to the military.

People whose houses had been smeared with 'PKI' were murdered and their houses burnt to the ground. People of Chinese descent experienced the same thing. Permadi's neighbours were beginning to disappear or be killed. A student from Gayo who was studying in Bali advised him, 'Brother, you must leave Bali. Everyone, especially the leadership, will be killed. That's for sure.'

Every morning Permadi woke up with his hand at his throat, giving thanks that he was still alive. He could not bear to just stay at home. He was prepared for the worst. He often went out of the house on his bicycle. He went to the market to buy food, while killing and burning was going on along the road. There was no one that he recognised. They were people from Bali – but who knows where they were from – carrying knives, wood, cudgels. Sometimes you would hear screams of pain, or yells to burn, to kill. When the road was full of people, he would get off his bike and wheel his bicycle through the crowd. In the midst of the chaos, no one recognised him.

But the time came for a gang in black and with black headbands to come to Permadi's house. That morning, Permadi was preparing his canvas and painting equipment. He was going to paint in front of his house. He had not yet sat down to paint when he saw a gang of about hundred people in the alley, some of them coming towards his house. His landlord was terrified and from the corner of the house he called out, 'Permadi! You're going to die, Permadi!' But Permadi himself felt calm. Incredibly calm. One of the black headbands came up,

'Are you Permadi? Permadi Liosta?' Asked the gang leader.

'Yes, that's me', Permadi replied.

'You're the head of Lekra?'

'I am not the head of Lekra, but I am head of the visual arts section of Lekra. There is a head of Lekra, but that is not me', Permadi answered calmly.

'Well we've come to do a search!'

'Please do' Permadi said. Then the gang went inside and ransacked his room, the kitchen, and then climbed up on the roof. They were there for about an hour searching Permadi and ransacking the house.

'Have you found anything?' asked the gang leader, speaking Balinese.

'No, nothing here', came the reply in Balinese from within. Permadi had no idea what they were looking for. Guns perhaps, who knows. Then the gang leader ordered his men to come outside and gather in the yard.

'We apologise if we treated you roughly', the gang leader said.

'That's alright. Thank you', Permadi replied. Then the gang left his house.

After this incident, Permadi felt the situation was increasingly unsafe. The Governor of Bali, Suteja, had already left Bali at President Soekarno's orders. Permadi heard that another Lekra artist, Raka Suasta, had been put into prison, and others had escaped by going into churches, or had secretly left Bali. The situation in Denpasar was extremely tense. The student from Gayo advised Permadi to go to Java as soon as possible.

'Go to Java, brother. You need to have travel papers. I know a policeman. I'll organise it', he said.

The relationship between Permadi and the student from Gayo (who was also an activist in HMI, the Association of Muslim University Students) was like uncle and nephew. The student would often ask Permadi's help in doing his assignments, and his lecturer was one of Permadi's friends from the Association of Indonesian Graduates (HSI, Himpunan Sarjana Indonesia). The student was worried about Permadi's safety and invited Permadi to go and stay with him while waiting for the travel documents from the police. He lived near the police station where people said to be political prisoners were being held. The student's room was right next to the prison wall. Through the ventilation hole, Permadi could clearly see the trucks taking the prisoners out of the prison. The truck had two large headlights, and small tail lights. The prisoners were pushed on to the truck where they sat crowded together. Every night between eleven and midnight, trucks full of prisoners would go out escorted by two jeeps in front and a tank behind. No one knew where the prisoners were taken. Some said to Kapal or perhaps other places.

Permadi stayed at the Gayo student's place for a week. As soon as he had the travel papers in his hands, he left Denpasar. He did not have much money, but gave his clothes, some jackets and a few other things to the Gayo student. The student gave Permadi some money for the trip. At four in the morning, the student took Permadi to the bus station by bicycle. They said their goodbyes and Permadi got on the bus.

On the way out of Denpasar, Permadi pretended to sleep so he could cover his face. He saw many terrifying scenes as the bus went through Tabanan, Gilimanuk and Banyuwangi. There were mobs yelling, fires here and there, piles of corpses, and even bodies hanging beside the road. Before all this tumult in Bali, Permadi had thought that this island was truly heaven on earth. Peaceful, calm, its people gentle and friendly and accepting of newcomers with open arms. How different now were the expressions on the faces of the people he saw surrounding the houses, or those on the roadside chasing and killing their own people, fellow Balinese.

At the Surabaya railway station, the train for Jakarta was about to leave. Permadi ran and jumped into the carriage just in time. He bought a ticket on the train. He remembers that it was 13 December 1965, and Soeharto had just revalued the rupiah (1000 rupiah became 1 rupiah).

When he got to Jakarta, Permadi went to stay with a relative. Unlike Bali, the situation in Jakarta at the end of 1965 was safe and quiet, there were no arrests. Permadi started painting again to earn money. Then there was a ban on the publishing or sale of any works by Lekra artists. Books and paintings were burnt. Luckily, Permadi was still on good terms with gallery owners like Adi Prana, so he could store his paintings there and get some money. Now he did a different technique, using a brush for painting and no longer the palette knife. He was no longer painting with his former idealism. His paintings were now done to order, with commercial themes according to the market.

But it was difficult to keep calm. Permadi was sure that at a certain time, sure enough something would happen. More than two years after the events of December 1965 in Denpasar, news went around of arrests of people accused of being involved with the September 1965 incident. These included people accused of being involved with the Communist Party and organisations affiliated with the Communist Party, or just people who had attended Communist Party activities and events, or people of Chinese descent. They were being arrested at home, on the streets and at their place of work. Those already arrested were being forced to mention names of friends or relatives who were often with them and at the same activities. At the very least, they had to give three or four names, the more the better.

It was in mid-1968, at midnight. A group of people in black jackets surrounded Permadi's house. They were called 'Kalong' (bats). One of them shouted outside the house.

'Permadi! Permadi!' Permadi came outside. 'Excuse me, are you Permadi?' asked the bat.

'Yes I am', Permadi answered calmly. He knew he was going to be 'taken'. The day before, someone he had once known from Kramat 81, the Central Committee of the Communist Party, had been spying on him. Permadi had seen him drinking coffee at the market near his house. Permadi knew he had come there to point out where Permadi lived.

The bat came up. 'You must come along with us. This is for interrogation purposes.'

'Alright', Permadi said. Then he got his clothes together. Unfortunately, Permadi's nephew who had just graduated from high school and recently arrived from Aceh was also taken.

When they got to the District Military Command (Kodim), Permadi and his nephew were interrogated. Luckily, Permadi's nephew was released a month later because he knew nothing at all about the events of 1965.

The interrogators used all kinds of methods to make the prisoners admit to involvement with the 1965 incident, or to admit to being Communist Party members. The prisoners were abused, hit, kicked, struck with barbed whips, and given electric shocks. When they could not come up with names of friends, they would be tortured some more. Permadi remembered a particularly cruel interrogator, a young man from a youth organisation, who interrogated him and forced him to give addresses of Lekra people he knew. The interrogator would mention many names of Lekra artists, but Permadi could not say where they were.

'How would I know? I have been living in Yogya and Bali. I know the names of friends in Jakarta, but I have no idea where they are! He was almost given electric shocks.

Permadi was more fortunate than many of his friends. He only suffered blows. His friend Martian had to crawl on his hands and knees out of the interrogation room, his leg crushed because he did not want to admit that he knew Permadi. Permadi himself managed to avoid 'dragging' his friends to prison, because many of them and the Lekra painters had already died in Bali, or he had no idea where they were or what their situation was now.

Permadi was held for a few months at the District Regional Command in Jakarta, the headquarters of the 'Operation Kalong'. Then he was moved to Salemba prison. He was held there for two years along with thousands of other detainees without any court process whatsoever.

There was one occasion when Permadi was summoned by the Commander of Salemba Prison, Sanigonjo. He was accused of being an escapee from a communist-affiliated organisation in Bali. They had the idea that the Communist Party and its affiliated organisations had all been 'pulled out by the roots' in Bali, so they were surprised to find that Permadi, a high ranking Lekra official there, had escaped. Permadi himself thought the same thing – to this day he is thankful that he managed to escape what happened in Bali.

'This is him. Permadi', Sanigonjo's staff said.

Then Sanigonjo himself questioned Permadi about why and how he had left Bali.

'I am not an escapee', Permadi said. 'I could not live in Bali. Back then, Bali was chaotic, there were no tourists, and I couldn't live. Who could I ask for money to buy food? So I went to Jakarta. Things were clear there, because I had travel papers.'

Permadi was soon returned to his cell.

In 1971, some of the prisoners were taken to Buru Island and others to Tangerang prison. Permadi was one of the thousands taken by boat to Buru. Before they were transported there, every prisoner was given a shirt and trousers clearly marked with their prison number, and a coolie hat made of palm leaf. The boat left from Tanjung Priok harbour in Jakarta and arrived in Namlea about eight days later. The official name of Buru island at that time was 'Buru Humanitarian and Location Utilisation Project' (Proyek Kemanusiaan Tefaat Buru). It was intended as a place to prepare and 'resocialise' the political prisoners before they returned to society after their period of detention. The other name was Badan Pelaksana Rehabilitasi Pulau Buru (Body for the Administration of Buru Resettlement and Rehabilitation), known by the acronym Bapreru. But the more familiar name was 'Inrehab', which was short for Instalasi Rehabilitasi (Rehabilitation Installation). Obviously the name had no relation to rehabilitation. Upon release, political prisoners had to have the symbol 'ET' for 'former political prisoner' stamped on their identity cards. This continued until the Minister for Security, Soesilo Soedarman, rescinded the regulation on 18 August 1995. Even then, the rescinding order was not applied evenly over Indonesia.

Soeharto copied the colonial and fascist model for the 'Rehabilitation Installations'. Just as in Dutch colonial times and during the Japanese occupation, the people considered enemies to be defeated, had their freedom taken away, were sent mad, or died in exile. The total number of prisoners taken to Buru was about 13,500, over a few stages.

The island of Buru is about 9,500 square kilometres in area, or about one and a half times the island of Bali. Its capital is Namlea. At that time, Buru was still part of the regency of Central Maluku. The prison camp at Buru was made up of 21 units, with each unit containing at least 500 prisoners. Each unit comprised barracks that were surrounded by barbed wire and closely guarded by young soldiers. The young soldiers were brought in from the Maluku area. The units were separated from each other by a distance of a few kilometres, with long grass, rivers or wild jungle.

The basic principle of the camp was that every prisoner had to be self-sufficient. Prisoners were given hoes, machetes, seeds and some basic crops, dried salted fish, sugar and rice. They were supposed to produce their own food in three months. So they had to clear the land for rice paddies and fields. The guards monitored their hours of work, waking and sleeping. In the initial stages when clearing the land, the prisoners worked themselves to the bone, from early morning until night. The guards in the barracks had fierce expressions, quite in contrast to their young years. Most of them were only in their teens or early twenties. But they had no problems hitting prisoners they saw chatting during work hours.

This cruelty was particularly true of the early period of detention on Buru. Prisoners were automatically denied books, paper and writing implements. They had to work, farm, plant and raise animals, and were not permitted to pursue any former occupation. Each unit also had spiritual advisors, including Muslim, Protestant and Catholic, to watch over the spiritual and psychological state of the prisoners. While Permadi was in Buru, he was in unit 12, barracks number 2, together with about 50 others. He was not shocked to see the jungles of Buru. He could remember the jungles of the interior of Aceh when he was young, which were as dense as this. Some things that other prisoners found difficult were relatively easy for him. He was used to hoeing, sawing wood and cutting through the undergrowth with a machete.

Because the prisoners felt they were sharing the same fate, a sense of solidarity was built between them, not only between inmates of one unit but between neighbouring units. Often prisoners planting cassava, bananas and peanuts would walk through his unit's work area. This was to make work easier for them, and so they could get some food from the existing crops. Permadi recalled:

> It was as though we had our own unspoken vow to watch out for ourselves, to watch out and help our friends, and to do as much as we could to keep alive. If we had to plant bananas, cassava and coffee, we could plant as much as we could wherever we could. The important thing was to eat. We could often plant beyond another unit. But then our friends from another unit would sometimes carry water in kettles, and hide it under the plants. When we went past we would see a glass on top of the kettle. Someone might boil up cassava and leave it beside the path. We would understand that these things had been left on purpose for us to eat and drink. But we had to keep it hidden from the soldiers. If they found out, they would beat us ... There was strong solidarity between friends. And everyone was certain that there would come a time when we would return [leave Buru].

The parish in Namlea helped a lot by supplying medicine. Often Permadi and some other prisoners were sent as a company to pick up army supplies or sacks of rice in Namlea, and then had to carry them on their shoulders along the paths through the jungle. In Namlea, people in the Presbytery would ask whether any of the prisoners were sick and needed medicine. This was Permadi's opportunity to get medicine for friends who were ill.

Unlike the solidarity between the inmates or the sympathy of the church people, the army often abused its powers over the prisoners. Often the unit commanders or the camp commanders going home to Java on leave would demand 'gifts'. Sometimes they would ask the prisoners to get them endangered birds, or a few sacks of their produce, or they would ask the prisoners to saw a few cubic meters of wood to take. There were many opportunities for self-enrichment, and it was accepted practice for the unit commanders to ask prisoners in their units to go into the jungle, fell some trees, then float the logs to Namlea down the Wai Apu River. In Namlea there was a thriving black market dealing in stolen goods. The proceeds went to the camp bosses of course.

In April 1976, Permadi and some other prisoners were moved from the unit to the Camp Command (Mako). There they were placed in one barracks. There was a special barracks for graduates, doctors, and artists. Permadi was put in a barracks with about 20 other people including the Lekra writer Pramoedya Ananta Toer, the actor and director Basuki Effendi, the painters J. Gultom and Isa Hasanda, and the sculptor Supeno. The camp commander relieved these prisoners from farming duties, and allowed them to pursue their different crafts. These political prisoners got special treatment and were like shop window displays. Indonesia, which was in the process of 'trying' thousands of political prisoners in this Buru 'rehabilitation' camp, invited international journalists and organisations like the International Red Cross and Amnesty International to visit. The prisoners were out clearing the jungle or hoeing the fields, bathed in sweat, but the visitors were treated to scenes of political prisoners free to write creatively, paint and sculpt, so that it appeared as though the camp was a true humanitarian project that did not inhibit the freedom its prisoners to create.

From the time he moved, Permadi began to pursue painting again, after five years of being prevented from touching anything to do with art. He and six other painters were given painting equipment. Their paintings were often exhibited when journalists, organisations or international bodies visited. It was a simple gallery. Permadi often got orders from the camp officials for paintings. Once the Camp Commander asked him to make a painting of the seven nymphs (from the Jaka Tarub legend), but wearing bikinis rather than their usual nymph robes. Who knows what was in the Commander's head, but this was certainly not the only time Permadi got rather 'strange' requests. In the same camp, Pramoedya Ananta Toer produced his writings like *Nyanyian Sunyi Seorang Bisu* (Mute's Soliloquy) and the Buru tetralogy. Pramoedya was even given his own room to make it easier for him to write. Or maybe this was the way the Camp Commander could keep close watch over Pram's work.

Permadi was also often interviewed during these visits. As best he could, in his English, he would translate the answers by the other painters to questions. At these times, Pramoedya Ananta Toer was always separated. Unlike Permadi and other political prisoners, who would always give the 'right' answers, Pram would always explode in protest at the injustice of his situation and that of the other prisoners.

'How can anyone live here! This is not a place for farming! This is jungle!' Pram would say.

There was one occasion when Permadi was brought to face the Camp Commander and almost put into a cell. The Red Cross had interviewed Permadi, and Permadi was accused of saying in the interview that the Camp Commander was exploiting the artists. Luckily, at that time there was an American-born doctor working there. He explained to the Commander that he had been present when Permadi was interviewed. And the doctor knew exactly what Permadi had said. So the slander was proven wrong, and Permadi escaped punishment.

It was difficult to keep one's sanity as a detainee on Buru Island. Thousands of political prisoners were not as fortunate as Permadi or Pramoedya Ananta Toer who had the freedom to create. Being moved to Camp Command and being able to do creative work kept up their intellectual and artistic spirits. But thousands of other prisoners suffered deep depression. Actually, not just the prisoners, but the army and even the high ranking officials were under severe mental tension. The difference was that the army had many ways to escape these tensions. Many of them had girlfriends or 'second wives' in Namlea.

There were a few soldiers and officials who were kind to the prisoners. Towards the end of the rehabilitation camp, there was a nice Camp Commander who brought a small television to the Camp Command, having first got approval from headquarters, and not long after that, every unit had a small television. The prisoners were also permitted to watch simple performances like *dangdut* music or traditional drama (*wayang wong*) performed by the prisoners themselves with young men playing the female roles. Permadi remembers in particular when there was a Camp Commander who liked to joke, and who was close to the painters.

'What's going on, Sir, with our friends here getting beaten up and so on?' Permadi protested to him.

'Well, don't become a political prisoner then,' the Commander joked, 'that's usually what happens to them …'

Permadi was in the Buru Rehabilitation camp for nine years in all. He was repatriated to Java in 1980, which was the last year of the releases from Buru. When he got to Jakarta, he went to the house of a relative. As a former political prisoner, he had to report every few days to the authorities. Permadi began to re-establish his life the only way he could, namely by painting. He went to the galleries where he had exhibited his paintings before he was arrested. He went to Adi Prana's place, in Bargas. He had earned a small amount of money from paintings that had been sold while he was in prison, but the money now, a decade later, was worth virtually nothing. Permadi went to collect the money, anyway, as it was his right. He recalled this time of collecting money, bit by bit:

> The gallery owner did not give me cash, he told me to get the money at the bank. I once went to Manhattan Bank, another time to Bank America. I would be picking up just 25,000 rupiah [approximately $10 in 1980, trs.] or 50,000 rupiah [$20] and for this I had to show my identity card or other documents. Sometimes people in the bank

> laughed at me, coming to collect such a tiny sum. But I went and collected every single bit. And then I started painting again.

Permadi worked hard, painting once more. It was like when he first went to Bali, before he was arrested, he painted to order. Adi Prana, a gallery owner and architect, often came to Permadi's house to show him photos of houses, so that Permadi could make pictures on predetermined themes and in certain colours.

'Could you make a painting of people harvesting rice? The room for it is green like this … so the rice fields must blend in', Adi Prana would request.

Permadi knew all about the market. The market wanted commercial paintings. This was far from the ideology of realistic art that he had followed. Now the yellow rice fields at harvest time were made green because that was what the buyer ordered.

In 1982, while still in Jakarta, Permadi met Siti Bendara, the woman who later became his wife. By now, his mother and his friends were urging him to marry. Siti Bendara's family knew Permadi's story and his status as a former political prisoner. Soon after, Permadi married Siti Bendara.

A year later, in 1983, Permadi bought some land in the area of Jagakarsa in South Jakarta and built a house where he lives to this day. He continued to paint on commission for galleries. He was often criticised by his artist friends, 'Adi Prana is using you. You are being exploited!' But he didn't pay much notice. Permadi sees that God has given him a second chance at life after he escaped death in Bali. So after his imprisonment, he is prepared to do anything at all. To remain faithful to his calling as a painter, Permadi had to adapt to the commercial market and make paintings that people like and will buy. He is no longer as idealistic as he used to be with his palette knife. It was enough for him and his wife to live without depending on others.

Over the last decade, Permadi has been in exhibitions with other Lekra artists, and has had single-man shows. His paintings have sold well, and he has become more well-known. So now he does not need to sell his paintings through Adi Prana. Buyers come to his house which doubles as his gallery.

His former artist friends from prison days sometimes come to his house, just to visit, check on the news, and tell stories. Many of Permadi's friends are not as lucky as he is. Some of them are no longer able to work because they are still haunted by feelings of wrong-doing, or from fear and terror of the past. Permadi, though, has been able to rediscover art as his life's path. Permadi and Siti Bendara did not have any children. Permadi's wife had three miscarriages. Permadi's friends used to say, 'ah, you need to take another wife'. But Permadi saw this as his destiny. It is his destiny not to have children.

He once went back to Takengon in Aceh, to meet his relatives still living there and to reminisce about his childhood. He settled matters to do with his inheritance from his parents. As he has no descendants himself, he gave his land to another family to be shared in a fair way.

Permadi lost his wife Siti Bendara in May 2008 after she had been treated in the Cipto Mangunkusumo hospital. Many of his Lekra colleagues came to pay their last respects. Permadi remembers that [the actress and TV presenter, trs.] Rieke Dyah Pitaloka came to the hospital. She wept and embraced Permadi. Not long after this she bought one of his paintings for 15 million rupiah (approx. USD 1500) to help him out as he had many costs to meet.

* * * *

Permadi's status as a former political prisoner has not isolated him from society. His neighbours call him with the affectionate Gayo title '*Awan*', meaning 'grandfather'. Probably many people are totally unaware of Permadi's status, but the local authorities know it of course. However, they treat him no differently to other people. They often ask him to talk about his experiences, especially when he was in Bali and on Buru Island.

Permadi now lives alone. His grand nephews and nieces live nearby and visit every day to help out with the housework, cook, chat and watch television. His nephews and nieces and their children, and his close Lekra friends often help him out and bring him things. He has not painted now for the past two years. After the death of his wife, his paintings no longer sold, he himself has no idea why, for when his wife was still alive many people used to come to his house to buy paintings directly from him.

'Does he miss painting?'

Permadi answered,

> Right now, I do have some desire to paint a bit, but I am waiting until this urge matures. It won't be tomorrow. I am tired. I don't have the strength. I find it difficult just to get my body to move. It's my health problems these days.

* * * *

Permadi Liosta considers everything he has experienced as part of the story of his life. He accepts all of his past. He does not have any regret for choosing to love art. This love brought him a wealth of experiences. Once he wanted to travel the world. Having been to Europe and China, he wanted to see America. But this did not happen because the political situation led him into prison and to be exiled on Buru Island. He is not vocal like his friends in demanding justice and rehabilitation. To him, it is enough to spend his old age in peace, every now and then remembering his past and laughing about it, and telling his experiences for the study of art, culture and history.

Interviewers and transcribers: Amangku Bhumi, Puti Yassmina.

Writer: Amangku Bhumi.

Chapter 11

Rahim Marhab

History will reveal the truth

My name is Rahim Marhab. I was born in 1941 to Marhab and Ntokea in the village of Bambelamo, Parigi, in the district of Parimo, the province of Central Sulawesi. The village of Bambelamo is on the main trans-Sulawesi highway that runs between Central Sulawesi and South Sulawesi. It is about 55 kilometers from the city of Palu, which is the capital of the province of Central Sulawesi. I was the youngest of three children. The eldest, my sister, was called Saho, and my older brother was called Hajasa. My father worked in Poso in handicraft, making gold and silver ornaments. He supported the family with this work. But my father died while I was still young, and so my mother and older sister had to work to support the family. Fortunately, my mother and sister could sew clothes, knit and crochet. After living in Poso for a few years, I returned to Parigi. When I got back to Parigi, my older brother fell seriously ill, and then he died. I was very sad to lose my brother who was also part of the backbone of the family.

In 1952, I started primary school in Parigi, and six years later I graduated as the top student. I then went directly to the junior high school in Parigi, but only for a few months, because my mother, who was my one and only support in life, passed away, leaving me forever. No choice. That is the phrase to describe when I had to quit junior high school. And so in 1959 I decided to go to Poso by motor boat, and ended up continuing my schooling there. It was in Poso that I met Yakob Lamajuda, the person who introduced me to Marxism. At the time, Yakob was the local head (*lurah*) in Kayamanya. He was related to my father's family, and so he invited me to stay at his house. And it was at his house that I first came across the books *ABC of Politics* (*ABC Politik*) about Marxism, and *How Society Develops* (*Bagaimana Masyarakat Berkembang*) which was about communist ethics and morals. These books introduced me to Marxist teachings, and I became interested in them.

In 1961, I decided to join the Communist Party in Poso. I had to wait until 1962 to be sworn in because I was not yet of membership age. Actually, in mid 1962 I graduated from junior high school, again with top marks, and my uncle suggested that I go on to maritime college, but I refused and decided to return to my home village of Bamalemo. There I met Bung [Brother] Hasan Tungenge from the Communist Party Sub-section Committee [committee at the sub-district or *kecamatan* level. Trs] of Parigi who asked me to establish a Communist Party committee in Bambalemo. This I did, and on 12 October 1962, the Bambalemo 'Resort Committee' [Committee at the *kelurahan*, sub-sub-district, or lowest level of representation. Trs] of the Communist Party was officially established, with me as Secretary and Simin B. Pulo as deputy.

In early 1963, another Communist Party Resort Committee was established in Central Parigi, covering the area from the village of Kampal to the village of Sidole. I was chosen as deputy secretary. Because the organisation was going so well, Dai Borahima was chosen as head of the Indonesian Peasants' Front (BTI, Barisan Tani Indonesia) on the East Coast in what is now the district of Parimo, and I then took over his position as Secretary. In early 1964, the Parigi Section (Seksi, district or *kabupaten* level. Trs) of the Committee of the Communist Party held a conference, and various people were chosen to further the party's mandate; Sidin Umar (secretary), Hasan Tungege (deputy secretary), Ukas Abdullah (head of the secretariat), and Maks Lumanto and myself as executive committee members.

I had many reasons for wanting to join the Party; one of them was what they called the '3M' method. This stood for: *Merangkul* (Embrace), *Membatasi* (Limit) and *Menggunakan* (Utilise). The Party also taught me that service to the community is the highest aim of all struggle. This was the essence of the vow we had to make when we decided to become part of the Party. It was the same aim as that taught by the figure for education, Ki Hadjar Dewantara; 'at the fore give example, in the middle work alongside, and at the back encourage.' I truly implemented these communist teachings, because I thought they were wonderful if implemented properly. I had to be prepared to help everyone, paying no heed to their social class. Party teachings said we must not differentiate between people, because man is God's creation. So when people say that the communists were anti-God, this is wrong, because I was never taught this in the Party. Actually, before the 1965 incident, many people thought that we communists did not believe in God and had no religion. This was totally wrong!

I could see that within the Party its members were prepared to 'go below' ('*turba*', *turun ke bawah*), to the grassroots, to see the social situation for themselves, so they would get a picture of social reality directly and not from others. They had to not only know and see social conditions for themselves, but also to change situations that were backward. Once I saw that the roof of the mosque at Siniu was leaking badly, so that every time it rained the floor of the mosque was full of puddles. This was a big problem for the people who went there to pray. So I proposed to the Village Head that we should repair the roof. I told him that friends from the Indonesian Peasants' Front (BTI, Barisan Tani Indonesia) were happy to repair the roof. There were many sago palms in that village, so I asked them to sew sago palms together to thatch the roof. After the Village Head gave his approval, we worked one Sunday to repair the mosque roof. Beginning in the morning, food started arriving, because I had told them to bring food.

The enthusiasm the BTI members displayed fixing the roof led members of PSII (Partai Sarekat Islam Indonesia, Indonesian Islamic Union Party) and NU (Nahdlatul Ulama, Revival of Islamic Scholars) to say, 'people say those guys have no religion, but look, they are the only ones doing this work'. Actually, there were many from other groups who wanted to help fix the roof, but they seemed to be embarrassed. Maybe because the ones who were doing the work were PKI people who they thought had no religion. After we finished fixing the mosque roof, we also fixed the roof of the village community centre which was in a bad way, like the mosque. The way we saw it, our practical work was an example of the Party's teachings of 'going below'. We had to be always prepared to help in people's daily life. That way, people could really sense the existence of the Party and that it was not just occupied with power. I never saw any other political party carrying out this kind of activity.

After I passed the short course for teachers in [Communist] Party schools (KKGSP, Kursus Kilat Guru Sekolah Partai) held at the house of Hasan Tungenge and also at the local primary school, I took the plunge and opened a Party school in Silanga. Unfortunately, at night people threw stones at the building. Even though on the first day 20 people had already enrolled. After that incident, I sent the tutors from Gerwani (the Indonesian Women's Movement), like Aminah, Sabiha, Pihu and Sapina, back to the main secretariat. I did not want them being the target of such rage. I myself was confused as to why people would act like this, even though all I wanted to do was help people who were still illiterate. And even after I was treated in this way, I still wanted to continue the Party school. When Lamunuri, the

Party head in Siniu, heard this he immediately sent an adjutant and ordered me to move the Party school to Siniu. He said 'the people in Silanga don't think, they even kill each other there'. This was a serious blow to the spirit of Party members.

The Party school in Siniu opened with just a few students, but gradually the number of students reached 300. We divided them into classes of 20. They came from all kinds of social strata and age groups, and some were still illiterate. We taught them Marxist teachings which had been summarised in a political primer or ABC. I did not have to provide the books, because they were freely available. All I had to do was help them understand the contents. And unlike formal schools which demanded long periods of study, the Party schools required only ten days. After this period of study, every student was given a kind of certificate which said, more or less, that they had successfully completed the course. Their faces were so happy when they received that certificate. It was indeed very basic, but nonetheless to them the education they got at the Party school was really useful, and I fully trusted that they would go back and put what they had learned into practice.

* * *

As for my love life, I had a rather unique experience. After pursuing relationships with a few women, I eventually married someone who had never been my girlfriend, Ida Nusiplo'o. And she is still my life partner to this day. It might sound strange, but actually I married her not for love as other couples did. I married her because of an instruction from the Party.

In fact, I already had a girlfriend in Ampibabo at the time, called Ibonia. She was rather short, with fair skin and long hair. I had already asked her family for her hand in marriage. We first met when I was looking for long grass for thatch. After passing each other and stealing a few glances, I felt something stir in my heart. It was love at first sight and I immediately decided I would make her my wife.

I pedalled the bicycle I had taken to carry the cut grass, trying to chase after her. I asked everyone I met, explaining what she looked like, desperate to find her. After quite some time, I did eventually find her house which was about one kilometre from where we had first met. Her family greeted me warmly. Once when I visited the house, her parents told me to stay the night because it was already late, saying it was dangerous to go home. I was surprised to discover that our families were related, something I found out when exorcism prayers were held for one of my family who had to be rid of an evil spirit, and members of her family were there too.

It did not take long for me to declare my intention of making her my wife. I went with my uncle to her house and she immediately accepted my proposal. We decided to wait six months before marrying.

But then suddenly a messenger from Bambalemo came and asked me to meet Maselo in Parigi. I told the messenger that I was going to get married soon, and he asked, 'Brother, do you want to be a champion of the family or a champion of the nation?' I said, 'champion of the nation'. 'So, what are you waiting for? Let's go!' the messenger said. I went to take my leave of Ibonia. We even had a photo taken of us together. This was our parting, because our wedding plans came to nothing. After our parting, Ibonia got news that I had been taken to Poso and shot. Someone told me that Ibonia had been devastated to hear this. She was ill for three months, and lost all her hair from shock at hearing this news. Later on, a messenger came once from Ibonia's family telling me to come and marry her, but my situation did not permit it.

After being interrogated by the Area Command (Korem) of the Military Police, and detained for about one month in late 1965 in Maesa prison, Palu, I finally decided to return to Ampibabo, Parigi. I had been detained because I was a member of the leadership of the Communist Party. This was the one and only reason that I was detained and interrogated. Because things were not going well for me, I decided not to get back together with Ibonia. But at that moment I met another woman who later became my sweetheart. Her name was Hamra. I felt the same love for Hamra as I had felt for Ibonia. But with Hamra, too, things came to nothing, because suddenly Yakob Lamajuda ordered me to marry Ida Nusiplo'o.

I remember the first time I met Ida, the woman I eventually married, when she came to the village of Bambelamo, Parigi, in late 1966 looking for her husband Ruswanto, who has not been heard of to this day. Initially, she wanted to go to Gorontalo via Parigi by boat to look for her husband, but she failed to find him. Prior to this, friends who were doing forced labour on the Coffee Plantation Mountain digging irrigation ditches, clearing roads and carrying away felled trees, had talked about Ida's coming. They said that the wife of Ruswanto, the deputy head of the Central Sulawesi Communist Party Committee [provincial level. Trs] was coming to Parigi and in the cause of Party solidarity I had to look after her. Ida stayed at Toli's house with her three children. While she was staying there I went back and forth checking on her and her children. I couldn't stay there all the time because I was working as a building labourer in Kopel.

At the end of 1968, Corporal Masmur took Ida to Palu. I could not follow because at the time I was still working on a building project. After one year in Palu, at the end of 1969, Ida returned. This was when Yakob Lamajuda encouraged me to marry her so that she would have someone to protect her. And so in March 1970, I went to the Village Head to announce my intention to marry her. At the time, marrying her was an obligation. I was concerned that she had three children, and I truly wanted to guard and protect her. So it was not wholly because of Yakob Lamajuda's instruction. In other words, I did not marry Ida out of lust but because of a sense of responsibility and my solidarity with the Party. We could not expect anyone or anything to help or protect Ida.

I saw my marriage with Ida as destiny and we lived peacefully. After my release from Maesa prison, Palu, in 1966, I took her with me wherever I went. Later I faithfully carried out my duties, as a husband looking after her and her children and also the duties that were instilled in me as a Party member. And on 1 January 1971 our first child was born, called Slamet Ria Akres. Our second child was Surahman, the third Murahman, the fourth Yanti Priyatni and the last one, Sunaryansa. I never for a moment considered ignoring my responsibilities or leaving her. I understood that love is a form of responsibility. It is not like the love of young people today which arises from sexual desire.

* * * *

The ripple effect of the political incident that happened in Jakarta in 1965 arrived where I was living. The accusation of the Communist Party as the mastermind of the kidnapping of the high ranking army officers was gathering strength, and this included me too as a Communist Party member. At that time, the security forces had begun their 'cleansing' of anything considered linked to the Communist Party, and this was going on right down to outlying areas. Probably they hoped this would ensure that the Communist Party would never cause any more trouble in Indonesia. On 16 October, we were assembled at the Military District Command (Kodim) in Poso and told that we were forbidden to carry out any political activity. On the night of 18 October, we returned to Parigi by sail boat together with the Communist Party Section (district, *kabupaten* level) Committee from

Poso. Yakob Lamajuda and I landed at Torue, and from there we walked to Bambalemo, which was 20 kilometres away.

By now the situation was critical. On 8 November 1965, while I was firing bricks at the factory owned by W Mambu who was a member of the local Parigi police, a mob of about 300 people from the village Pelawa arrived. They captured me, my older brother Hajasa, my uncle Harati and my cousin Agi. Suddenly they started beating us with pieces of blackwood, beating my entire body except for the soles of my feet and my toes. They hit my head until it bled. After I passed out twice, we were taken to the Parigi district police station and held there for ten days. When we were let out of the cell we had to go and report to the district police station 1306-09 of Parigi and Military District Command (Buterpra) in Parigi.

Then in December 1965, I was picked up by Corporal Efendi and staff from the Central Sulawesi Military Area Command (Korem) and taken to Maesa prison in Palu. The conditions there were terrible: we were given miniscule food rations, and often any rice we did get was mixed with bran. There were 20 people crammed into a cell measuring 3 x 4 metres, so none of us could sleep properly because we could only sit on the floor. I was taken from there to the Military Area Command for interrogation. For four full days I was interrogated by the local interrogation team (called 'Teperda', tim pemeriksa daerah) from Menado. I remember that I felt like a lecturer, because I was made to sit on a high chair, while all nine members of the interrogation team who were sitting in a circle around me, interrogated me in turn.

They asked me when I had joined the Communist Party and what positions I had held. I told them I had been secretary of the Resort Committee, then promoted to secretary of the Sub-Section committee. They asked what 'sub-section' was. I told them this was *kecamatan* (sub district) level. Then I said that I had also participated in Party Schools (Sekolah Partai, SP), Courses for Party Teachers (KGP, Kursus Guru Partai) and Party Schools at the provincial level (SPDB, Sekolah Partai Daerah Besar). I had learnt about Marxism at these courses. Something I remembered well was studying How Society Develops (Bagaimana Masyarakat Berkembang, BMB). I gave a long explanation about this, from man's beginnings in the Garden of Paradise in Heaven through to man's development in this mortal world. The interrogation was always the same, from Palu to Parigi, and I would always give my long explanation in reply. After being held in the Maesa prison in Palu for one month, I was finally allowed to return to Parigi.

I was also made to do forced labour on Coffee Plantation Mountain (Gunung Kebun Kopi) for 20 days. This entire area had been planted with coffee during the Japanese occupation [1942–45], but today there are no longer any coffee plantations, although some coffee trees still grow wild in the forest. The coffee plantation road links the western coast of the city of Palu with the eastern coast of Parigi regency. The area is very hilly, and the road through the steep hills is about 48 kilometres. To the left, going from Palu, is a steep, deep ravine, and to the right there are hills that often have landslides. The forced labour consisted of clearing the road, digging ditches, carrying away felled logs, clearing landslides, and cutting grass. I was one of the fortunate ones because I only had 20 days of this work, but other friends of mine had to do it for a full year. We had to cook our own food, and were given only some uncooked rice, with nothing else. We were not paid anything at all. We were merely provided with hoes, shovels and sickles as work tools. We also had to sleep on the roadside, as no place had been prepared for us to rest.

It was not only me who was arrested, but other members of the Party too, and anyone at all suspected of being part of the Communist Party. In early January 1966, after being held for a month, some friends and I, including Paliudo, Gerson Goni, Gusti Camang, Sapina, Samsiar and Gusti Made were released. My friends and I who had been held in Maesa prison walked from Palu to Parigi. When I got to Parigi, I had to report to the Village Head, to the Parigi district policy, and to the Military District Command in Parigi. Even though I had been released, I had to report regularly. In the beginning, officially it was four times a week, but actually almost every single day I had to report because officials were always calling me in. It was only finally in 1978 that I was freed from this obligation to report.

It was exhausting going through this endless interrogation, from one place to another, from one town to another. The interrogators often punched me in the face, and when I was finally moved to Maesa prison, the interrogation came with torture. The interrogators were always looking for something I had done wrong, but I knew that I was not wrong, and nor were the Marxist teachings I had got from the Party. Not a single teaching disadvantaged others, or society. And it was through the Party that I came to understand how to build a society with social justice. Nor could I accept the accusations that the Communist Party was atheist. After all, we had fixed the damaged roof of the mosque which no other Party had done, even though they claimed that their guiding principles were religion or nationalism. So, wasn't this enough proof that we were not atheists?

I was not the only one treated so unfairly by the State and society. Later, my innocent children were affected by the 1965 political events. My two sons, Slamet Ria Akres and Surahman, later had to leave high school just because they were the sons of a former Communist Party member and political prisoner. They were victims of the ongoing stigmatisation of the Communist Party, even though I knew that they did not really understand what had happened to them.

When I no longer had to report regularly to the authorities, I could finally heave a sigh of relief because society could now accept me once again, and the stigma of being a former member of the Communist Party slowly began to fade. My family, especially my children, began to have their rights and freedom restored. Sunaryansa was able to complete his education at the Aliyah Madrasah (Islamic school), and Yanti Priyanti completed her education at the Muhammadiyah high school. They were able to attend school with no intimidation at all.

The burden I had to bear was extremely heavy. All the terrible accusations made of me really hurt me deeply. Had I not been able to face these trials wisely, I would probably have gone mad. Fortunately, I am able to face things calmly. I always joke with people I talk to, and I do this to lessen the pain and memories of the past. Even now, in my 70s, I love to chat with my son-in-law, Yanti's husband, until late at night. Chatting like this helps me to forget the pain I went through. Joking with others is like a balm to the pain of the bitter memories of the past.

* * * *

After Reformation and I regained my freedom, society accepted me again. I was no longer reticent to work with the Village Head in Bambelamo. To this day I still use the methods the Party taught me. Every day I mix with people, and am able to get close to them. There was a time when no one could write wedding invitations, so I gladly offered to help with this. People were not afraid to come up and ask help from a former political prisoner and former Communist Party member. And finally I felt that people really accepted me again.

These days people often ask me to be an advisor for weddings. Once, the Village Head said in front of the District Head that it was better governing one thousand Communists than one hundred 'good' people. This was because the Village Head knew for himself that it was people like me who had initiated the development in Bambalemo. We Communist

Party members had been trained to give our complete service to society, because we were aware that we are part of society and must make a positive contribution. And all the intimidation ceased, along with the stigma that had stuck to me.

But I also knew that this reformation was one-sided – it advantaged only the group in power. There were no real meaningful changes in society. After the fall of the Soeharto regime and the reformation that followed, I was no longer afraid to be politically active. I was once a supporter of Megawati Soekarnoputri's party [PDI Perjuangan] but when I saw that the party supporters in Parigi were not truly committed to furthering the causes of the people, I switched my allegiance to the Democrat Party (Partai Demokrat). They accepted me openly, with absolutely no reference to my links to the Communist Party. But I refused any position in the Democrat Party because I wanted to be just a regular member.

Apart from being active in a political party, I was also part of the backing team for one of the candidates for *bupati* (regent) in my area. His name was Longki Janggola. Longki never met me directly to ask me to be part of his team, but other members of his backing team in my area asked me to join. So I did – not mindlessly, but because I saw that his methods and his way of working were really good. His team of supporters in my area considered me to be their leader. Members of Longki's support team were once beaten up by some irresponsible types – probably members of a rival's support team, when they were putting up banners. But the minute someone said that I was one of Longki's team, they panicked. My position as an important figure in Bambelamo was enough to frighten them off.

I am no longer involved with any party. The way I see it, there is no point in supporting any party, it is totally futile. Parties are no longer of any benefit to the people they supposedly defend. It is just a waste of time to become a party member. I see that people who become members of parliament are often acting merely on instructions from their superiors, and their actions are not based on people's needs. Those party people are not stupid, they know the rules. But people with any conscience at all are probably very few and far between.

Another proof of the loss of stigma attached to families of former communists is that two members of the regional parliament from my area, Parigi, are children of 1965 political victims. They are also smart people, so I have never felt any need to give them advice. I have faith in their capabilities.

* * * *

It makes me sad when I have to remember the past. It feels like my heart is being sliced. Why did communists like me have to be treated so inhumanely? I am fortunate in that I am still alive, whereas so many of my friends are dead or disappeared. I once heard that a Gerwani member, called Ruhia from Playa, was raped by the police. I find that utterly incredible. How can those who are supposed to uphold the law rape a woman just because of her ideology? I can still remember how she cried until her eyes swelled as she told the story of being raped. Now that I am in my 70s, the only thing left for me to do is be of service to society. The only work I am capable of is tending the plants around my house.

It is my children now who support me. They are all independent. I give thanks to God for the blessings to me and my family. My marriage to Ida, which happened because of a Party order, has endured to this day. Even now that I am old, and my body stooped, Ida still wants to be with me and care for me. I can still see traces of her pretty face and fair skin. She often spoils me, calling me *uwa*, which is Gorontalo language for Granddad. We live peacefully and harmoniously, no longer having to deal with various forms of intimidation and social stigmatisation. Now we are accepted with open arms. I am even considered to be an important figure, and people often come to me for advice. But I always refuse all invitations to take on any social positions, including Kaili customary positions, where I now live. I know that at my age there is not much I can do, and I do not want to get in the way.

Even though people treated me so badly just because I was a Communist Party member, I do not harbour any revenge. As a Muslim, I know the story of the Prophet, who, when he began teaching Islam, was hated by those around him so he had to move to Madinah for safety. If people can treat even the Prophet in this way, then the same thing can happen to me, a mere communist. These days, I spend most of my time gardening, especially fruit and vegetables. Apart from that, I raise chickens. I am not able to do much more. With my decrepit body, and with conditions like hernia, diabetes, and cataracts, I can perform only light tasks.

Wrinkled and toothless as I am – I lost most of my teeth as a result of the mass violence in 1965 – I fit the name *Uwa*, Grandpa. But even though I am old and fragile, my spirit gets fired up when I listen to political news, and news about efforts to further the truth in this country.

But my hope is that the matter of the 1965 incident can be settled properly, because there were so many transgressions. Like the violence and intimidation I experienced. Personally, I hope that the government can give proper compensation, and rehabilitate the good names of those who were victims. My final hope is that there will never again be a tragedy like this in this land that I love, Indonesia. History will reveal the truth!

Interviewer and transcriber: Nurlaela Ak. Lamasitudju.

Writer: Akhmad Zakky.

Chapter 12

Rukiah

Undying loyalty

Where is there a mother prepared to hand over her baby to a stranger? This is what Rukiah had to do when she did not want to raise her child in prison.

Rukiah was born in Ujung Pandang, South Sulawesi on 7 March 1940. She came from a modest family. Her father was a sailor and her mother ran the house. Rukiah did not excel at school, she was average. But in her subsequent life journey, she proved to be an amazing organiser. She had a fierce drive to improve the lot of her gender.

Rukiah began to get involved with organisations when she was in sixth class of primary school. It was Ibu Salawati Daut who introduced her to organisations. Ibu Salawati, who was then in her 30s, was a well-known figure in Sulawesi. She came from Menado, but moved to Makassar and lived near Rukiah's house. Initially, she invited Rukiah to chat about the situation at her school and also about her family. Rukiah began to get close to Ibu Salawati through these chats. She often went to Ibu Salawati's house to ask about things she did not learn at school. Ibu Salawati would teach her how a girl should behave and mix with people socially. At this time, most girls concerned themselves only with household chores. Ibu Salawati advised Rukiah to venture beyond the house, for in this way she could also bring in a little extra income for the family.

Rukiah also often mixed with other women activists. They frequently came to her house to explain basic Party principles, one of which said that Gerwani (Gerakan Wanita Indonesia, the Indonesian Women's Movement) was anti-polygamy. As a young woman enamoured with ideas of emancipation, Rukiah fully agreed with this. She thought that Gerwani was an organisation that could protect the rights of women. She wanted to avoid the shackles of polygamy which was common practice in her social circles. Among the aristocratic strata in Makassar, polygamy was common. People accepted it as something normal. Domestic abuse and oppression of wives were common, and victims of this abuse were powerless.

When Rukiah was 14, she joined the Makassar branch of the Indonesian Women's Movement, Gerwani. She was then only in the second class of junior high school. Actually, to become a member of Gerwani you had to be 18 years old or above, or already married. However, the Makassar branch of Gerwani was short of members, and most of the members were from Java. So Rukiah was eventually allowed to join. At least she was proficient at reading and writing. 'Of course, the fact that I was close to Ibu Salawati was a factor that allowed me to join and become active on the organisational side,' Rukiah said. Her first duty was to help in the secretariat.

Rukiah's parents did not make much fuss about her activities. Her father, a fervent nationalist and Soekarnoist, allowed her do it. Her mother did not interfere. She left everything up to her daughter. 'My mother was the obliging and unassuming type of woman, what in Java they say '*suarga nunut, neraka katut*', 'faithfully following to heaven or to hell', Rukiah said.

Falling in love

Around 1959 in Makassar there was a Holden car show, with some attractive models dressed in bikinis posing in front of the cars. This offended the local people. The women protested because they felt this was not in accordance with Eastern custom. 'Why do you have to degrade women just to promote cars? Indonesia is not a Western country!' Soon members of People's Youth (Pemuda Rakyat, PR) and Gerwani hit the streets, demonstrating against the show. They all thought that the event organisers' actions were a deliberate infiltration of Western ideas to Indonesia. The demonstrators painted slogans on the streets, walls, and strategic places.

A few days after the 'Holden' incident, many of the People's Youth members behind the graffiti were held at the police station. Seeing this, some People's Youth and Gerwani activists discussed what they should do to get them released. Rukiah was one of those delegated to go the police station.

The activists' negotiations for the release of the detainees were successful. On the way back from the police station, a young man from Java who worked in the Bulog office (Badan Urusan Logistik, Body for Logistic Matters) in Makassar approached Rukiah and whispered, 'Thankyou, sister. It's thanks to you that my friends and I were freed.'

That was the first time she met Marsaid, her first love. Rukiah was suddenly overcome with shyness. She blushed. She hid her head. But her heart was racing. She was elated. She felt happy and proud.

'It was love at first sight for us', Rukiah recalled.

From that moment on, Rukiah and Marsaid were close. As they became inseparable, their friends encouraged them to marry. Their friends even went to visit Rukiah's parents to ask for her hand in marriage, on behalf of Marsaid's family who lived in Java. The proposal was accepted. And so the pair of sweethearts married in March 1963. It was their friends and colleagues from their organisations who organised the whole wedding.

Rukiah decided to do away with some aspects of the traditional wedding ceremony. According to her, there were some rituals that were no longer relevant to the times. For example, the ritual of throwing offerings into the sea, hitting gongs, and so forth. Apart from being impractical, she considered these traditional rituals a financial drain.

'The important thing was that our marriage would be strong', Rukiah said, grateful to her parents for accepting her decisions.

After her marriage, Rukiah joined the Gerwani staff in Makassar in Central Sulawesi. At that time, the leadership of Gerwani for South Sulawesi and Central Sulawesi was not yet split between two branches. As an organiser, Rukiah had to be skillful at dividing her time between her duties inside and outside the home. Her husband remained active in his organisation, so he totally understood his wife's enthusiasm, as they were both fighting to safeguard the ideals of the Great Leader of the Revolution, Bung Karno. In his speeches, Bung Karno always said that the revolution was not over. This duty was now passed to the young generation.

Apart from her organisational activities Rukiah taught at the Melati kindergarten which was right behind her house. Rukiah herself donated the land on which the kindergarten was built. While teaching, she also continued her studies although she was pregnant with her second child.

An unforeseen change of fate

No one ever knows what the future will bring. And so it was. The political and economic situation in Indonesia suddenly worsened. In September 1965, seven high ranking army officers were murdered in Jakarta. The news broadcast on national radio (RRI, Radio Republik Indonesia) truly shocked all Indonesians. According to the news, the murders were masterminded by the Communist Party. 'I was immediately shocked, deeply questioning, and in disbelief. But I tried to understand the situation calmly.'

The situation became increasingly unstable because other youth organisations were then linked to the Communist Party and what had happened, including Gerwani and People's Youth. Rukiah and other staff called a meeting to discuss the situation, which was becoming increasingly critical. Those leading the meeting called on members to remain calm.

'I managed to discuss the situation and ask for directions from Jakarta. But they told us in the regions to remain calm, and to wait for directions from the Leader of the Revolution, namely President Soekarno. So we did not think further than this. You could say that we kept calm. We had no idea that the situation would then get so bad. At that time, my husband was told to report to the police station for his own safety. Absolutely not to be arrested and detained,' Rukiah recalled.

In this confused situation, days felt oppressive. Rukiah's anxiety peaked on 15 October when her beloved husband did not return home. 'Please, please no ...' Rukiah thought. She immediately imagined the worst. She had been hearing about many Party members who had been taken for their 'safety'. 'No!' she said to herself. 'This cannot happen to my husband.' But facts proved otherwise.

The evening is still clearly etched in her memory, when at around seven at night, a group of youths from the Makassar branch of the Association of Muslim University Students (Himpunan Mahasiswa Islam, HMI) and others came to her house situated on a main road in Makassar, near the Mumi cinema. They forced entry into her house, looking for a member of Gerwani, who was none other than Rukiah herself. She instinctively escaped through the kitchen door and jumped over her neighbour's wall into the garden behind. She paid no heed to the fact that she was eight months' pregnant. From here she could see what was happening in her house. A group of about 30 people ransacked her house. After an hour went by and they had not found Rukiah, they started taking anything of value: watches, the radio, clothes, even crockery. Rukiah's legs were shaking. Her belly felt tight. She did not want to think about the meaning of what was going on. She did not want to think of this as looting.

In Makassar there were many demonstrations by students and others attacking the Communist Party, which was considered to be the mastermind behind the 30th September Movement. They were provoked into capturing and even torturing Communist Party members and also members of organisations considered to be 'under' the Communist Party. The demonstrations involved painting slogans along the streets and putting up anti-communist banners, like 'Gerwani sluts!' 'Communist Party atheists!' 'Communist Party: Your wife is my wife!' and 'Arm the workers and farmers following the Communist Party coup d'etat and their murder of the generals!' This was the kind of provocative tone of the slogans in Makassar at the time.

Rukiah was afraid to return home that night. She had to sleep in her neighbour's yard. Absolutely nobody was prepared to take her in, even for a moment. They were all terrified of being labelled as involved with the communists, so even the fact that Rukiah was heavily pregnant meant nothing. But what can one say? It was the situation that forced people to act in this way. Rukiah herself understood. She had to accept this treatment without rancour. It was only her desperate resolve to protect the child in her womb that kept her going. Fortunately, her mother was already caring for her first child. That certainly helped.

Rukiah, now on the 'wanted list', tried asking for help from one house to the next, but no one at all was prepared to take the risk. There was just one old servant who helped her in the house. Even to get her help, Rukiah had to sell anything of value that she had left.

Then she read a notice saying that all Party members and members of its support mass organisations should turn themselves in at the nearest police station for their own protection. If Party members did not turn themselves in, then the police could not guarantee their safety. Rukiah began to waver between continuing to hide and turning herself in. But if she turned herself in, what would happen when she gave birth? She despaired.

Finally, on 28 November 1965, she turned herself in at the nearest police station. Quite beyond her wildest dreams, she found that her husband was there. She was overjoyed. But only for a moment. Her husband signed to her to keep her mouth shut. 'Ruk, when they question you, say you don't know anything. And don't let on that I am your husband,' he whispered to her. Rukiah nodded. And then came her turn to be called for interrogation. As her husband had instructed her, she answered 'I don't know' to all the questions. She was held for almost a month, until her labour started. Then something amazing happened. The officer called for male detainees to carry Rukiah to the car, but no one came forward. It turned out that Marsaid had orchestrated this. And then he himself came forward. So Rukiah went to the hospital with her husband. During the journey Marsaid never took his eyes off his wife. Her husband's loving gaze gave Rukiah strength. She was immediately taken to the labour room. Marsaid could take her only as far as the door and then had to return to the police station. Although this was terribly hard, Rukiah was able to accept her husband leaving. All she could do was pray that the birth of her baby would go smoothly.

Rukiah's prayers were answered. Her second child, a daughter, was born safely. After staying a few days in hospital, Rukiah was sent back to the police station. Not long after, she was moved to the Makassar Military

District Command (Kodim). There were about 300 other detainees there. Then she was moved again to the office of Administrative Body for Food Affairs (Badan Pelaksana Urusan Pangan, BPUP). When the police could not get enough evidence, Rukiah was released, but on the condition that she report regularly to the authorities.

Rukiah immediately returned to her parents' home. For almost two years she worked as a seamstress in a garment factory. Even though she tried to keep resolute, every now and then she would be gripped with fear when she thought about the fate of her friends who had been detained. This included Javanese migrants who knew absolutely nothing about organisations, but had become the victims of arrest.

Realising that the condition was uncertain, she thought about leaving the town of her birth and moving to Surabaya in East Java where her husband's family were, and where she thought it would be safer. She asked her husband's permission. He was still undergoing interrogation at the local interrogation centre. He agreed. 'Be careful, Ruk. Take care of yourself. Don't bother thinking about me. I will be fine here,' Marsaid said, holding Rukiah's hand tightly.

Rukiah went to visit her parents to ask for their blessing. She asked them not to mention her departure to anyone at all, for safety.

To Java

Rukiah immediately sold her husband's Vespa motor bike and used the money to leave for Java. She left with her baby by boat. Her mother looked after her older child. During the journey she had the chance to think – what if she was arrested on the way? While staring at the sea, she tried to calm herself. She thought this would be better than being arrested in her own neighbourhood. At least there would be no family members who would know she had been detained.

When she got to Surabaya, she looked for a house to rent. Even though many of her husband's family lived in Surabaya, she tried her best to be independent. She opened a small business selling stuffed fried soya bean cake. It produced enough to cover daily costs.

But then, the situation that seemed to have calmed, suddenly changed. In 1968, on 23 May, the day of the Communist Party's anniversary, the army instigated their Operation Swoop (*Sambar Nyawa*) to hunt down all party members not yet arrested. This led to another operation called *Sambar Laga* (Swoop and Fight) which was even more intense, to hunt down Communist

Party figures. It turned out that Rukiah was on the list of Wanted Persons. Her photo was distributed all over Surabaya. Among her listed features was a mole on her forehead and the fact that she had a baby with her.

Rukiah was worried. She had noticed a man in plain clothes hanging around her house for the past few days. And what was strange, he was asking the neighbours questions about her. He even once approached Rukiah and asked, 'You seem to be alone. Where is your husband?'

She replied, 'Oh he's out of town right now. He's in Solo collecting some batik.'

Then he said, 'I am a friend of your husband's. Be sure to tell him I am looking for him.'

'Oh yes, I will tell him', Rukiah answered.

'Your husband's name is Marsaid, isn't it?' probed the man.

Oh no, my husband's name is Sumarno', Rukiah answered, spontaneously.

The man then took his leave with a knowing smile on his face. When he had left, Rukiah suddenly felt scared. She knew it was no longer safe where she was. That very evening she left and went to her husband's family. But when she got there she was dreadfully shocked to see three men sitting on the terrace, and one of them was the man who had spoken to her earlier. She quickly hid and ran away, making a sign to her cousin to keep quiet.

> That night I did not go back home to the house I rented. I preferred to sleep in the graveyard which was one kilometre from my house. Lots of graves have shelters, so I slept there. It was better to sleep in a graveyard than go home sick with worry. And lots of beggars sleep in the graveyard.

The next morning she went back home. Her neighbours told her that the previous night two cars of soldiers had come to her house. Rukiah was not too surprised as she had already suspected this would happen. So she immediately packed her things and said goodbye to her landlady.

'Be careful, child. Take care of your health', she said to Rukiah on parting.

Rukiah looked for a new house to rent nearer the city. As she had skills as a tailor, she found work at a clothing factory that made uniforms for the navy. She worked there for a month. But because of the terrible work conditions, she got a lung condition and had to go to hospital for treatment. On her way home, she noticed three men following her. One of the men arrested her and took her to an army interrogation centre. It was in a former doctor's surgery because there was a laboratory there. Rukiah was not alone. There were about 30 other women there. Rukiah felt her hair stand on end when she saw a woman tied up, with her blouse open. Her small child was tied up beneath her feet. The child was crying because it wanted to nurse at its mother's breast. The woman was being tortured because she would not say where her husband was.

Rukiah had a coughing fit. Her chest felt tight. She could not imagine how it would feel to be tortured like that. She also saw one of her husband's relatives there, but they pretended not to know each other. If it was known that there was any relationship between them, then Rukiah's identity as a Gerwani official on the run would also be known.

The detainees were moved from this illegal interrogation centre to the Tiperda (Tim pemeriksa daerah, local interrogation team) office in Surabaya around 1973. Her duty was to cook for the guards. It was there that she met a kind-hearted policewoman working for the Military Police Corps (Corps Polisi Militer, CPM). Rukiah did not know why, but suddenly she felt she should give her cute little daughter, Gestina Patriani, to her. Rukiah just could not rid herself of the image of that mother being tortured with her child. What's more, she had no idea what was going to happen to her. This is what led her to make that decision.

So she immediately wrote a letter of authorisation of adoption. When it was completed, Rukiah handed over her own daughter to her new adoptive mother who changed Gestina's name to Watiningsih. Rukiah did not object to this, as long as Wati was loved.

Time passed. In 1975, after being held at the Military Police Corps headquarters in Surabaya for nearly two years, one day Captain Awari, who she had known in Makassar, arrived. 'Ibu Rukiah! You're Marsaid's wife, aren't you?'

This time, Rukiah could not deny it, 'Yes, I am.'

Captain Awari said that Rukiah's husband was dead. He forced Rukiah to return to Makassar. With a heavy heart, because she had to part from Watiningsih, Rukiah left Surabaya. When she arrived in Makassar she was taken to the prison. Imagine her joy when she then found that her beloved husband was still alive. Even though the male and female detainees were separated, the prisoners organised it so that the husband and wife, who had been separated now for eight years, could meet.

A new page in Nanga-nanga

A few months later, the male detainees were sent to Maros prison, and the female detainees to Gunung Sari prison in Makassar. In 1977, Marsaid and Rukiah were sent to Moncong Loe. Not long after this, Marsaid was released, but Rukiah was still held. The Commander for the Restoration of Security and Order Operations (Panglima Komando Pemulihan Keamanan dan Ketertiban, Pangkopkamtib) for South Sulawesi recommended that the prisoners still in detention agree to be sent to the internment Camp in Nanga-nanga, Kendari. They would be given two hectares of land per family. Rukiah decided to accept this offer in order to forge a new life. Her husband agreed to join her. There were around 41 political prisoners who went. But it turned out that conditions there were far from favourable. The house that had been promised turned out to be no more than jungle. There were floods in the rainy season. One of the women detainees who was pregnant miscarried because she could not walk the four kilometres to shelter.

There were already 14 other political prisoners at Nanga-nanga who came from Ameroro Camp in Kendari. The detainees had no problems mixing. Each person was given the promised allotment of land. They were given tools, an axe and a sickle. They worked together to clear the forest for agriculture. Rukiah and Marsaid, who had always lived in the city and worked in offices, found this extremely hard. But they had to do it, like it or not, or die of hunger.

Finally, in 1980 Rukiah was officially released after 15 years of detention as a political prisoner. She and Marsaid decided to stay on at Nanga-nanga. In 1982 they received the official titles to their land from the Military Area Command. By then, there were 56 houses measuring 6 x 6 metres there, and the land was planted with fruit trees.

But their peace was momentary. In 1983 there was a drought that ruined almost all the trees and crops. Many of the former prisoners gave up and moved to Lepo-lepo in Kendari, about five kilometres from Nanga-nanga. They rented houses there. Marsaid tried to find office work. Because of his education, skills and experience he was offered work in a business owned by an acquaintance in Makassar. Over time, he was able to save and buy some land.

People in Lepo-lepo accepted them without question. They did not pay much heed to their status as former political prisoners. Rukiah and Marsaid's financial situation was now quite good, and they were independent. But even with all this happiness at Lepo-lepo, still something gnawed away at Rukiah's heart. She remembered her daughter who she had left behind in Surabaya. She must be a pretty young woman now. Whenever Rukiah thought of her, she couldn't sleep. Sometimes she wondered, was she still alive? How was she now? If they met, would she even want to acknowledge

Rukiah as her mother? The questions went round and round in her head. Finally she decided to go to Surabaya to find her.

So with just enough money, she returned to Surabaya. She asked one of her husband's friends to help. He worked as civilian staff in the Military Area Command office, archiving all the files. Through him, Rukiah managed to find the address of the woman who had adopted her daughter. But it was not easy to find an address in the huge city of Surabaya. And it turned out that the woman had already moved. Rukiah did not give up. With a lead from a neighbour, she was able to track down the new address. Rukiah walked from one neighbourhood to another in the heat of Surabaya, and finally found the new address.

Her heart was pounding when she walked up to the front door. All kinds of things were spinning in her head. Knock, knock, knock ... Rukiah finally dared to knock. A woman opened the door. The minute she saw Rukiah's face her expression changed. But she politely invited Rukiah inside. The woman seemed extremely nervous. She had never imagined that Rukiah was still alive, and would come looking for her. After the usual polite greetings, Rukiah got straight to the point.

'First, I apologise for coming here without prior notice. The reason I am here is just to see my daughter who I entrusted to you. I have been so disturbed, because I can't even imagine what she looks like now.'

Hesitatingly, the woman explained, 'I must first beg your forgiveness. Watiningsih, your daughter, has not lived here for a long time.'

'What happened to her?' Rukiah snapped.

The woman explained in detail her family situation after Watiningsih came to live with them. At first it all started out well. But over time, there was a drastic change in her son's behaviour. He was jealous of Wati, and was always mean to her. He was afraid of losing his family's love because he thought that they gave Wati more attention and loved her more than him. He used to hit her. Finally, the woman decided to give Wati to a friend of hers who was longing to have a child. The woman explained,

> Please do not be too worried, for Wati's adoptive mother loves Wati as her own daughter. The couple was desperate for a child on whom to shower their love. When they saw Wati, they immediately wanted to take her and asked for my permission to bring her up as their daughter.

Rukiah calmed down. She tried to understand. As a mother, she could not bear to hear that her daughter had been tormented by her adoptive older-brother. 'Would you please give me the address of the family?' Rukiah asked.

The woman gave her the address. Very soon thereafter, Rukiah went to find the place. This was not easy. When she got there, the family had moved. So once again she had to find a new address which was not clear. When she found the address, it turned out the family had moved from Surabaya to the countryside, not long after the man's retirement.

After almost a month of searching in Surabaya and nearly giving up, Rukiah's husband's uncle managed to find the place where Wati's adoptive parents had moved. They were in a village about 40 kilometres away. The family greeted Rukiah in a friendly way. Rukiah was not afraid to tell her whole story and her bitter experiences. Wati had not yet returned from school, so this was a good opportunity for Rukiah to chat with the family.

When Wati got home from school, her adoptive mother called her over. 'Come here for a moment, child. I want to talk to you.' Wati came over. The adoptive mother patiently explained that Rukiah was Wati's mother. As Rukiah observed the way she talked to Wati, she felt relieved. It seemed that her daughter had ended up with good people. She had been brought up to be a good and obedient child. Hearing all this, even though in her heart she probably did not believe it, Wati did not resist. Politely, she walked over to Rukiah and hugged her warmly. They were lost for words. They wept. And even though no words were spoken, the warmth of Wati's hug was enough to convince Rukiah that her very own daughter still had some inner connection with her. Fifteen years is a long time for separation. But this is what Rukiah and her second daughter experienced.

And there were countless other families who had similar or even worse experiences, courtesy of the New Order regime. Many families were split apart. Children were made orphans, because their parents were murdered or tortured to death. If no family members came to help, then they had to survive as best they could. Some performed on the streets, or became beggars, worked in food stalls, at the harbour, anywhere they could. And these innocent children lost their childhood and adolescence and had to face a bitter life.

Rukiah learnt many lessons during her time as a political prisoner. She learnt that Indonesia, renowned for its friendliness, could, at that time, change into an inhumane nation. People were free to torture, murder and rape their fellow citizens just because that person was a member or sympathiser of a Party now banned. And hundreds of thousands of people who knew absolutely nothing at all also became victims.

Rukiah endured her sufferings with determination. She has aged. Her body is more fragile. But her spirit is still strong. She is thankful that the

New Order that oppressed her collapsed. Soeharto stepped down in 1998. Rukiah and her husband, along with victims of the 1965 incident, welcomed the new era. The era of Reformation. There was a spark of hope that the new government would uphold justice. But to this day, justice has not come.

The succession of governments in the Reformation era have not dared to face the dark history of 1965. But Rukiah is certain that God will not remain quiet. There will come a time when the real truth will appear.

Interviewer and transcriber: Resma Nanga.

Writer: Ika Mustika.

Chapter 13

Sutarni

A story of family survival

This morning, like other mornings, the sun was shining. It was early September, still the dry season. Inside the house, there were the usual signs of life. Tarni, the wife of the man of the house, was busy organising her six children. She had to get the three older children ready for school. Svetlana, the oldest, was in 4th class of primary school. Wawang and Timur, the second and third children, were both in second class of Cidurian primary school in Cikini in Jakarta.

The house in Jalan Malang was large with a spacious yard. It had once been a ballet school for Dutch girls. The Dutch ballet teacher used to live there. Tarni did not know exactly how her husband managed to get the house, but she remembered that a number of people were interested in it, including people high up in the government. Her husband, Nyoto, was a member of parliament at the time – after the 1955 general election.

As usual, Tarni took her children to school. The three little ones stayed at home with her sister-in-law and the domestic helper. The drive in their Fiat car from Jalan Malang to Jalan Cidurian took no time at all. In those days, the streets in Jakarta were empty, and it was nice to drive. Then she went on with the driver to Cikini market to buy some vegetables, after which she returned home.

Svetlana, the oldest child, was clever and independent. She was nine. Her complexion was rather dark, and she was pretty like her mother. Her younger brother Wawang was exactly a year younger, also born in February. He was the one who caused Tarni the most trouble. He was shy and lacked confidence, and often cried at school. When he was in first grade, Tarni often had to wait outside the classroom, and when Wawang was acting up, she had to join him in the classroom, sitting with him at the back of the class.

After just six months, Wawang refused to go to school. He was very happy when he had to repeat his kindergarten year and could be together with his younger brother Timur. Timur was born in August 1958, so was eighteen months younger than Wawang, but was more confident than his older brother. Timur did not like eating rice. The brothers attended the kindergarten at the main office of Lekra (Lembaga Kesenian Rakyat, Institute of People's Culture) in Jalan Cidurian, Cikini, Jakarta. This is why, despite the age difference, Wawang and Timur ended up in the same class at primary school.

Wawang and Timur were the only boys. Tarni's other children were all girls. Apart from Svetlana, the oldest, there were the three youngest children: Risa, aged five, Irina aged three, and Atun who was just one year old. Risa was born in a leap year, on 29 February 1960. Three of the children were born in February – Svetlana, Wawang and Risa. Irina, the fifth child, was born on 30 June 1962, and Atun on 14 April 1964.

It is not easy minding six children alone. They all need attention. Tarni's sister-in-law, Untung, also lived in the house. The children called her Aunty Win. Her husband was Uncle Yan, whose family was Chinese. Uncle Yan – his full name was Tan Yan Gei – worked at the Irama recording company. Tarni's sister-in-law helped look after her nephews and nieces. Tarni also had a domestic helper who did all kinds of chores. Every day was busy.

When Svet, Wawang and Timur finished school, usually they did not go straight home, but went to their Aunty Marto's house in Jalan Surabaya. Aunty Marto had only one child, a daughter named Budi, and she and Svet were good friends. Aunty Marto was not really the children's aunt, but they called her that because the family had known the Nyoto family for such a long time that they were like relatives. It was not far from Jalan Cidurian to Jalan Surabaya, just a short walk across the Cikini railway tracks.

Sometimes, Svet and her two younger brothers would go to school with their father, if he was not too busy. Nyoto took this opportunity to pop in to the Lekra office which was close to the Cidurian primary school. If the children saw their father's car outside the Lekra office after school they knew their father was there. The children would run to meet him and he would take them out for a ride. Usually he would treat them to an iced drink called Es Shanghai, or he would buy them a cake at Tjan Njan shop on Jalan Cikini Raya.

The children called their father '*bapak*' and their mother '*mamah*'. It was a happy family. Bung Nyoto (as he was known) was rarely angry at his children, just like Tarni. They were both warm hearted and patient. Every now and then the children would do something to annoy them or would cause trouble. Wawang's health was not good. He had a skin condition, and often had to be taken to the doctor for injections. This ritual of going to the doctor caused big problems, because Wawang hated the injections and the medicine.

Time moved on. Nyoto was busy with all kinds of activities. Apart from being a Minister, he was also Second Head (Ketua II) of the Central Committee of the Indonesian Communist Party, editor of the *Harian Rakyat* newspaper, and a leading figure of Lekra, but he was also head of a household with six children. Everything had to proceed in tandem. Outside the house, the political temperature was heating up, and there was much friction. Tarni did not understand much of the political upheaval. Her duty was to support her husband and bring up their six children.

And the end of September came. As Minister, Nyoto was often away from home. This time he was accompanying the Deputy Prime Minister Soebandrio on a tour of Sumatra. Towards dawn on 1 October 1965, a group of army officers carried out a swift action. They took some generals by force to meet President Soekarno, the Great Leader of the Revolution. But things did not go according to plan and there were casualties. It was truly a morning from hell.

That's when the storm broke.

Tarni and her six children were at her younger sister Tari's place in Mampang Prapatan at the time, where there was a family event. The house was in the precincts of a piping factory owned by the Bakri family. Totally out of the blue, the shocking news came by telephone. Jakarta was in crisis! Tarni and the children were told to go back home at once. It wasn't yet clear what exactly had happened, but Uncle Koen Li, the Nyoto family's driver, said that a number of generals had been kidnapped by an army brigade.

You can imagine Tarni's worry. She had no idea where her husband was. She had no idea when he would come home. The only news was from the radio and the television. The situation was chaotic, uncertain. Every minute was terrifying. Tarni could only hope that the worst would not befall her family. Luckily the next day the entourage accompanying the Deputy Prime Minister Soebandrio returned to Jakarta from Sumatra.

Nyoto arrived back home late at night. He immediately took his wife and six children away from their house in Jalan Malang to a house in Jalan Tirtayasa in Kebayoran Baru in South Jakarta. This was a large two-storey house. Nyoto and his family often stayed there on holidays. The house used to be owned by a Chinese family that had returned to China, and was then bought by the Party.

Tarni remembers that they stayed there only for a few days. While they were there and Nyoto spent his time reading, their house in Jalan Malang was ransacked by a mob. All their furniture and personal effects were thrown into the street and set alight. The newspaper also reported that things had been found at the house: army fatigues, complete with guns and grenades. But actually those army fatigues belonged to Wayang and Timur. They were children's costumes that Nyoto had bought in Singapore, and indeed were complete with metal helmets, rifles, pistols and hand grenades. All just toys.

There was more ridiculous news saying that the mob had also found in Nyoto's house a tool for eye-gouging. But what they called an 'eye gouger' was actually just a back-scratcher, the type sold everywhere as souvenirs in Solo and on Jalan Malioboro in Yogyakarta. However the saddest thing of all was that they burnt Nyoto's entire book collection of thousands of books. Nyoto had painstakingly built up his collection, buying books from all the countries he visited. He had also been given many books as gifts.

Nyoto's second child Wawang remembers his father's book collection. There were thick volumes, most of them in foreign languages like Dutch, Russian, English, French and German. The books were stored in Nyoto's study on specially-built bookshelves that went right up to the ceiling. This was an old Dutch house, so the ceilings were very high – about four metres high. There was also a big bookshelf dividing the sitting room from the family room. And apart from this, in the back garden there was a sort of shed that was separate from the house, and this was full of books neatly arranged on bookshelves. To the side of this were the rooms for the driver and the domestic helper.

One night, a group of soldiers came to the house on Jalan Tirtayasa. Luckily, some friends of Nyoto's were staying there that night. A dialogue took place between the two sides. Nyoto said that as State Minister, his duty was to assist the Deputy Prime Minister Soebandrio carry out his duties. They left Nyoto alone, but took his pistol (which he owned himself) and took with them some of Nyoto's friends. According to Tarni, from that moment her husband knew that he and his family's safety was at risk if they stayed on in that house. They had to leave at once and find another place to stay that was safer.

And so began the episode of being refugees, or on the run. It was not an easy thing to find a place to sleep the night. Everyone was looking for safety, and to take in the family of the Communist Party leadership was a reckless act. Taking in one person seeking shelter might be possible, but to take in a whole family with six children was something else indeed. And some of Tarni's children were still very young. There had to be baby food and milk. Not to mention clothes. Not to mention the children complaining. It was a huge imposition.

When they first left the house, fortunately one of Nyoto's friends agreed to shelter Tarni and the children. Nyoto himself went elsewhere. But after just a few days in the Kebayoran Baru area, Tarni and the children had to move again. For a while, Wawang and Timur were separated from their mother and the four girls. But after the whole family had been moving around the city of Jakarta, they finally ended up at the student hostel of CGMI (Consentrasi Gerakan Mahasiswa Indonesia, Indonesian Student Movement Concentration) in Gunung Sahari. Tarni no longer remembers exactly when this was, but it was definitely 1965. She does recall that she often heard Christmas carols from the neighbour's house.

The student hostel was a temporary construction. The walls were half brick topped with woven bamboo. It was set in the middle of a plot of land, and there was a large yard in front of the house. To the left and right of the house was about 2 metres of land. There was a high bamboo fence around the house, although it was not very compact. The hostel had a verandah at the front, then a sitting room, dining room, three bedrooms, a kitchen, bathroom, toilet and a manual pump at the back for water. There were two entrances to the house, one at the front and one at the back. The hostel was situated in a densely populated neighbourhood where many people of Chinese descent lived.

There were a few students still living at the hostel. Tarni's children called them Uncle Gorma, Uncle Robert, Uncle Pardede and Uncle Kaligis. Many of their friends came and went, some of them staying overnight. Usually they discussed the latest developments and shared information. Gorma was from the Hutajulu clan, and was a student activist. He was strict and rigorous. He was made hostel leader. Even so, he often went shopping in the market and he could also cook. Pardede was the youngest of the students, and he was close to the children. But if the children did not take their showers, he would chase them with a reed broom.

Wawang talks about how he and his younger brother Timur had lots of friends when they stayed at Gunung Sahari – the neighbourhood children. He loved to play mock battles, hide and seek, bamboo sword fighting, and kites. Wawang was nine and Timur was turning eight. They used to make guns from match boxes, make their own kites, and the older kids taught them how to smear the kite strings with powdered glass. If they got bored with their games, sometimes they would wander around the neighbourhood and go out to the main road of Gunung Sahari Raya.

Svet and Wawang also loved reading comics. They don't remember where the comics came from. Maybe those Sumatran uncles gave them the comics. There were stories from the Mahabharata and Ramayana. There were also stories about heroes created by Indonesian writers. It was also around this time that Timur, who previously would never eat rice, began to like rice. There was a radio at the house in Gunung Sahari. This is where they got the latest news updates. And there were also songs popular at that time by singers like Titik Puspa, Lilis Suryani and Fety Effendi. A real hit song that used to be played constantly was 'Gang Kelinci'.

Sutarni's belly got bigger by the day. She was pregnant. She remembers that when they were at Gunung Sahari, her husband visited her and the children twice. This was towards the end of 1965. And then her labour pains began. She was taken to a birthing clinic near Gunung Sahari in Jalan Kartini. And here her daughter was born, who she named Esti Sayati. The young Batak man called her Butet. Butet was born on 23 July 1966. This same date has now been named national children's day. Butet was the only one of Nyoto's children not named by their father, and she was also the only one who never met him.

Not long after Butet was born, the army came and ransacked the house at Gunung Sahari. It was still very early in the morning, but everyone in the house was woken. Tarni sat on the edge of the bed holding the baby. Captain Suroso, the army commander sat beside her. He asked her questions, speaking Javanese but in a rough way. Maybe this was his way of intimidating her. Meanwhile the other army personnel searched the house, even going up on the roof. They managed to find some books that Gorma had hidden in a hole under the rubbish. The search went on for ages.

When they came to search the house, Timur happened not be at home, as Gorma Hutajulu had taken him to North Jakarta where they stayed the night. So they escaped being taken by the army. Tarni and the other six children were taken away by car. The young men had already been taken first via the back door. The neighbours lined the alley way to the main road, and others peeped out from behind their windows. Wawang remembers that he was told to bring a rolled up mattress. Maybe the army was thinking about the newborn baby. All of them were then taken and detained at the Military District Command (Kodim) on Jalan Budi Kemuliaan. Today this is part of Bank Indonesia.

Tarni and her six children were put in a tiny room which was already full of women prisoners. You can imagine how it was when this room had to accommodate seven more people, even though six of them were children. There was one bathroom and toilet right beside the room, which often stank. Across from the bathroom were two rooms used for interrogating prisoners. The one on the western side was bigger than the main interrogation room, and was only about seven or eight metres away from the women's' cell. And in that room horrific episodes took place day after day. Screams, shouts and howls along with the sounds of beating and whipping were constant.

The brutal soldiers used all kinds of torture on the prisoners. This was also the case with the female detainees, who were sure to endure sexual abuse, especially the young ones. The army used any means at all to get the confessions they wanted. The most piercing and terrifying cries were heard when detainees were tortured with electric shocks. Some of them, because they held out from giving information, or were forced to confess, were later taken to the beach and shot. Many of the detainees were naked when they were tortured.

Wawang remembers how he once saw a man wearing only underpants thrown out of the room, covered with blood. He had received such a savage beating that he smashed against the door so hard it opened. The man was unconscious. Usually the torture victims would be returned to their cells, and there their cellmates would tend to them as best they could. They used cooking oil, shallot onions or just a rinse of warm water. The prisoners used to cook in the cell to supplement their meagre rations.

Then, one day Gorma Hutajulu was arrested. Like the other prisoners, he was interrogated and tortured. You could hear his loud screams when he was being given electric shocks. Tarni and the children recognised Gorma's voice, but they could not utter a word. All they could do was hope that Timur was safe. Tarni was dreadfully worried about her third child, and just hoped someone was caring for him. Something else that made Tarni panic was when little Butet was accidentally burnt with hot water from the thermos. Fortunately Tarni was permitted to take her to the clinic, under guard of course.

In early 1967, around mid January, the military operation called Operasi Kalong (Operation Bat) had a big success when they captured Brigadier General Supardjo, one of the leaders of the 30th September Movement. Captain Suroso and his men were all promoted as a result. Captain Suroso was now major. When they began the interrogation of Brig. Gen. Supardjo, many people crowded around him. They came to get a close look at him, but this also put psychological pressure on him to confess.

Not long after the arrest of Brig. Gen. Supardjo, Tarni and the children were released from the Military Resort Command. Tarni's younger brother Sutarwo gave a guarantee and took responsibility for them. The release was also because of Sutarwo's personal efforts, through meeting President Soeharto's wife, Ibu Tien Soeharto, at her home to ask for permission to take Tarni and the children to Solo in Central Java. There was a family connection between Tarni's father Soemosutargiyo and Ibu Tien Soeharto's father, Soemoharyomo. They were cousins, descended from Mangkunegara III. For people from Solo, this is considered close family. But sadly politics had severed this link, and they had to pursue separate paths.

Tarni's brother Tarwo lived in Baturetno, a town between Solo and Pacitan in south Wonogiri. He worked in the Tasikmadu sugar factory in Karanganyar, Solo. As a relatively high-ranking employee, he was allotted a moderately large official residence. He was in charge of supplying the sugar factory with limestone from the hills of Selomarto to the south of Baturetno, which was taken by rail. The limestone was taken by truck to the station at Baturetno, and then in cattle wagons by train. Today those railway tracks are gone – all submerged by the Gajah Mungkur dam.

Needless to say, the arrival of Tarni and her children in Baturetno attracted much attention. In such a small town, everyone knew everyone. And Tarni had young children with her, none of whom could speak Javanese. Tarwo's position as Limestone Controller at least kept the local people from gossiping. But many local figures knew who Tarni and the children were. Namely, a family affected by the incident of 1 October 1965.

Uncle Tarwo (as the children called him) had nine children of his own. Three boys and six girls. On top of this, there were relatives and nephews and nieces. So it was a big extended family even before the arrival of seven more. It was lively and happy there. But even though Tarwo was relatively well off, these were difficult times. The economy was in a mess. And everywhere people had to queue for rice and kerosene.

Everyone, Tarwo and his extended family included, had to tighten their belts and live as best they could. Svet, Wawang and their younger brothers and sisters had to learn how to live frugally. For breakfast, they would usually eat rice porridge or broken-rice porridge, namely the 'second' broken grains that were much cheaper. Sometimes the children would eat steamed cassava cake (*getuk*), with palm sugar or soy sauce. For lunch they would have boiled corn husks, or boiled cassava with chilli vegetables and soya bean cake.

Because Baturetno was a rural area, it was not too difficult to get basic foodstuffs because locals still produced their own food. There were all kinds of plants in Uncle Tarwo's large garden including coconut trees, *turi* bushes, lead trees, papaya, banana, cassava, chillies and tomatoes. Out the back he kept goats, chickens, ducks and geese. There was also a fish pond. And you could always also buy vegetables cheaply in the market.

All the children, Tarni's children and the cousins, played in the large yard. The girls liked to play house or market, as well as knuckle bones and a counting game with seeds called *congklak*. The boys liked to play with kites, marbles, cards, and do drawing. Together, boys and girls would play a ball game called *kasti*, chasing, hop-scotch, and walking on stilts. They communicated in a mixture of Javanese and Indonesian. And if at times they did not understand one another, they found this funny and laughed about it.

Uncle Tarwo's house was directly across from the primary school. Svet and Wawang attended school there. Svet was in fifth class, Wawang in third class and Risa in the first class. They immediately attracted a lot of attention from the teachers and the other pupils. Lessons in Javanese language, arts and literature were completely new to them. They had never learnt to write the Javanese alphabet. It was not easy. Nor was the Javanese language which has seven different levels, or three main levels, the everyday language of *ngoko*, the more polite level of *krama lugu*, and the extremely polite *krama inggil*.

The Javanese language has a rich vocabulary. Every flower and plant has a separate name, as do animal offspring. For instance, a baby buffalo is called a *gudhel*, a baby lizard is called *sawiyah*, a chick is *kuthuk*, a puppy *kirik*, and so on. In the culture lessons, they learnt traditional Javanese sung poems, all the twelve different verse forms, like *pucung*, *dandanggula*, *pangkur*, *mijil*, *megatruh*, *kinanti* and so on.

Even though Svet and Wawang were born in Jakarta, they already had some familiarity with Javanese art forms. They knew about gamelan music, *wayang kulit*, *wayang orang*, *ludruk* and *ketoprak*. Their father Nyoto's role as a driving force in Lekra was extremely important in introducing the children to art forms from all over Indonesia. Nyoto used to have a large record collection. Apart from national songs, classical music, jazz and popular music, he also had a lot of *kroncong* and Javanese traditional arts like gamelan, *wayang orang* and *ludruk*.

Wawang talks about his primary school days in Baturetno as a really happy time. There were lots of practical lessons in village skills. He learnt crafts, like how to make door mats and brooms from coconut fibre, reed brooms, feather dusters, and limestone ash trays. There were other crafts with wood, coconut shell, bamboo, fungus, coconut husks, roots, chicken feathers and all kinds of things. He particularly remembers learning to draw wayang kulit figures and cut them out on cardboard, with all the decorative incisions and painting.

Another typical village activity was to look for grass and firewood, and to herd ducks and goats. Sometimes he would walk with his friends along the railway tracks and go swimming in the river. There were often all night *wayang kulit* performances, and he would stay up watching, tucking a sarong around him as protection from the mosquitoes. They could not watch the *ketoprak* drama performances, though, because you had to buy tickets. He could only peep through the cracks in the walls.

One year later, in 1968, Timur arrived from Jakarta. Tarni was very relieved. At last her third child was together with them again and he was healthy and well. But Timur did not go to school in Baturetno. He went to stay with his aunt in Solo, Tarni's older sister called Sutarminah Djusen. Uncle Tarwo was number seven in that family of 12 children, and Tarni herself was number eight. Timur attended the Tegalharjo primary school which was close to his aunt's house. She had a huge house. This was because her husband, Djusen, was an architect and a contractor. He helped build the campus of Gadjah Mada University in Yogyakarta, the Daksinapati University campus, and the campus of the Indonesian Institute of the Arts in Solo.

In 1969, Svet and Wawang also went to live with their Uncle Djusen in Solo. Svet had finished primary school and now enrolled in junior high school (SMP Negeri III) in Solo. She was in the same class as her cousin Rita, Uncle Djusen's fourth child. Wawang entered class 5 of the same primary school as Timur, Tegalharjo school. The younger girls all stayed at Baruretno. Wawang and Timur remember their time in Solo fondly. They got to know every nook and cranny of the town, and can remember all the names of different areas and places to this day.

This was the time when everyone was crazy about the band Koes Plus, and then other bands like Mercy's, Panbers and Favourite Group. The top singers in Solo were Titik Sandhora and Waljinah. There were many youth gangs too which often caused trouble. Street fights and brawls, skipping school, graffiti, racing in the streets, sex, staying up all night and getting drunk were the gangs' daily rituals. But in response to this, many martial arts clubs of varied persuasions arose, such as karate, *pencak silat* and kung-fu.

But that year Uncle Djusen died, after a long illness. His only daughter was not with him at his death because she was with her husband in Pekanbaru, Riau. Crowds of people came to his funeral and joined the procession to the graveyard. Afterwards, there were many problems concerning his business to do with management and also his many business assets. His wife did not want to have anything to do with all this, and asked all her late husband's relatives to sort it out.

Then, in 1969, something dreadful happened. The army arrested Tarni, accusing her of secret meetings with 'communist remnants'. Even though what they were referring to was when Tarni attended her niece's wedding in Solo. The new commander at the Military Area Command (Korem) wanted to make a name for himself. So he found a pretext to take Tarni for 'further processing'. She was taken to Solo together with her youngest daughter, Butet. She refused to leave Butet behind, because she was too young. Tarni also did this deliberately because she thought that the army would not act as irresponsibly if she had a small child in her arms.

Tarni was detained and interrogated at the City Hall in Solo. She refused to acknowledge that she had ever had secret meetings with Communist Party people. To most of the questions she answered 'I don't know', or 'I forget'. But this was the truth. Tarni had never been active in the party, in any organisation, or in Gerwani. She was truly a housewife whose focus was the family. Of course she knew many party people and officials, but this was because they were her husband's colleagues. After a short time, Tarni was moved from the City Hall in Solo to the Women's' Prison in Bulu, Semarang. Butet was still with her.

Butet was a favourite with everyone at the prison, with both the women prisoners and the guards. She lightened their hearts and entertained them. When families came to visit the prisoners, they always gave Butet snacks like cakes and bread or other food. Luckily, Butet never caused any trouble in the prison. She used to ask why there were so many women there. She also missed her older sisters, who did not come to visit. Tarni's youngest brother came to visit a few times. Aunt Djusen and Uncle Tarwo came to visit the prison in Semarang only once.

In prison, Tarni worried constantly about her other children. She was desperately sad to be parted from them. The political and military upheaval had completely changed her life and that of her family. But she hoped that all her children were safe with their relatives. Their willingness to help was truly astounding, especially when they themselves were interrogated and detained for short periods, needless to say because of their family relationship with Nyoto. Nonetheless they continued to generously offer support and to help as best they could. And this is how things should be.

Unlike other women prisoners, Tarni was always treated well in prison. The guards showed her respect. But some of the officers were malicious, complaining, quarrelsome, or acted tough. Well, they were just human beings. It is understandable. The women prisoners, to combat boredom, were given various activities. There was physical fitness, badminton, and ping pong. There was also sewing, weaving, crochet and knitting. The results were various pieces of handiwork 'made in Bulu prison'.

Time marched on. In early 1970 Tarni got news that her three daughters in Baturetno, Risa, Irina and Atun, were now together with the other three children in Solo. It was not good for them to be separated from both their mother and their older brothers and sister who were safe in their widowed Aunt Djusen's care. The children helped to liven up that big house. There was also a relative called 'Wo Wir' living there, a domestic helper called Mbok Nem and the driver called Kasimanto.

After the death of her husband, Aunt Djusen's health declined. Her stomach enlarged and it felt as though she was being pierced by something sharp. She went to the doctor and was also examined in hospital, but nothing helped. And then, at the suggestion of a relative, she decided to go to a traditional healer in Purwodadi. His diagnosis was that Aunt Djusen was the inadvertent victim of black magic. She had been affected by a spell that was not meant for her. Because she was in a weak physical and mental condition, the spell had entered her.

As soon as she got back home from Purwodadi, the healing ritual began. Every morning, Wawang and Timur had to go and buy a chicken egg at the Gilingan market near the house. They rubbed the egg all over Aunt Djusen's body, and then they cracked it open. And, incredible! In the yolk there was a rusty needle. This went on every day for 40 days, and that was exactly the number of needles found in her body. After that, her health improved, although she never fully recovered her former health.

Aunt Djusen's daughter, Isnaeni, worried about her mother's health, and decided to take her to Pekanbaru. Isnaeni's husband worked with Caltex where there were good medical services. And Isnaeni had two sons aged four and five. They were very happy to be close to their grandmother.

Aunt Djusen asked her youngest sister, Tardi, to look after the house and Tarni's children. Tardi and her family were living in the area of Jebres, to the east of the city. But they now moved to Aunt Djusen's house. Tardi also had many children – six at this time. The oldest, Heru, was 12, the same age as Timur. And so now the big house was full of children. They all got on well, even though there were the normal quarrels and fights here and there. Like all children.

This was the period when the economy was unstable. Everyone was still living hand to mouth. In Solo, people had to queue to buy rice or kerosene. Every now and then the government would distribute cracked wheat (bulgur). But it did not taste good. Many people preferred corn to cracked wheat. People in the city were much worse off than people in villages like Baturetno. In the villages, people could still grow their own produce. But even with this, conditions worsened when a national lottery called NALO was introduced. Who knows whose crazy idea this was. The people were told to live on false hopes alone!

The national lottery had a terrible effect on social life. Everyone suddenly went mad gambling. And not only men, the housewives also became addicts. From high officials to becak drivers, from farmers to students, everyone turned into a gambler. Suddenly there were fortune tellers everywhere, called *dukun* or *paranormal*. Many families were destroyed, all their worldly wealth gone, along with their dreams. Many changed to a lesser form of gambling, for instance betting on the last two, three or four numbers of the lottery. The lottery was drawn weekly. And that's what happened. The poor got poorer.

Towards the end of 1970, Wawang was preparing for primary school exams. Three subjects were examined at a national level, namely Indonesian, arithmetic and general knowledge. He studied in a group of five. Every day they would move from one person's house to the next. Finally, the examination day arrived. The exam was held at a different school. This was a good system. And it turned out that Wawang's hard work had not been in vain, because he got good marks. He scored 10 for every subject. He hoped his good result would please his Aunt Djusen, because it was she who had cared for him and put him through school.

Uncle Tarwo now entered Wawang in junior high school (SMP Negeri III) in Solo. The headmaster of the school, Maryadi, was Uncle Tarwo's friend, and all his children went to this school. For some reason, many children from the Surakarta palace, sons and daughters of Paku Buwana XII, also went to this school. One of them, Tedjowulan, was a classmate of Svet's, and it was he who later came to be Paku Buwana XIII, replacing his father. Two other sons of Paku Buwana XII, Suryo and Bandono, were classmates of Wawang.

And time moved on. Every day, Aunt Djusen's financial burden grew. Her house was large, and cost a lot to upkeep. Costs of electricity, water and maintenance were high. Not to mention the costs of food and school fees for all her nephews and nieces. Her only income was her late husband's savings. So to reduce the financial burden, with the agreement of her children, it was decided to sell the house on Jalan Wolter Mongisidi.

The person given first option on the house was Dr Kwik, her neighbour. He had once said to Aunt Djusen that if she ever wanted to sell, he would buy the house. He wanted to turn the house into a hospital. With the proceeds from selling the house, Aunt Djusen was able to buy a small house in Jalan Madyotaman, near the Batik Semar factory. The house had a living room, five bedrooms, a bathroom, toilet, laundry and kitchen. Wawang and his younger brother and sisters moved there too.

The head of the house at Madyotaman was 'Wo Wiro', a relative. Apart from her there was Wawang and Kasimanto's cousin Utiek, and Aunt Djusen's driver. Tardi and his family returned to their house in Jebres. Svet had completed junior high school and went to Jakarta for her high schooling. She lived with her aunt, Tari, at the Bakri Brothers' factory housing complex in Mampang Prapatan.

When they had some spare time, Wawang and Timur often went to the lending library. Wawang loved to read the silat stories by SH Mintardjo called *Nagasasra Sabuk Inten* (Nagasasra with the Diamond Belt) and the serial *Api di Bukit Menoreh* (Fire on Mount Menoreh). Timur liked to borrow comics popular at the time like *Si Buta dari Goa Hantu* (The Blind One from Ghost Cave), *Laba-laba Merah* (Red Spiders) and so on. The two of them often played badminton or football. There was a badminton court near the house. At night they liked to watch television at the neighbour's house. Their favourite program was the serial *Mission Impossible.*

But the time at Madyotaman did not last long. Only just over a year. That house too had to be sold. Aunt Djusen needed money to help her daughter build a house at Pasar Minggu in Jakarta. Her son-in-law had left Caltex and was now working for Pertamina in Jakarta. Economic conditions in Solo were so bad by this time that no one wanted to take in five children. So they had to be split up. This was not something that anyone wanted, but they had to accept it.

So Wawang went to live with Aunt Wigno, one of Nyoto's cousins. Timur went to live with Mas Wahyudi, a cousin who lived in the Air Force complex in Panasan. Risa, Irina and Atun went to live with Uncle Tarso, their mother Sutarni's younger sister (child number eleven) in Kadipiro, in

North Solo. But after just a few months, Wawang and Irina were also taken to Jakarta. There, their Aunt Tarko met them to take them both with her to Sumatra. Aunt Tarko was their mother's older sister, the fifth child in that large family. She had lived and worked in Sumatra for a long time.

Aunt Tarko lived in Kayuagung, the regency capital of Ogan Komering Ilir in South Sumatra, to the south of the city of Palembang. She had three children, Pebsi, Oki and Novi. They spoke the local Palembang language to each other. Much of the vocabulary was foreign to Wawang and Irina. They also found the accent strange. So Wawang and Irina used Indonesian. In Sumatra at that time, the use of Indonesian was more common, because there the local language was Malay.

But there was something interesting. It turned out there was also a local language at Kayuagung, and it existed in two versions. Between the 'town Kayuagung' (*Kayuagung kota*) and 'original Kayuagung' (*Kayuagung asli*) was a kampung across the Koerming river which had a different language. Areas that were very close to each other had their own languages. The language of Palembang was the unifying language. This is part of Indonesia's invaluable heritage.

Uncle Tarko lived in a traditional Sumatran house, a wooden house raised on stilts. It measured about 6 x 11 metres. There were many supporting wooden pillars set on big stone blocks. The floor of the house was three metres above the ground. There were only two bedrooms in the house, one dining room and a kitchen at the back. The bathroom was under the kitchen, and the well and toilet were separate at the back of the house. Underneath the house there was a ping-pong table. The middle section beneath the house was used for a chicken coop and to store firewood.

At her uncle's house, Irina's daily job was to clean the house, help with the washing, and boil water. Wawang had many jobs. Early in the morning he had to go shopping in the market. When he got home from school he had to take a lunch box of food to his uncle's workplace at the petrol station. After that he had to tend to the chickens. There were many different kinds of chickens, including leghorn, red brown and australop. In the evenings he would do the ironing using a charcoal iron. Sundays were gardening days when they planted cassava, taro, banana, pineapple, bitter melon and peas.

Most Sumatran cooking uses coconut cream, turmeric and chilli pepper. The basic everyday staple is fresh water fish. There are many different kinds of fish. At Kayuagung the most common snacks were fishcakes, fish crackers, fried bananas and a red bean ice drink. Every area of Indonesia has its food speciality.

Wawang stayed at Kayuagung until 1976 when he graduated from high school (SMEA Negeri) specialising in librarianship. Then he returned to Jakarta to look for work. Irina stayed longer in Kayuagung. After completing primary and junior high school, she went on to study at a high school for training teachers. Graduates from these schools could teach in primary school. Wawang and Irina had many experiences when they lived in Sumatra, all of which were good preparation for their lives that lay ahead.

Back to Solo now. When Timur finished junior high school in 1974, he and his younger sister went to live with their aunt who lived in Medan. She was Aunt Henny, Nyoto's youngest sister. She had married a dentist from the Sitorus clan called Hakim. Henny and Hakim had met in Surabaya. Hakim was a graduate of Airlangga University where he had shared accommodation with Fadli, the dentist who was a well-known film star. Henny had four children, two boys and two girls. All four were still very young, and so Timur and Atun helped look after them.

Hakim's work as a dentist meant that the family was relatively well off. He had many patients, and a large house. But later on his career went off on a tangent. He was made Head of the Coordinating Body for Family Planning at Tebing Tinggi in North Sumatra. This led to a political position as head of the regional government (DPRD) of Tebing Tinggi. Who knows what connection there is between dentistry and family planning. But, well, this is Indonesia where anything can happen. Just imagine if anyone had found out he was Nyoto's brother-in-law!

Timur continued his study at a technical high school studying car mechanics. At school, though, he had always been good at art. He was very good at drawing and painting. His writing was also good. At junior high school he painted decorations on big pots and paper parasols to decorate the school. He also made models from papier maché and drew portraits of heroes. When he was at Uncle Hakim's house he helped out with the patients' files. He also learnt how to make false teeth.

Timur, though, is the quiet type. Sadly, it is extremely difficult to get him to talk about his life. There seems to be something in the past he wants to forget. He has many friends. He is clever and smart, so it is not surprising that his friends like him. His laugh is just like his father's. He also has a great taste in music, just like his father, and he can play all kinds of musical instruments. His music collection includes jazz, progressive pop, fusion and so on. He does not like politics, but is crazy about football, also just like Nyoto.

Timur was lucky in that when he entered technical high school, mechanics was a new department. Graduates were sought after by businesses. Timur graduated in 1977 and immediately got a job with a heavy industry business called Trakindo in Medan. Trakindo sent him to Jakarta many times for training courses. This was a good opportunity for him. When he was there he was able to meet his brother Wawang and sisters Svet and Risa. Timur was relocated from Medan to Lhoksemawe in north Aceh. Many businesses there needed heavy equipment. Atun, Tarni's sixth child, was six years younger than Timur. When she finished junior high school she went on to a school for dental nurses. She hoped that she could work for her uncle when she finished. During the day, she helped her aunt with the housework, and also cared for her little cousins. Timur and Atun, like their uncle's family, communicate in Indonesian with a heavy Medan accent. But they never learnt to speak the Batak language, just a few words here and there.

Timur and Atun were the only ones of Tarni's children who were cared for by Nyoto's family. The rest were all brought up by Tarni's own family. This is because Nyoto had only three siblings, whereas Tarni came from a large family. Tarni felt relieved that none of her children was left stranded. They were all well cared for and educated well, by their own relatives. Not by other people. Not like herself, 'cared for' by the State. Or her husband, given special 'disappearing' treatment by the army!

When Irina and Atun left, Risa, Tarni's fourth child, went to live with Isnaeni, the only child of Aunt Djusen, who lived in Jakarta. Unlike the other children, Risa never completed her schooling. The separation from her mother and brothers and sisters deeply troubled her. Even though very slightly built, she is a master of female skills. She followed in her mother's footsteps, clever at cooking, baking, sewing, make-up and hair dressing.

Isnaeni taught Risa interior design and flower arranging. But Risa always had health problems. She had a severe stomach ulcer and often had headaches. Skills are not only obtained sitting at a school desk, one also learns extremely useful things in other ways. Learning by asking, reading, watching, listening, remembering, trying and putting into practice is another model.

Tarni herself, after almost two years at the Bulu Semarang prison was moved to the Bukit Duri detention centre in 1971. Her youngest child, Butet, was not permitted to accompany her mother. She had to be given to someone to care for her as she was now five and when children turned five they were no longer allowed to be cared for by their mothers in prison. Tarni was extremely sad about this. Now she was completely on her own, with none of her seven children. Where is there a mother in the world who would not be sad, thinking about all her children having to live without their parents' love?

Tari, Tarni's younger sister who lived in Jakarta, took Butet at first, but then Tarti, Tarni's immediate younger sister and number nine in the family, 'adopted' her. Tarti's husband, Heryono, was head of the Office for Meteorology, Climatology and Geophysics and lived in Ronodigdayan, Yogyakarta. Butet was enrolled in kindergarten. From then on, she was called Tetty, (from her full name, Esti Dayati). Heryono had two children, a girl and a boy. Esti was dearly loved by the whole family.

Tetty spent all her childhood in Yogyakarta, from kindergarten until she graduated from university. Her adoptive mother Tarti died in 1983 when Tetty was still in senior high school, and her adoptive father died in 1988 when she was in her last year of university. She obtained her bachelor's degree in Development Economics from Gadjah Mada University. Tetty is the only one of all Nyoto's children who obtained a bachelor's degree.

Tarni's younger sister Tari often visited Tarni in Bukit Duri prison. She would usually bring food. When Svet moved to Jakarta she could also visit her mother. But to visit political prisoners was not easy. You had to have a letter from the local authorities where you lived (kantor kelurahan) and a special permit from the Guntur Military Police Corps in Jakarta. And to get this permit was not just one visit – you sometimes had to go many times before the permit was forthcoming. Risa and Wawang regularly visited their mother in prison.

Tarni was held in Bukit Duri for a long time. Finally, at the end of 1977, she forgets which month, she was moved yet again, this time to Central Java to Plantungan, Sukorejo. Three busloads of women prisoners were taken from Jakarta to 'exile' in Plantungan. Who knows what was behind this decision, why the women were moved there. Was it because they were considered to be so dangerous to the State, or was it just because they were considered no more than trash, so that for more than a decade after the 1965 incident they still had to be punished in prison, without any legal process, and without any sentence in a court of law.

Plantungan had been a leper colony in colonial times. It was situated in a valley beside a flowing river with large rocks. When Tarni arrived, the place was neat and well organised. This was not the case for those who were first sent there, though, when conditions were shocking. It was like jungle, overgrown with weeds and frightening. The living quarters were damp, dirty and stank. It was snake infested. The first group of women had to work extra hard just to make the place liveable and safe.

Tarni's relocation was sudden and without any prior notice. The family lost track of her. After asking around, they found just the name of the location, Plantungan. They had no idea where this was. No one knew. Tari gave Wawang the task of finding the place where the army had taken his mother. It was not easy to get to Plantungan. Wawang had to go to Solo first to ask his family to help find this place called Plantungan. They left from Solo for Semarang.

From Semarang they went on to Kendal. The journey was not over yet. They still had to change buses and go on to Sukorejo via Weleri. They had to wait a long time to find a car to take them there. There was no public transport to Plantungan. It was evening. Finally Wawang had to charter an illegal taxi to get there. It was a long way, and they were exhausted. And it was very expensive.

At Sukorejo, Wawang and his relative, Mas Wardi, met a female prison officer who happened to be returning to Plantungan where she worked. She asked, 'Who do you want to see at Plantungan?' Wawang said he wanted to see his mother named Tarni. Luckily the officer knew the Tarni that Wawang was referring to. And it was because of her help that Wawang was finally taken to meet his mother.

The meeting was extremely short, just half an hour – absolutely nothing compared to the half day's journey there from Solo. But Wawang was relieved to see his mother healthy and her face bright. He gave his mother news of the family in Jakarta and Solo. Tarni was extremely moved that her son had come all this way just to find out how she was. Even though the meeting was brief, it was like balm to her pain of longing for her family. Tarni's group was the last intake to Plantungan. The first group was sent there in 1971, when Tarni had been moved from Bulu Semarang to Bukit Duri in Jakarta. And when Tarni arrived in Plantungan, some of the inmates had been moved back to Bulu prison in Semarang. To use contemporary terminology, this was to maximise 'operational funds'. The army's behaviour is the same from one period to the next, it never changes!

It turned out that Plantungan was the last detention place. Plantungan was another entry on the female political prisoners' long curriculum vitae. It was the most beautiful place that the Soeharto regime gave to those who had been used for the birth of the New Order, those made scapegoats to justify all his political manoeuvring. In mid 1978, the first Plantungan female prisoners were released. Then the others followed, in batches. Tarni was released at the end of 1978 from Salemba, Jakarta.

Tarni's younger sister Tari and brother-in-law Sambodo came to collect her. The family was relieved. For the time being, Tarni stayed with Tari in Mampang Prapatan. Only three of her seven children were living in Jakarta. Timur and Atun were still in Medan. Irina was at school in south Sumatra, and Tetty, the youngest, was with her adoptive parents in Yogya. It took quite some time for Tarni to adapt to normal life after life in detention. There was also a psychological barrier for her to communicate freely and openly, even with her own children.

With many people's help, Tarni was able to rent a small house in Rawamangun, east Jakarta. She spent her days sewing, with her skilled daughter Risa helping her. Over time, she got more and more customers. But she had problems with arthritis in her fingers and knees. She had to have regular physiotherapy at the hospital, and acupuncture from a friend who was also an ex-political prisoner. Svet, Wawang and Risa came to live with her. Later on, when Irina finished school, she too was able to come and live with her mother. She became a primary school teacher and taught at a school near her mother's house.

There was something strange about the social acceptance of ex political prisoners. Protestant and Catholic groups were able to accept them with open arms. But the majority who were Muslim gave the impression of keeping a distance. The reason was not clear. It could be because this group was directly involved in the campaign to annihilate the 'communists'. Rather than embrace the returnees, give them sermons or religious teaching, the Muslims seemed to actively reject them. There was only one Muslim who wanted to communicate with them and to apologise to the victims, and that was Abdurrahman Wahid.

Soeharto's politics continued. There was the issue of 'latent communists' which was used to attack his political enemies. The Soeharto regime even had the gall to ask the ex political prisoners to vote for Golkar in the 1982 election so that Soeharto would remain in power. As an ex prisoner, Tarni was once called up to the local administration office (kelurahan) together with newcomers who were becak drivers and so forth. They were all registered and instructed on how to ensure that the 'yellow' party (Golkar) would win the election. Incredible! Soeharto and his Golkar collaborating with people branded as communists! For real!

Tarni was overjoyed when her oldest child, Svet, married a young man from Yogya. Not long after, Timur married a girl he got to know in Aceh.

Her family knew nothing at all about Timur's background. Wawang's father-in-law, though was a military man. He was a member of the Military Police army (PUSPOM ABRI) intelligence. He knew exactly who Nyoto was. But he allowed his daughter to marry the son of a Communist Party boss! Risalina, the fourth child, married a painter who was also an ex political prisoner from Kroya, central Java. And Atun married a work colleague, also a Javanese born in Jakarta. The youngest, Tetty, married a Yogya man, the son of a dentist.

Tarni is a grandmother now, her body aged. Her youthful beauty is replaced with wrinkles. She walks with difficulty because of the decades of calcification on her knees. Her memory is also fading. But she does not forget her experience in detention. She has 12 grandchildren. Svet, Wawang and Timur each have two boys. Risa has one boy. Atun has two girls. Tetty has three children, one boy and two girls. None of them ever knew their grandfather, Nyoto. Not even where his body lies buried!

Tarni and her family's experience was not as dramatic as that of other victims. The most painful thing was the disappearance of Nyoto, the head of the family; the loss of a father who deeply loved his family. Someone who was deliberately disappeared so as to muddy and bury history. Disappeared by his own relative, who was now The Boss [Soeharto. Trs], so that a new history could be born, so new heroes could be born. But history cannot be manipulated, it will fix itself and bury those who manipulate it.

Interviewer and transcriber: Ilham Dayawan.

Writer: Ilham Dayawan.

Chapter 14

Ibu Tachrin

Triumph over oppression

Surabaya, 1968

The sun was burning down when shouts were heard in front of a house, ordering the inhabitants to come out at once and report. The elderly owner of the house, doubled over, came out to face the man who the other three called 'Dan'. Without waiting for a word from the house owner, the Commander (Komandan) ordered his men to search inside.

A few metres away, a woman could be seen covering herself in a piece of batik cloth she had just taken off her neighbour's washing line. She hastened away from the scene. But then she saw some of those men in black coming to the house in front. Someone whispered for her to escape through the back door. She walked away quickly, with no idea where she was heading. Between her gasps, memories of the past came flooding back.

Kesamben Blitar, 1939–1965

On 2 January 1939, Raden Martodihardjo, the Irrigation Officer at Kesamben Blitar, was blessed with another daughter. The newborn baby completed the family. Tinah, as she was named, was the youngest in a family of seven children.

Tinah was raised in a four-roomed solid house together with her brothers and sisters; two other girls and four boys. There was quite a gap between her and her older siblings, who spoilt her. She was the little princess in the house, and always busy. She loved cooking, and spent most of her time in the kitchen. There, her mother taught her how to make all kind of cakes. Her older brothers and sisters would dutifully try all her cooking. If her cakes were a failure, Tinah would go and sulk in her room. When it was the season for the *duku* trees behind the house to bear fruit, she would spend her time there. She was clever at climbing the *duku* trees which grew among the stink bean trees, coconut palms, and wild spinach. She did not eat all the fruit she picked herself, but liked to give it to the neighbours.

As a colonial civil servant, Tinah's father was a man of status and respected. In his spare time, he used to take his youngest daughter on horseback around the kampung, checking the people's rice fields. Kesamben was on the main road between Blitar and Malang in East Java. This strategic location should have been of great advantage to the local people to carry out various activities. But back then they lived very simply; some were farmers, others were ironmongers. From a young age, Tinah was familiar with another kind of life beyond her cosy, sturdy house. This was a great influence on her later in life.

When Tinah was twelve years old she joined IPPI (Ikatan Pemuda Pelajar Indonesia, League of Indonesian Youth and High School Students). As in other places in Indonesia, young people in Kesamben were enthusiastic about youth organisations. IPPI arranged all kinds of activities: scouts, badminton competitions, football, *wayang orang* performances and fundraising for charity. IPPI members would often go on bicycle tours around the villages.

Tinah took part in this; although short and slight, she was nifty on her bicycle, her long hair flying in the wind, her round face smiling with joy. She had a wonderful adolescence. She also led the youngest level of scouts at IPPI, and taught in the Melati kindergarten.

Involvement in the world of activism led Tinah to meet her future husband. He was called Nuryanto, and was a young man of 24 years, a graduate of the senior high school for teacher training (Sekolah Guru Atas, SGA). Nuryanto came from a relatively poor family, which made many people doubt whether his relationship with the 'official's daughter' would go anywhere. But in Tinah's eyes, a man who was patient, clever and hardworking was the right type for her life partner.

So, just a year later, they married.

While Nuryanto was occupied with the non-politically aligned Indonesian Teacher's Union (PGRI, Persatuan Guru Republik Indonesia, Non Vak Sentral), and the National Youth Front (Front Pemuda Nasional), Tinah was just as busy with her organisations.

One of the activities of Gerwani (Gerakan Wanita Indonesia, the Indonesian Women's Movement), an independent organisation for women, was running the Melati kindergarten. Not just anyone could join Gerwani. Even though their focus was the lower classes, it was extremely rare for a woman from a peasant or labourer's family to become a member. One of the conditions of joining Gerwani was that you had to be at least 18 years old or already married.

As Tinah taught at the Melati kindergarten, was 19 years old and married, she automatically became part of Gerwani.

As a women's movement, one of Gerwani's basic guiding principles was, 'We are all mothers and wives.' Gerwani's actions were related to issues of morality, children and nutrition, and women's rights. Gerwani opposed prostitution and the practice of polygamy, defended rape victims, and opposed the destruction of morals through the influence of foreign culture. In Gerwani's view, women needed help to oppose their abuse as a result of tradition and social conditions. So while Gerwani acknowledged that women must fulfil their primary service in their role as wives and mothers, they still promoted the concept of 'militant motherhood'. Gerwani's image of militant mothers was not limited to housework, but spread to social activities and to the political arena. Their symbol was Srikandi, the warrior wife of Arjuna, and not Arjuna's other wife, the meek and mild Subadra.

Because Gerwani's activities often overlapped with politics, it was frequently linked to the Indonesian Communist Party (PKI). The Communist Party was indeed developing very fast. In Indonesia's first general elections in 1955, the Communist Party came in fourth place. But Tinah truly understood that Gerwani was an independent organisation. Even though it was true that many Gerwani members' husbands were members of the Communist Party, this did not make Gerwani a Communist Party organisation, because Gerwani had its own separate articles of association and bylaws.

The people of Blitar did not pay much attention to the political talk anyway. They were just enthusiastic about the activities that the Gerwani women carried out. Apart from the Melati kindergarten, Gerwani set up Banish illiteracy programs (Pemberantasan Buta Huruf, PBH) in every sub-regency, organised monthly savings clubs (*arisan*) with rice as the prize and gave arts and cooking classes. The cooking classes were for cakes that were easy to sell, so that women could earn some income of their own. Tinah played a part in all these activities. In the morning she taught at the kindergarten, and in the afternoons she either taught at the Banish Illiteracy program or gave cooking classes. In the weekend, sometimes there was still time for gamelan practice in the village (kelurahan). And when the *duku* or lychee season came, she would revert to her childhood hobby of picking them herself and giving them to the neighbours.

Gerwani did not operate alone. For national day celebrations or for voluntary work, Gerwani often worked together with police women or religious organisations. They would set up joint committees and they all worked well and harmoniously together. They differed only in their uniforms. The Gerwani members had duck-egg blue shirts and white skirts with *parang* design.

Tarni wore her Gerwani uniform when she taught the women. The women had no problems following her cooking class, but the literacy classes were another story. Many of the women would cry with frustration because they could not do their tasks. Then others would tease them. Tinah would calm the students down. Most of them were much older than her, but she had to treat them like children. After class, they would stay close to her, following her home. Tinah's life was good.

This all ended when the 30th September Movement happened.

Hundreds of kilometres away from Blitar, some high-ranking army officers were murdered by the Cakrabirawa Regiment. The Indonesian Communist Party was named as the mastermind. Everything linked to the Communist Party was leftist and now banned in Indonesia. It had to be cleansed.

It did not take long for the wave of 'cleansing' to arrive in Blitar. At the beginning of October everyone was ordered to report to the Military District Command and to sign a register every morning and evening. All social activities were virtually paralysed.

The Blitar Police searched Tinah's home. The police chief, who came to the family house where Tinah, her husband, children, and one of her older sisters lived, was a distant relative of Nuryanto's. He apologised for the search, but said he had to carry out his duty. There was nothing Tinah and her husband could do.

It was unclear what exactly they were looking for. Tinah did not understand. The only things in the house were her and her husband's teaching materials. In this crazy situation, they were almost accused of planning a revolt just because there were some spears in the sitting room. Even though they were only decorations Tinah's father had given her. The police finally went away without taking anything or anyone.

Then finally, in mid October, Nuryanto was 'taken' when he was queuing to report in. And after that, one by one, some of his teacher friends were also arrested. Tinah heard people saying that killing had started in Blitar. She did not ever see the killing herself, but every day, as the number of people who disappeared increased, she began to work out what was going on. The number of victims soared because many people just took advantage of the situation. Personal grudges played a part. All you had to do was shout, 'So-and-So is a Communist!' and that was it. He or she was disappeared or dead. If you heard dogs barking as they accompanied people carrying sickles wrapped in white cloth, you could be certain that there had just been some killing going on.

When her husband did not return, Tinah moved from one neighbour's place to the next every night. Until one day, a month after they took her husband, one of her colleagues at the kindergarten came over.

'Today, we have to collect our salaries at the office.'

'Sure, I'll come along soon', she answered.

But she didn't go. After leaving her third child with a relative, and now five months' pregnant, she left to go to her older brother's house in Malang, taking her oldest two children with her.

She decided to take the train. In the train she met two people who she recognised. One was her friend from People's Youth (Pemuda Rakyat) and the other was a friend of her husband's from the Nadhlatul Ulama Youth movement, Pemuda Ansor.

The Ansor youth asked her, 'Where are you off to?'

'I have to go to the doctor, because of bleeding', Tinah lied.

She did not wish to engage in conversation. She closed her eyes, but she was too much on high alert to sleep. She held her two children tightly at her side.

'Old Malang, Old Malang', called the conductor.

The call jolted Tinah to get prepared. She went to get off the train, but realised that the Ansor youth was following her. In the crowd pushing to get off the train, she and her two children managed to escape the eyes of their pursuer, and they got off the train on the left hand side. When she was sure that their pursuer had got off the other side of the train, Tinah managed to board again with the help of her friend from Pemuda Rakyat, and then stay on the train until the next stop, New Malang.

It was late afternoon when they arrived. It felt deserted and tense. A few people were passing by, with anxious faces. The journey from the station to her older brother's house was not very far, but Tinah decided to take a *becak* (pedicab). When she arrived at the front door, she fainted.

A few days later, the house opposite her brother's was ransacked. This created an atmosphere of fear in her brother's family. It was quiet. The radio was turned off. No one spoke, and everything was done in silence. Not wanting to be a burden, Tinah took her leave of them to go to Surabaya.

When she arrived in Surabaya, she went to Jetis-Ponorogo to look for her brother-in-law. She found him. But there, too, she could only stay for a few days and move on. With no destination, with no plan. Tinah and her two children wandered for days sheltering in the porches of buildings.

* * * *

In the evening light, a woman wearing an old, faded dress is sitting in front of the Wayang Orang theatre for the Pande Giling group in Surabaya, watching the pink sky redden and go dark. She is holding a tired child on her lap close to the one in her womb. Another child comes to look at the sky and turns to say, 'Mummy, I'm hungry. Please get us something to eat, Mummy'.

Surabaya, December 1965

To feed her children, Tinah went to a gold shop to sell some jewelry. She had brought with her almost all the jewelry her mother had left her. She sold the bracelets, earrings, necklaces, pendants and rings one by one. On this day, she sold her necklace. And the very next day, 13 December 1965, the rupiah was revalued. One thousand rupiah became one rupiah. Tinah could not afford to buy her children the soup they asked for. She could only afford boiled cassava at 25 rupiah, without any vegetables or chilli sauce. Just one big handful of boiled cassava for the day. One handful to be shared by three.

But she almost spat it out, when she got a slap on the back.

'It's you, Tinah, isn't it?' said the tall man of Chinese descent who looked at her rather hesitatingly.

'Yes, I'm right', he said, his face brightening.

'Come inside, sister. Don't stay outside. Come inside, for the children's sake', he went on.

Tinah followed. She went in to the old Dutch-style theatre, away from the leafy yard.

The young man came from the same kampung as her in Blitar. He was a member of Lekra, the Institute of People's Culture now being accused of being an arm of the Communist Party. He was also on the run, and was hiding in the building where there was a nightly *wayang orang* performance.

He gave his room to Tinah and her two children to sleep in. He himself slept on the floor with the other actors. And so began days backstage. The *wayang orang* performances were held every day from seven until nine at night. They were always full. If Tinah had not been pregnant, maybe she would have joined the performance, at the very least she could have played in the gamelan, using her skills from the regular gamelan practices she used to attend back home. The performances helped lessen her nightmares. But she often wanted to cry.

'If you cry, people will know you are afraid. They will take you away. You will die', her inner voice whispered.

She did not cry.

* * * *

In March 1966, heavily pregnant, she built up the courage to return to Malang, to her older brother's place, bringing her two children. There was no reason for her brother to refuse his favourite younger sister. Fortunately it was safe. And on 23 March 1966, Tinah gave birth to a girl at a private maternity clinic. No one asked any questions, because Nuryanto's cousin came and said he was Tinah's husband. One of Nuryanto's in-laws sent money to cover the clinic costs. He was a member of the Malang branch of the Railway Workers Union (Serikat Buruh Kereta Api, SBKA).

In June 1966, Tinah's older sister, the third child of the family, came to visit. She had just lost her job as Head of the Banyuwangi pawnshop because she had sheltered the head of the Banyuwangi branch of Gerwani. She was fortunate to lose only her pension, and not her life.

She was married but had no children, so she invited Tinah to come and live with her. That very day, Tinah and her three children moved to South Malang. There they opened a snack stall that sold Tinah's delicious cakes.

After a few months, Tinah's parents-in-law arrived. Their house in Blitar had been set on fire and burnt to the ground. They heard that Tinah was in Malang and followed her there.

'How about my house?' Tinah asked, meaning the house that her father Raden Sukemi Martidihardjo had bequeathed her.

They ransacked the house again, child, but thank God they did not destroy it', her mother-in-law replied. 'It is empty now'.

Her mother-in-law then asked Tinah to go with her to the Margosono cemetery area in Malang where they would build a new life together. Tinah agreed. But after just a few days, she decided to return to her sister's place.

'But please leave your daughter Riri with us, to keep us company so we are not lonely', her father-in-law asked. Apart from his son Nuryanto, he had also lost his second child in the wake of the 30th September Movement.

And Tinah did not see her three-year-old daughter Riri again. When she went back to the cemetery just three days later, the shack was empty, and no one knew where its inhabitants had gone.

No news ever came.

* * * *

When the baby, her fourth child, was about four months old, Tinah returned to Surabaya. Before leaving, she entrusted her oldest child with her older brother in Malang. In Surabaya, she met up with a distant relative who worked in the Navy Hospital (Rumah Sakit Angkatan Laut, RSAL). He invited her to stay with him. Tinah was there with some other young men in hiding, who had been members of CGMI (Consentrasi Gerakan Mahasiswa Indonesia, Indonesian Student Movement Concentration). Her relative then found her some work sewing navy uniforms. She lived there for two years, supporting herself and her daughter from the money she earned sewing.

But Tinah's nomadic life, like a wandering cat, was not yet over. After a while, her brother-in-law asked her to return to Malang. There Tinah reunited with her older sister, the one who had worked as the head of the pawn office in Banyuwangi and lost her pension. Two weeks later, one of her husband's cousins, a student at the Malang teacher's college (IKIP, Institut Keguruan dan Ilmu Pendidikan), took Tinah to a house rented by her husband's younger brother in a kampung in Buncitan. Tinah's older sister, wanting to save Tinah the trouble of moving her child here and there, asked Tinah to leave her youngest with them.

The house where they stayed was a place for pounding rice. During the day they would pound the rice, and the next morning the husked rice would be sold. Tinah helped with threshing, and carried the produce to the market. She also helped with planting in the rice fields.

Tinah's cousin-in-law gave her a one meter long garden plot and said to her, 'whatever grows is yours.'

In her spare time, even though her hands were blistered from pounding the rice, Tinah still managed to crochet or to weave borders on to remnants of cloth she collected, to make handkerchiefs. She would give them to the neighbours' children to sell to their friends at school. Tinah's interaction with her neighbours did not extend beyond that. She kept her distance. The people there knew her only as coming from a navy family, like most of the other people who lived there. But she did once recognise another former teacher who was also in hiding. Tinah entrusted her with a pendant to sell.

Tinah used the money she had managed to save from selling the handkerchiefs and the pendant to leave Buncitan after the younger brother of her husband's cousin made sexual advances towards her. He took advantage of Tinah's status as a guest, and said she must be 'lonely', and suggested she take the place of his wife who was out of town having just given birth. Tinah answered his disgusting advances with a kick.

She returned to Surabaya, to the same house she lived in before, and went back to her job sewing navy uniforms.

Surabaya, 1968

And that is where she is now.

She has just stolen a piece of cloth from a washing line.

Night fell, and Tinah walked back home. Her second family there greeted her warily. All the GCMI students living there had been arrested. Luckily the owner of the house, Pak Hadi, was released. The atmosphere was confused. Still wearing the piece of batik cloth as a veil, Tinah went to the kitchen. The washing-up was still in the kitchen sink. Tinah added water, and washed the plates and glasses one by one.

Questions were running around and around in her head.

'When will things get better?'

'When will this game of hide and seek end?'

'Since their father disappeared, the children have never asked where is. Have they forgotten him?'

'Will I ever be with my children again?'

She finished washing the last glass.

'Should I return the piece of cloth I took?'

She smiled bitterly to herself. She looked at the cloth, still wrapped around her, then folded it carefully and put it on the table in the sitting room. Pak Hadi came up to her and asked what she was going to do now. Tinah was silent for a moment.

'I will continue with my sewing', she said.

No, that is not a good idea. It is not safe here anymore. I will get you a ticket to Jakarta. You'd better leave', Pak Hadi advised.

Two days later Tinah returned the piece of batik cloth to its owner, the wife of a navy soldier.

'So that's what happened! Well I am glad all is well. It was just as well I washed that piece of cloth that day', the woman said, laughing.

'Thank you. I must also say goodbye now. I have a ticket to Jakarta. Pray for me', and Tinah took her leave.

Tinah left for Jakarta by train. In the midst of the chaotic scene at Gambir Station in Jakarta, suddenly two tall men approached her.

'Tinah?' one of them asked her.

'Yes'

'Please come with us'. The man who had asked the question took her bag that contained just a few clothes and a small amount of money.

Like a buffalo being led by the nose, Tinah followed. She had no idea who these two men were, how they recognised her, or where they were taking her. But for some reason she had no urge to ask. And the men did not engage in small talk.

'The important thing is that my children are safe. Now it's just me, so whatever happens, happens', she thought to herself.

They took Tinah by car. From the window she could see shop signs with the names of the areas they passed.

'So, this is Jakarta …' she whispered, amazed at the capital city.

After passing a billboard saying JAWA MOTOR Senen, which was in central Jakarta, the car turned right, and stopped right in front of an entrance to a garage.

The building was owned by Inkopal (Induk Koperasi Angkatan Laut, Central Navy Cooperative). Tinah's brain was in overdrive – browsing data to search who was connected to all this. She asked for a moment to rest and eat. Then she was told she had a guest. It turned out to be Eko, Pak Hadi's son. Eko was also on the wanted list. He had escaped to Jakarta and was working here at Inkopal.

'Oh … so Pak Hadi told Eko I was coming to Jakarta. Then Eko asked his friends to meet me …' Tinah was piecing together everything that had happened to her that day.

She was relieved. At least she had escaped the uncertainty of life for one more day. Eko then offered her some work.

'But not here. Probably in Bandung. Do you agree?'

To get another chance, Tinah felt she could not refuse. She agreed.

She only had one night to rest after the 14 hour ride on a bumpy train. The next morning she left for Bandung. She was taken to an air force housing complex in Bandung. They passed rows of neat houses, each the same as the next. They arrived at a house immediately in front of a little stall that sold odds and ends.

It turned out that the work she was being offered was as a domestic servant. The madam and master of the house were Javanese, and in fact there was a faint family connection with her. They were very distant relatives. And distant they were in more ways than one: distant physically, and distant emotionally.

Tinah was treated as no more than a servant. She had to start work at five in the morning: do the washing, sweep, wash the floors, cook, do the ironing, sell kerosene, and look after four boys and one girl – the same ages as her own children.

Tinah got thinner day by day. The clothes she wore when she first arrived got too big for her. She had sunken cheeks. She was constantly haunted by thoughts of her own children. And on top of that, her boss never stopped demanding this or that, yet always forgot to pay her wages. Tinah kept herself going during this trial in the Javanese way – by fasting, a total of 40 days in one year.

One day, after Tinah had been working there for nine months, Madam hit her. She accused Tinah of stealing salted eggs which were on the menu for that day. She lashed out with abuse. Master of the house then came and joined in. Tinah had no one to defend her. All she could do was cry. She was fired and not given a single cent.

Fortunately, Madam did not know that Tinah had been earning a bit of money. Every night she would burn incense with a neighbour who was a medium, and ask for the lottery code. Tinah's customers were air force people. If some of her recommended numbers came up, she would get a commission. And this was the money she now used to leave Bandung.

She could think of only one destination, to return to Inkopal in Jakarta. She went as quickly as she could to the Bandung railway station. But there was a checkpoint. Everyone entering the platform had to show their papers. Since the 30 September 1965 incident, anyone travelling from one area to another had to show their identity card and a travel permit. And Tinah? She did not even have an identity card.

She eased herself out of the queue waiting to enter the platform, clutching her stomach as though she suddenly had an attack of diarrhoea. She walked towards the toilet, but at the last minute walked out of the station and went straight to the Cicaheum bus terminal.

Luckily, there it was clear. Tinah had no difficulty getting on the bus. But she was physically exhausted. She vomited all the way to Jakarta, and her body was weak. When she finally got to Jakarta, Eko took her to stay temporarily with a friend of his.

Tinah was still extremely weak. For a whole week she could do nothing at all, and because of this, had no money. She sold what clothes she had just to get some food in her stomach. When she was well, she tried to find work in a clothing factory, but the pay was too low. One whole week's pay was only enough to buy two servings of rice, without side dishes, per day.

After about three months, Eko came to take her back to Surabaya. The route had been decided: depart from Jakarta by train, overnight in Yogya, call by Kertasono in Nganjuk and then on to Surabaya.

Then, in Yogya, someone snatched her bag with her money.

* * * *

Tinah and Eko stayed in different hostels, Tinah near the station and Eko at Patang Puluhan. They arranged to meet at five in the morning in front of Tinah's losmen. While waiting there for Eko the next morning, a man approached and started chatting in a friendly way. When he had gone, Tinah realised that a small bag that was together with her bag of clothes behind her had disappeared.

Eko had no extra money on him, so once again Tinah had to find a second hand stall and sell some of her clothes.

At Kertosono, they called in on a relative to ask for help. But it turned out that just two days previously the man of the house had died. He had been murdered, accused of being involved in the 30th September Movement. So they changed their destination to Kediri, where another of Tinah's brothers, number six in her family, who worked head of Irrigation for Malang, lived. After selling some clothes, all the money she had left was 750 rupiah. Tinah did not know if this would be enough to pay for the two of them to get to Kediri. She went up to the bus conductor and came out with her weapon of last resort: honesty.

The bus conductor took pity on them and let them get on.

They got off the bus near the Gudang Garam cigarette factory, not far from the Brantas River. The bridge over the river was being repaired, so they had to walk to find a *becak*.

Then there was a new problem. Tinah could not remember the full address of her brother's house. They asked a few *becak* drivers, one by one, to see who could take them to this 'almost' address. And one of the *becak* drivers passed the test. He was prepared to take them for 50 rupiah, an exorbitant price considering the usual price was just 20 rupiah.

After going round and round, they found the general area.

'Which house is it?' Eko asked.

'Let's see … this one … no, that one, with the blue motor bike', Tinah answered, 'at least I think so …'

This time her guesswork was right.

Her brother and sister-in-law were eating lunch. Their faces showed their astonishment. They could not believe that their youngest sister who was in hiding was there on their doorstep.

'Where have you come from?' her brother asked.

'From Jakarta. I have come to you as a beggar, Brother', Tinah answered softly.

'Why?'

'Someone stole my bag in Yogya. I've lost everything.'

'Well, let's worry about that later. Come and take a bath and have something to eat.'

Half an hour later, her brother was waiting in the sitting room with a pile of clothes, some dark sunglasses, and an envelope.

'The people in the house across the road were taken away by the police not long ago', her brother said.

A pause.

'Here's a bit of money, 10,000 rupiah', her brother said, emptying a white envelope with red and blue borders. 'Are you staying the night?' he then asked.

'No. I think for the safety of us all, Eko and I will go directly to Surabaya', Tinah replied.

Her brother did not try to stop her.

As soon as it got dark, Tinah and Eko continued their journey. Four hours later they arrived in Surabaya. The plan was for Eko to take Tinah to his friend's place in Tambah Sari, but Tinah refused and went with Eko to his house.

The next morning she discovered that Eko's father, Pak Hadi, who had been so kind to her and his son and had also helped the CGMI students, had been arrested.

* * * *

After Soekarno was sidelined and Soeharto emerged as the one in control, the regulation called Tap MPRS/XXV/1966 appeared, banning the teachings of communism, Marxism and Leninism. The cleansing campaign against leftist remnants was enforced through the requirement for people to have certification that they were 'clean' (Surat Keterangan Bersih Diri) and also 'from a clean circle' (Surat Bersih Lingkungan). Being 'clean' oneself meant that you were not directly involved with the

30th September Movement (now called G30S/PKI). Being from a 'clean circle' meant that none of one's family – father, mother, in-laws and close family – was involved.

Tinah had learnt her lesson at the railway station in Bandung. She knew she had to make a new identity. It was absolute suicide to go around without documents. Because this new certification started with one's identity card, Tinah scratched her head wondering how she could get a new identity. Using the money her brother had given her, she left the house wearing a veil in the Islamic style, just in case she came across someone who knew her.

God was on her side.

Just when she did not know what to do, she met a relative. He was an army officer called Captain Basuki. He took Tinah to Buncitan Sidoarjo, where Tinah had once worked pounding rice.

Captain Basuki knew the staff in the administration office there. He got a new name for Tinah. It was 'Pinah'. Tinah never knew what Pinah looked like, or whether she even existed. But what was clear was that the administration staff then got to work.

Her new identity card changed only her name. But that was enough to get Tinah – well, Pinah – a brand new certificate saying that she was 'clean'.

New name, new hopes

After she got her new identity card and documents, Pinah returned to Jakarta and her work at the garment factory. Because the wages were so little, she found new work as an assistant tailor. After a while, Eko brought his friend Agus to stay. Agus's father used to work for the *Harian Rakjat* newspaper. After the 30th September incident, *Harian Rakjat* was shut down, and almost all of the staff were accused of requiring 'cleansing', including Agus's father. When Agus's mother heard Pinah's story, which was similar to that of her husband, she took on Pinah as her adopted daughter. She then moved in.

In mid 1969, a neighbour who was a civil servant offered Pinah work in a logistics office in Cipinang where they needed some extra staff. Pinah got the job there easily.

Life was improving.

Two and a half years later, she was offered the chance to become a civil servant herself. The first requirement was to attach copies of educational qualifications. Pinah's hopes were dashed. When her nomadic life had begun six years earlier, she did not bring a single copy of any of her certificates. And even if she had them now, she could not show a certificate with a name different to the one on her current identity card.

She decided to resign.

Jakarta, 1971

They say that to have good neighbours is a blessing. Pinah does not doubt it. In Blitar, it was her neighbours who helped eat the *duku* and lychees from the trees that seemed to never stop bearing fruit. When the terrifying nights of the cleansing began, it was her neighbours who sheltered her. In Surabaya she had been 'saved' by her neighbour's washing on the line. In Jakarta she got a job in a government office because of her neighbour. And now, love came her way once again, through her neighbour's matchmaking.

* * * *

After the 30th September Movement, some new social groups were added to Indonesia's diversity. People who had been arrested and accused of being involved with communism were divided into three groups. Group A were those who had planned, helped to plan, or knew about plans for the 30th September Movement but did not report it to the authorities. This category included those who were actively involved. They were the ones tried by Extraordinary Military Tribunals or the state judicial system in various places in Indonesia.

Then there were people in group B who were those who agreed with the September 30th movement, or who obstructed official efforts to crush it. Officials of the Communist Party and organisations considered to be affiliated to the Communist Party were included in this category.

Group C included people who had been involved in the 1948 communist uprising (C1), former members of mass organisations that supported the Communist Party (C2), and people whose grandparents, parents, children, or uncles, aunts or relatives were involved with the Communist Party.

* * * *

Tachrin was a teacher and also an activist in the Cooperative Bank for Farmers and Fishermen (Bank Koperasi Tani dan Nelayan, BKTN) who was a 'graduate' of Salemba and Tangerang prisons, with the label Group C. His married status had also changed because when he was in prison, his wife had asked for a divorce. He was now single again. Fortunately when he was released he was not unemployed for long, because he got a job as a driver for a newspaper editor.

Then, through a neighbour, he was introduced to Pinah who it turned out was the adopted daughter of one of his good friends. After a while, he decided to propose marriage.

'Perhaps the idea of marrying again, and marrying someone labelled a communist sympathiser, is frightening?' Tachrin said after Pinah had already accepted.

'Not at all. I don't think anything about that. I don't feel I did anything wrong. And I know for a fact that my former husband never did anything wrong. And with you it's the same, isn't it?' Pinah asked.

The proposal went smoothly enough, but the wedding plans hit snags. The bride-to-be did not get agreement from her local official, the neighbourhood head (RT). The official the next level up (RW) also refused to give permission. Eventually, with the help of a relative who was a neighbourhood head in a different kampung, they managed to get permission from the top level, the Lurah. But this was only after he wrote in black and white that he did not take any responsibility if anything happened to Tachrin and Pinah.

Now Pinah got her third name: Bu Tachrin. Her new second life had just begun.

Jakarta, 14 January 1974

The Prime Minister of Japan, Kakuei Tanaka, landed at Halim airport to begin a four day visit to Indonesia.

The next day, thousands of students marched in the streets from the University of Indonesia campus on Jalan Salemba to the Trisakti University campus in Grogol, Jakarta. This was the climax of a series of demonstrations by young people that began in mid 1973 demanding the disbanding of two extra-constitutional institutions – the Command for the Restoration of Security and Public Order (Komando Operasi Keamanan dan Ketertiban, known by the acronym Kopkamtib) and the Assistant to the President (Asisten Presiden, Aspri) – criticising the corruption in the national petrol company, Pertamina, and protesting against the construction of the Indonesia in Miniature Park (Taman Mini Indonesia Indah).

However that day, suddenly the Proyek Senen site, the Coca Cola factory, the Toyota Astra show room and a few other places in Jakarta were set alight, destroyed, and looted by the mob.

This was the explosion that was named the '15th of January disaster' or Malapetaka Limabelas Januari, known by the acronym Malari.

There are various theories about what happened. One view is that 'Malari' was merely a student demonstration against foreign investment, particularly Japanese capital. Some saw the incident as an expression by intellectuals of their dislike of President Soeharto's assistants (Ali Moertopo, Soedjono Humardani and so on) who held tremendous power. Another theory was that there was conflict within the military, namely rivalry between two generals: Soemitro and Ali Moertopo.

As a result of the incident, at least 11 people died, around 300 were wounded, 775 were arrested, and thousands of cars turned to melted steel. More than a hundred buildings were badly destroyed and 160 kilos of gold went missing from gold shops.

* * * *

The Malari incident also deeply affected the new Tachrin family when the newspaper that Tachrin's boss was editor for, was banned. The newspaper known for being critical, anti-corruption, anti-tyranny, and for supporting the common people, was now closed forever and as a result all its staff were out of work.

The night of the Malari incident, Bu Tachrin's husband did not return home. Tinah had no idea of the conditions in the streets, and she waited. Usually her husband came home bringing the unsold newspapers. She would store them on the floor under a cupboard. When she had a pile, she would tie them together and sell them as recycled paper. But from that night on, there were no more old newspapers to sell.

A friend helped Pak Tachrin find work. Ironically, although he had lost his job because of anti-Japanese sentiments, he managed to get a new job with a Japanese multinational company. As Charles Darwin said in the theory of evolution, the ones who survive are the ones who can adapt. Pak Tachrin's good English language skills and his knowledge of the Jakarta streets led to him being employed as a driver for the Director of the largest glass production business in Southeast Asia. This later led to an opportunity for him to become a member of the administrative staff in the company. And his new family crawled upwards with him as his life improved. They moved a few times in rented accommodation until finally they lived together with Pak Tachrin's parents. Bu Tachrin helped the family finances by taking in sewing and making cakes.

But even with all this, their journey was still full of obstacles. Every pay day, Pak Tachrin's older brother would arrive and ask for a share as payback for having often come to visit Tachrin when he was in prison.

And the local Military Command, when they knew that Pak Tachrin had got work, also asked for a cut. Pak Tachrin was often called in on a work day to report. Bu Tachrin would then have to go to her husband's office to explain his absence. She could only ever think of a single excuse, 'there is a family funeral'. One day it would be the older brother of his mother's uncle who died, another day it would be the mother of the older brother of his uncle.

The Military Command did a deal with Pak Tachrin about how much he had to pay. It was unfair. In short, every month Pak Tachrin had to pay 7,500 rupiah. Then they called in Bu Tachrin for her to give her 'agreement'.

'Excuse me sir', Bu Tachrin said using very polite Javanese to the First Lieutenant who had called her in. 'My husband's salary is only 20,000 rupiah a month. If he has to pay you 7,500 out of that, how can we live on the rest? If it were you, would you agree to it?

'I would like to invite you to visit our home. Please come and see our living conditions', Bu Tachrin said, ending her diplomacy while straightening the piece of *lurik* cloth carrying her youngest child.

And two days later, the First Lieutenant really did come to their house. He could see for himself how Tachrin and his wife and their six children lived. The eight of them lived cramped in a house with earth floors and a door that could not be closed properly because the hinge was just attached with wire. The First Lieutenant went home without making any comment. But from then on, there were no more demands for payment. This was an exception made for the Tachrin family alone, that's for sure.

* * * *

The dry season replaced the rainy season, dry season, rainy season, dry season again.

Very slowly, life was falling into place, but there were still some scattered fragments. With faith that God always protected her, that her mother's spirit was always with her, and that she had never done any wrong, Bu Tachrin began to gather those scattered fragments in order to build her second life.

The first fragment: Srikandi. Bu Tachrin returned to her woman soldier role by becoming a volunteer at the Cathedral of Mary of the Assumption in Jakarta. The Cathedral offered social services to the underprivileged, particularly to victims of conflict, and especially former political detainees from the 30th September movement. Services offered included the provision of micro credit for business, and looking for employment opportunities. Unfortunately for former political prisoners, the only kind of work offered was as building labourers or coolie type work. Teaching or any other work where they would interact with many people was basically out of the question.

Bu Tachrin was given the task of supervising the loans, and giving classes in making cakes. The baking classes were held in different places. She went all over Jakarta, from Saint Mark's in Cililtan and Saint Mark's in Klender, East Jakarta, to the convent at Sunter in Central Jakarta. She would carry cake tins and cooking bowls of all shapes and sizes, scales, spatula, and egg beaters in a big bag. Bu Tachrin is of slight build – only 1.5 metres tall, and she was dwarfed by all the things she carried. So on days when he did not have to work, Pak Tachrin would offer to be her assistant, and accompany her when teaching.

Because of Bu Tachrin's volunteer work, the cathedral, which worked in partnership with the Christian Children's Fund, gave the Tachrins' first child a scholarship until graduation from senior high school.

The second fragment to be put in place was Nuryanto's children. Bu Tachrin had four children from her first marriage, but none of them lived with her. Eventually, one day her son, her third child from her first marriage came to visit. Bu Tachrin had entrusted him to her older brother before she left for Surabaya. He was about fourteen years old when he came to Jakarta looking for his mother. The very first question he asked her was, 'My friends say that Gerwani women were prostitutes. Were you one too?'

This was the question of a child brainwashed by the New Order.

* * * *

The New Order Regime had its own story about Gerwani. It went like this: 'On the night the generals were murdered, Gerwani members were having an orgy, dancing and singing the song '*Genjer-genjer*.'

The song *Genjer-genjer* then became the most legendary Indonesian song after *Indonesia Raya*. But whereas *Indonesia Raya* was given exalted place as the national anthem, *Genjer-genjer* was given the label 'banned'. No one could sing it.

The song had been composed in 1942 by an artist from Banyuwangi, inspired by the resilience of people during the time of famine in the Japanese occupation. People turned a water weed into a tasty dish. The prolific weed was lightly fried or boiled and mixed with a sweet and sour peanut sauce.

Bu Tachrin liked the song. She would often sing it as a lullaby for her children. The song told of the simple pleasure of a husband and wife as they picked the *genjer-genjer* to eat.

The words, in Javanese, went like this:

Gendjer-gendjer neng ledokan pating keleler
Emake thole teka-teka mbubuti gendjer
Oleh satenong mungkur sedot sing tolah-tolih
Gendjer-gendjer saiki wis digawa mulih

Gendjer-gendjer esuk-esuk digawa nang pasar
Didjejer-djejer diunting pada didasar
Emake djebeng tuku gendjer wadahi etas

Gendjer-gendjer saiki arep diolah Gendjer-gendjer mlebu kendil wedange umob
Setengah mateng dientas digawe iwak
Sega sa piring sambel penjel ndok ngamben
Gendjer-gendjer dipangan musuhe sega

Genjer-genjer everywhere
Women and children come to pick
A basketful and straight back
And now it's here at home

Early morning it's taken to the market
Neatly in bunches on display
Lined up side by side
The women buy it and put it in their bags

Now it's cooking time
Into the pot of boiling water
Just lightly cooked to make a tasty dish
A plate of rice with chilli peanut sauce
Delicious with a plate of rice

Muhammad Arief, who wrote the song, later joined Lekra, and the song then took on new associations. It was a hit in the 1960s and associated with Lekra and leftist ideology.

During the 'cleansing' after the 30th September movement, the song was also 'cleansed'. The main reason given was that the song was written by communists. Secondly, after the 30th September incident, the student daily newspaper KAMI (Kesatuan Aksi Mahasiswa Indonesia, Union of Indonesian Student Action) ridiculed the song, changing the words 'Genjer-genjer' to 'General-general'. And so the injunction against the song became even stronger.

This was their version:

Jendral – jendral nyang ibukota pating keleler
Emake Gerwani, teko teko nyuliki jendral
Oleh sak truk, mungkir sedot sing toleh-toleh
Jendral Jendral saiki wes dicekeli
Jendral Jendral isuk-isuk pada disiksa
Dijejer ditaleni dan dipelosoro
Emake Gerwani, teko kabeh milu ngersoyo
Jendral Jendral maju terus dipateni

Generals in the capital everywhere
The Gerwani girls kidnapped the generals
Got a truckful and straight back
There they are all tied up
Early morning it's torture time
Lined up, tied up, tortured
All the Gerwani girls join in
The generals come forward to be killed

* * * *

Bu Tachrin could not reply. She was too deeply hurt. All she could do was stroke her son's head.

This experience with her third child from Nuryanto made her keep a tight lid on her past, never discussing it with her children, neither her children with Nuryanto nor those with Tachrin. It was enough for them to know their mother in the same way as her neighbours knew her, as someone who baked cakes, no more than that.

But God has His own ways.

A good opportunity for her to meet with her 'first edition' children arose when her son, her third child with Nuryanto, married in Malang. Bu Tachrin was reunited there with her lost daughter, who disappeared in the Margosono cemetery in Malang when she was only three. It turned out that her grandparents had taken her to Nuryanto's family. She lived with them until she married a soldier who was also a former 1965 person on the run.

Bu Tachrin's son-in-law, her second daughter's husband, knew Bu Tachrin because they had once lived in the same sub-regency in Blitar. So they knew each other's status in relationship to 1965. On top of that, he was once stationed in Pamekasan and often met Bu Tachrin's older brother who used to be the Irrigation Officer there before he moved to Malang.

After that reunion, Bu Tachrin's 'first edition' children began to know their mother's story, even though it was incomplete.

Tebet, January 2011

In a 5 metre square space with pink, green and yellow striped walls, Bu Tachrin spends time with four of her children from Pak Tachrin (the four still living at home), watching a Korean TV show on their 27 inch LCD screen. This room is multipurpose: sitting room, dining room, TV room, workshop, and storage place for all the handicraft and cake orders.

The prayer call comes from the mosque. Bu Tachrin has just finished making an orchid frame out of white piping. She tidies up the scissors and pieces of cloth and puts them in a plastic box so that her little grandson Satrio will not play with them. From behind her brown-framed glasses that hide some of her wrinkles, she watches Satrio run about carrying his toys, his cute little mouth chewing the rice his mother is feeding him.

Her children built this house around ten years ago for their parents. They paid if off in instalments, but truly built it themselves, from mixing the cement, lifting the stones, making the foundations and walls, and doing the painting. Bu Tachrin knows that her children have inherited their parents' spirit for hard work.

She remembers a conversation a few years ago with one of her daughters …

'Mother, why do you never speak up when people call us 'hobos'? You should say something. Defend yourself', her daughter protested when one of their rich neighbours called the Tachrin family 'hobos'.

'Well, the truth is we are just hobos ... why get upset about it? The gap between them and us is huge. But you just wait and see, one day they will need us.'

Justice seems to work in mysterious ways. It turns out that even someone labelled rich needs someone labelled poor. Her daughter understood this only when one day the neighbours who had looked down on them came to ask for help with the preparations for their son's engagement. So, it turned out their rich pride could melt.

The Tachrins always taught their children to be independent, hold their heads high and be honest and courteous. Bu Tachrin herself is grateful that in these crazy times, her children have become well-rounded people. They managed to further their education, get degrees, work and have their own families. Their lives are not glamorous, but also not lacking.

Bu Tachrin herself keeps to her long-held Srikandi principles. Although now in her seventies, she is still active – extremely active – in various things. Apart from organising catering and taking cake orders with her youngest daughter, she makes plastic flowers out of drinking straws. She takes them with her when she attends exhibitions. She also makes routine visits to the Waluya Sejati old people's home which was established by Ribka Tiptaning. Most of the people in the home are former political prisoners. Their get-togethers provide times for these women marginalised by history to allow themselves to remember the past. Bu Tachrin often reminds them not to waste time regretting the past. 'That's enough. If you keep on thinking about it, keep on regretting things, it will eat away at you and cause an early death.'

It is not easy to forget what they experienced. Even for Bu Tachrin herself. Sometimes at night the black and white film of her past begins to play, without her wishing it. She remembers when she could not even cry. Now that she is sure she is more accepting of the past, she feels the need to let the tears flow.

The fact that she did not go mad was not a miracle, but because she worked at it. So she tries to maintain her mental health that she fought so hard for, by remaining productive. She has now started to write her story, and wants to complete her autobiography. The doctor who helped restore her health after she was diagnosed with diabetes once told her, 'biographies are not only of famous people, are they?'

She wants to give her writing to her children and grandchildren. She wants them to really know their grandparents, and to learn that this country where they live has another side to it that perhaps they do not know.

Then her old friend, Putu Oka Sukanta, invited her to be involved in a writing project of stories about 1965. Stories from various makers of 1965 history. Bu Tachrin saw this as a real step in the restoration of people's reputations, something that government after government has promised, but never actually done.

Bu Tachrin often takes part in discussion forums about human rights and 1965. There she puts forward the demand for compensation through a public acknowledgement to the whole world that they – the victims – were not evil. This compensation, a correction of history, is more meaningful than any financial compensation. 'And after all', she says 'where would the state get enough money to compensate us financially?'

* * * *

A mobile telephone buzzes.

Her oldest daughter hands her the phone.

'Hello?'

'Is that Bu Tachrin?'

'Yes it is. Who is speaking?'

'This is Puti, Bu'

'Hello Puti.'

'Bu, keep the 10th of February free, won't you? There will be the launching of Putu Oka's film at the Goethe Institute. It is still a while away, but I am booking you now because I know how busy you are. We would love it if you could come and help mind the stand selling books and films.'

'Of course. I'll note the date.'

'Okay. We will get in touch again later on. Oh, and by the way I am really craving those steamed cakes with palm sugar you make. If you happen to make any, please bring them. This is a special order ...'

'Yes, yes, February 10th at Goethe, to mind the stall and bring cakes. Anything else?'

'No, that's all. Thank you so much. Until then, Bu Tachrin.'

Click

Interviewers and Transcribers: Puti Yassmina, Amangku Bhumi.

Writers: Ibu Tachrin, Puti Yassmina, Amangku Bhumi.

Chapter 15

Wardik

New Order survivor

Wardik, born in 1949, was named by his mother. She was from Majalaya in West Java, and when she was twelve years old, she was taken by her aunt to Sumatra to work on a plantation. Six years later she met her future husband, Wardik's father. He came from Ponorogo in East Java. Their son Wardik later married Elya in 1980 and they had four boys and a girl. Now 62 years old, [2010, trs.] Wardik is still fit and strong with a thick moustache. His gaze is sharp, but conveys disappointment and suspicion. His friends find him rather daunting.

You can tell at a glance that he is a hard worker who has found success. He lives in the area of Helvetia in Medan, in a well-built, sturdy house, with marshes behind the back yard. The people nearby often fish in the marsh ponds. In the past, this land used to be a tobacco plantation, but in the 1990s the people took it over and now live there.

To get to Wardik's house from Polonia airport in Medan is a long and expensive taxi ride. It takes more than an hour at the best of times. You have to go through the city centre of Medan, to a flyover heading towards Belawan harbour, then turn left into a dense housing area where there are many children running around, and finally come to an alleyway about 300 meters long which is inaccessible to public transport, and there you will find Wardik's house. Nowadays he rarely travels far from the house because his health is not so good.

He built the house with the proceeds from his work as a contractor for the Malibu Medan housing complex in 1999. It has four bedrooms; three for the family, and one especially for his old friends from Padang Halaban Rantau Prapat if they come to Medan.

He has never forgotten these friends, because they are an integral part of his life. They forged their friendship fighting for the rights to their land, and in surviving the bitter journey under New Order rule.

* * * *

When Wardik was just 18 years old, some soldiers came one morning to where he was helping out someone holding a celebration, and arrested him. This was on 30 May, 1967. He had time to go home briefly and then was taken to the Merbau Military District Command in the Labuhan Batu regency. There he was interrogated and tortured and shortly afterwards moved to the Military Command 021 headquarters at Pantai Timur Pematang Siantar. After further interrogation there, he was moved to the prison on Jalan Sutomo. He still vividly remembers that interrogation, and in 2010 told the story like this:

> They interrogated me with the accusation that I had hidden a large cache of weapons. According to them, only my older sister San knew where I had hidden them. When I was taken from the prison on Jalan Sutomo, all I could think of was torture and death. I cannot remember how many times they interrogated me, but the questions were always just the same kind of thing. And my answer was always 'I don't know'. This was because I truly did not know. Then they gave me electric shocks, three or four times, then I was lashed with a piece of rattan as thick as your big toe, all over my body. And then they specially brought over a three-edged barbed kind of whip called a 'sting ray tail' (*ekor pari*) from Tanjung Balai Military Resort, which left deep red scars on my back.
>
> When I was first taken in to be interrogated by the 'Section One' at Military Command 021 headquarters, I saw my eldest sister San there, sprawled on the floor. She had black eyes, a bleeding mouth, and her long hair had been completely cut. I was ordered to sit and they took off my handcuffs. The Assistant First Lieutenant, Meta Ginting, sat behind a desk that was in front of me. He said 'How can you not own up? Look at your sister – don't you feel any pity for her? This is all your fault.' Then a pause, as though he was thinking. 'If you confess, you and your sister will be released. And you will get a medal from the State for exposing a network of rebels'.

As Wardik was telling this story, he paused here, as though the pain returned. Then he went on, imitating the interrogator's voice.

'But if you insist on being obstinate, you will see for yourself what happens. So, tell us where you hid those weapons.'

'I don't know, Sir.'

So he was tortured some more, kicked, fell, dragged up and kicked some more, until he passed out. Two months later he was interrogated again. This time it was a new technique. He was ordered to sit on a table and put his legs out straight on another table in front of him. Then the interrogator, an assistant First Lieutenant wearing heavy army boots, stamped on Wardik's legs until they broke. Wardik passed out and when he regained consciousness he was in hospital. His right leg was in plaster and balanced on a wooden bench.

'When they brought you here, you were unconscious' one of the nurses told him. Wardik was kept at the hospital until his leg healed and he was strong enough to walk. There were some particularly caring nurses at the hospital, and Wardik made friends with them. He told them all about his torture, and also exactly where he came from. The nurses often gave him extra food, like bread and milk, as well as their sympathy. Wardik still remembers their names: Malijarwati, Sundari, Kartini Sebayang, Kartini bd Sinaga and Ginem. The doctor who treated him was of the Siagian kinship group, wearing army fatigues, with the status of Major. That was how Wardik knew he was in an army hospital. Six months later he was declared healed and taken back to the prison he had come from. Wardik remembers a snippet of conversation he had with one of the nurses:

'Actually, brother, where did you come from, and what did you do wrong to end up like this? Tell us, so we can know you better. But if you want to keep it secret, that's fine. You don't have to tell us anything', Malijarwati said, as though she understood.

> Is it wrong when someone tries to save another person's life? You were talking before, Nurse Malijar, about humanity, about saving lives. That is so beautiful, so noble to hear. But when I saved the lives of people who were nearly murdered, I was arrested and thrown into a cell. Given 'free accommodation', incarcerated and tortured, and eventually I came here where you are nursing me.

Back in prison, Wardik was put in a cell in C block which used to be a leper colony. The room measured 3 x 4 meters square. There was one wooden bench, one small cupboard and two stools. He lived there – rent free – for six months.

Apart from the kind nurses, Wardik also made friends with a boy called Supriadi who lived near the hospital. In the afternoons after school, Supriadi would go around the hospital selling a sweet cassava dessert, and would always stop by and keep Wardik company. On Sundays or on holidays, his little friend would be busy selling all day long. He was about twelve years old.

Wardik also talked to the nurses about how in March 1966 he hid someone on the run called Cak Muso, who was in the army that was based at the Military Resort Labuhan Bata, because he was going to be killed. He stressed that he did this out of a sense of humanitarianism.

> He and my father were arrested and taken to the Military Command headquarters. They – the army that is – took my father and some of his friends out of the holding cells there. They killed them. Why didn't I save them? My father, my father's friends, my neighbours? I could not save my father.

After Wardik's return to the prison at Jalan Soetomo, he was moved with nine others to Medan. There were two detention centres in Medan, one at Jalan Gandhi and one at called TPU C (Tempat Penahanan Umum, General Detention Centre C) in Jalan Binjai, at Kilometre 7. It turned out he was taken to the Jalan Gandhi centre, which, from what he had heard, meant that he was going to be detained for a long time. When he arrived, his heart was racing. He was met by guards who searched all this things.

Wardik talked about this detention centre in this way:

> It was quite a large building. When I got inside, I realised this it was some kind of hall or performance place. I remembered a school in Rantau Prapat, Sin Min School, which was similar in construction to this building. On the left, through the large door to the hall, were rooms like classrooms, all closed. This certainly used to be a school. A school that had been magically converted into a place to lock up detainees, a prison for detainees.
>
> Conditions were better here than at Siantar prison. The detainees were allowed to have cooking stoves, or to make stoves to boil rice and water. Their food ration was just one coconut-shell full a day of rice mixed with corn, with watery spinach that tasted like drain-water, and a tiny piece of dried fish the size of a chicken feather. But at least family members were allowed to visit, and to send ingredients twice a week. The solidarity between the detainees was much better than in the Siantar prison.

Hendrik Napitupulu was detained here together with his wife Supriati. Both of them had been activists with CGMI (Concentrasi Gerakan Mahasiswa Indonesia, Indonesian Student Movement Concentration) at a university in Yogyakarta. They had to bring their little daughter Niken into prison with them. Niken was a lively little thing. Everyone liked her, everyone loved her. It was Hendrik who informed Wardik that his two older sisters were both alive and held at the other detention centre (TPU C) at Jalan Bingkai.

Every working day, people were summoned for interrogation, morning, noon and night, right through to the next morning. The detainees could hear the screams of pain coming from the interrogation room. There were eight rooms at the centre, plus the hall and performance space. The seven former classrooms were used to lock up people considered dangerous. The room right at the back was for female prisoners, and the hall and performance area were for prisoners considered to be less dangerous. This is where Wardik was.

Under the stage was a storage area which was used to keep broken equipment. Every now and then the interrogators also used this space to put detainees who would not confess to what the interrogators wanted them to confess to. This two-functional space was dark, airless, and damp.

Pak Marto, a retired soldier (assistant Second Lieutenant) in Indonesia's revolution who had defended the Pangkalan Brandan area, and whose last position had been at the Inter-Regional Sumatran Command (Moanda, Komando Antar Daerah Sumatra), was held in this space for a while. For twenty one days, his companions were rats the size of cats, cockroaches and lizards. When they finally let him out, he could barely walk, and was weak and emaciated.

Before he was thrown into this former storage space, Pak Marto had been in one of the classrooms, room Number 7. The room, which measured only three and a half metres square, housed 14 prisoners. They never saw the light of day. The former storage area, magically transformed into a prison isolation chamber, was right beside room Number 7.

Not all the guards were cruel. Corporal Sujati, for instance, often gave Wardik sugar, coffee, and his own take-away rice meals, and even passed on his old clothes. He said that Wardik reminded him of his younger brother in Java.

Eventually Wardik was moved to the other detention centre on Jalan Binjai which housed 2000 prisoners. There he met his older sisters and his neighbourhood friends from Labuah Batu. Until then, Wardik had thought all of them were dead. They had thought the same thing about him. His two older sisters, San and Yus, together with the head of Gerwani for Labuah Batu, called Nurhaida Lintang, came and brought him corn-rice with dried fish and spinach.

Their children were with them at the detention centre. They were forced to join their parents there because there was no family outside to take them in. Some people had their houses confiscated, their fathers murdered. Some of the children in the detention centre learnt reading and writing, taught by the prisoners. Some were permitted to go outside the prison and sell things, like cakes their parents had made.

The prisoners made all sorts of handicraft to keep them going. Wardik studied painting with Jono, a member of Lekra, the Institute for People's Culture. Wardik studied for months, and made ten paintings, but did not manage to sell a single one. The small amount of money he had earned at the Jalan Gandhi centre cleaning the guards' rooms and doing ironing all went on buying canvas and oil paint.

Then he was offered work outside helping to clear the Chinese cemetery in Petisah. He got this work outside the detention centre only through bribing his guard. The cemetery was being cleared to build the fun park 'Taman Ria'. This is how Wardik described his experience:

> The contractor was a member of the Military Police Corps. The rate was 1500 rupiah for each grave we broke up. But the prisoners got only 1000 rupiah the other 500 rupiah went to the contractor.

His two older sisters were happy that Wardik had got work outside the barracks. Wardik gave them whatever he earned. San asked for permission to go home to see their mother. Wardik was very upset when he heard how his mother was suffering. He also asked permission, via a female prisoner who was on very good terms with the Commander, to go and visit his mother. If he himself ever asked for leave, he was never given permission to go. Wardik said the authorities had razed his village to the ground. Nobody in the village had dared to protest. They just had to accept it. Nobody was given any compensation.

> Mother had to move to some fields near the jungle. This was my mother, who during Indonesia's revolution for independence had been head of a revolutionary kitchen to feed the fighters, and now here she was going hungry.

Wardik then had to do forced labour on the Blangkahan plantation together with other prisoners from the detention centre on Jalan Binjai. They had to work for the bosses of P.T. Telaga Sari Indah at the Blangkahan plantation in Kwala subregency, in the regency of Langkat. Prisoners had been used there as forced labourers since 1969. These prisoners greeted Wardik and his companions warmly. One prisoner, Ngamen, who had been leader of People's Youth in Tanjung Keling, warned them:

> No one supervises what goes on here. We are just slaves, so don't expect any pay. We have to leave the barracks at 5:30 in the morning. The plantation overseer arranges what work has to be done, and the barracks supervisor then divides up the tasks among the prisoners. Our guard, Second Lieutenant Sungkono from Brigmob (police mobile brigade) comes here only once a month. We get food rations only twice a day, and even those are not enough. There is no breakfast. Everyone has to try to find something to eat for breakfast.

Wardik described one of his experiences in the plantation in this way:

> It was burning hot. The first day of this forced labour was torture. We had to clear wild sugarcane grass that was six meters high. I was drenched with sweat. I hadn't used a hoe or scythe for ages. The cane scratched my arms, and the scratches itched and hurt. The plantation assistant and the overseer meanwhile never let up with their orders. None of us had shoes. We trod on sharp thorns that pierced the soles of our feet. We were parched with thirst. We realised no one had brought any water. I tried to find a spring. The overseer, Saidi, said there was no spring in this plantation. There were only irrigation ditches, and they were right in the middle of the sugarcane grass to be cut in front of us. After cutting four hectares of the grass, we still had not found any ditches. Bastard, we thought, that was a trick! But no, we shouldn't rush to such conclusions.
>
> Selamat told me to dig a well. I looked around for a place that was a bit damp, and began to dig. My efforts were not in vain. After digging for just half a meter, there were signs of water. Ribut, who was with me, encouraged me to keep digging. I was totally exhausted, totally. All of us were dying of thirst, remember, especially me. But there was nothing else to do but keep on digging. Until at last, a spring gushed forth. I shouted, my voice croaky. I remembered that Tukimin had carried his lunch in a small metal container. So I went and got it. And so my little

> well saved us all from thirst. The assistant and the plantation overseer let it be. Senen drank too much and almost passed out.
>
> That first day of forced labour was a lesson. At one o'clock we were allowed to return to the barracks. It was a four kilometre walk. At the plantation quarters there was a small stall run by a Chinese who the workers there called Banglae. We stopped by and bought a five litre jerry can. We were not going to be thirsty again tomorrow!
>
> We worked cutting that wild sugarcane grass for fifteen days solid. My skin, already dark, turned black. Some of my workmates got sick because they had not done heavy work like this for a long time, or because they had never been farmers. But there was no choice except to work and go on working. Like a buffalo pulling the plough. It would have been bearable, even though we got no pay, had we been given enough to eat.

Over the time of working there, Wardik and the other prisoners found ways to endure their forced labour. They befriended the villagers living around the plantation, who often helped out and gave them extra work for money. Wardik got to know a village girl called Surtini who asked him to help her in her rice field, and she became a close friend. Wardik often went to help her. After a while, he accompanied the girl home and met her parents. They received him politely, and their friendship continued.

When Wardik was finally given permission to go home for four days to see his mother, he had no money for the journey. It was Sutini who gave him the money so that he could go. Together with some other prisoners who had been given leave, he was taken from Blangkahan plantation to Sukamulia prison. After being given advice and lectures on good behaviour, he went with his friend Antaran who came from the same village, to Timbangan, which was a two minivan ride away. From there he hitched a ride on the back of a truck. The truck driver knew they were prisoners, because it was written clearly on their travel papers, which they showed him. The truck driver helped them, even giving them lunch on the way and then a bit of money. During their conversation, it turned out he too had been detained for three months at Siantar.

When they arrived at the Padang Halaban turnoff, the truck driver got out of the cabin and gave each of them 1000 rupiah. Wardik now went to look for his mother who was no longer living in the old village, but in a field. This is how he told of his reunion with his family:

> From a distance, I could make out my mother and younger brother Susanto hoeing in the rice field, and I called to my mother. They both turned around, and my brother screamed out, 'Mum! Brother has come back!' He threw down the hoe in his hands. My mother came running, stumbling through the muddy rice field, shrieking, howling, 'Son, son, you've come home son!' You could hear her sobbing and yelling all the way to the house. She grabbed me and hugged me close, not caring that she was covered with mud. The neighbours arrived, wondering what was going on. I led Mother in to the house. She just hugged and hugged me as though she would never let me go.

Wardik sent his nephew to buy some rice with the money the truck driver had given them. Wardik used his two-day homecoming to meet his friends and relations, all of whom were oppressed by intimidation and poverty. Even so, some of his friends including Arfan and Bero gave him some money to cover the transport costs of returning to the prison. Wardik left his mother some of his money.

Arfan told Wardik what was going on there at the plantation, and what the people living at the complex were doing.

> That Second Lieutenant Aritonang, for instance, just because he was made officer supervising the plantation, he evicted all the people living there just like that. These were people whose land had been in the family for generations. What will they do in their old age? And no one dared complain. Anyone who complained would be accused of being a rebel and branded communist. And if you are branded communist, you lose everything, including your life.

The night before Wardik returned to Blangkahan plantation, they exchanged stories about the bitterness of life, and also about ways of enduring their suffering. Wardik asked Arfan to look after his mother. They parted with tears.

After two years working at Blangkahan plantation, Wardik was moved to a detention centre in Tanjung Kasau, in the regency of Asahan bordering the regencies of Simalungun and Deli Serdang. It was about 19 kilometres from Tebing Tinggi on the way to Kisaran. In Dutch times, it had been a rubber plantation with a hospital which was later used as a police school. This complex – the former plantation hospital –what was now 'General Detention Centre for Group B'. Wardik – who used to be in category C – had suddenly been moved to group B without any process of any kind and without him being notified.

Wardik and about 200 other prisoners were sent to be forced labourers on the Suka Luwei rubber plantation in the Bangun Purba sub regency, in the regency of Deli Serdang. It was very cold there because it was up on the slopes of Mount Barisan. This is how Wardik described his experience on the rubber plantation:

> We were given a hoe and a scythe. We had to clear the jungle and hoe. Each person had to finish four plots called *gawang* which measured four by six metres. So that meant one person had to clear and hoe 96 square metres. When it was done, you were paid 25 rupiah per *gawang*. If you did only this and no more, you were given only two ounces of rice. So prisoners had to work extra hard to get any extra.
>
> After working for six days, hunger mixed with exhaustion. There were absolutely no plants growing in the jungle that we could eat. Luckily there were centipedes and scorpions as big as your hand which tasted delicious. If you put them over a fire they were like barbequed prawn. We got rice only by working extra hard.
>
> One day I got an idea. Every morning, I would move the marker that the plantation people had placed back four *gawang*. That meant that if I cleared and hoed eight *gawang*, it was counted as 12. Six was the basic requirement, but the other six would be counted as extra 25 rupiah per gawang, so I would earn 150 rupiah a day. Not all of the other prisoners wanted to copy what I did. They were afraid of being found out, for indeed the punishment would definitely be extremely severe. One of the prisoners was once too weak to finish just his required six gawang, so then we were all made to run back to Suka Luwei carrying our hoes and scythes on our backs. This was a distance of eight kilometres.
>
> Rats and snakes were also a source of food. If we chased them together, we usually managed to catch between four and eight rats.
>
> I was a forced slave labourer at Suka Luwei for three and a half months. I had had enough. I approached the new guard and asked if I could be sent back to Tanjung Kasau prison. He said I had to have a reason. I had to find a reason. I had no answer to this, so I asked him, 'like what?' He suggested that the next day I resist the plantation assistant who helped supervise our work.

> Hit the assistant, Mesin Tarigan, if necessary. He is bound to report. And then you are bound to be punished. Only then can you be sent back to Tanjung Kasau, for hitting the assistant.' I followed his advice to the letter. Twenty other people were also accused of joining in the fight. Twenty of us were summoned and punished. We were beaten and had to crawl 100 metres, and told to walk back to the barracks. I was punished by being moved to Tanjung Kasau.

* * * *

Wardik was back in Tanjung Kasau for only two days before 30 people, including him, were listed to be moved yet again. The Camp Commander said it was only as temporary replacement workers. Wardik explained.

> The Naga Timbul plantation was in Deli Serdang regency. The nearest city was Tanjung Morawa, about fifteen kilometres away from the plantation. The pay at the plantation was 100 rupiah a day for clearing the plantation ditches. They had not been cleared for eight years. There were no barracks there, as was usually the case. We prisoners were housed in three empty cabins.
>
> The Contractor, Menghong, had bought the prisoners' labour from the authorities. Dirt cheap. Cheaper than slaves. We ate wild green plants like fern, swamp cabbage and water lettuce that grew beneath the oil palms. There were lots of different kinds of fish, eels and even soft-shell turtles in the irrigation ditches that were delicious to eat.

Every day, the prisoners would have to walk at least five kilometres. At five thirty in the morning they would have to leave and would not finish until five thirty in the evening. Rain or sickness were no reasons not to work. It was day in and day out as the contractor ordered.

There was a village near the plantation, called Naga Rejo. In the past it had been a large village, but in 1969 half of the area of nine villages had been seized by the plantation and planted with palm oil. According to the villagers, they were given no compensation. The fate of Naga Rejo was the same as Wardik's village. Wardik recounted,

> I often traded the fish I caught for cassava or coconut. Almost every afternoon when we went through the village, someone would give us bananas, cassava or vegetables.

> One day we were ordered to leave for the area of Galang. It was still early morning mist as the truck went through the Batu Lokong plantation towards Petumbukan. As we went over a bridge, Legimin leaned in close and said that there were hundreds of friends buried in the river bed. "This is Snake River", he said, "they killed my uncle here. Over there is the village of Pulau Gambar. All the people taken from Pulau Gambar were killed right here in this river."

Wardik and the other prisoners were often sent to work on other plantations, doing Menghong's contracted work. Even though they were working elsewhere, in the evenings they would be taken back to Naga Timbul plantation.

Four years passed like this, moving from one plantation to the next, doing forced labour. In October 1974, all the prisoners who had been sent to work on the plantations had to return to Tanjung Kasau detention centre. Wardik was moved from there to the Sukamulia detention centre. After seven months there, he was moved back to Tanjung Kasau again, this time as preparation for release. Before his release, he was permitted to visit his mother who was extremely weak. She asked her son Wardik to feed her. Five days later Wardik's sister, San came and brought the news that their mother had died. San told him his mother's last words for Wardik were, 'don't give up easily.'

On 20 December 1977, the first batch of prisoners was released at a ceremony attended by Sudomo, Commander of the Kopkamtib (Komando Operasi Pemulihan Keamanan dan Ketertiban, Command for the Restoration of Security and Public Order). Wardik was not included in this batch, but he attended the ceremony as a spectator and then had to go back to prison.

In April 1978, there was a second batch of releases, this time all those from north Sumatra, except for those who had been tried. Wardik had no desire to return to his village after his release. His friend suggested that Wardik go to his brother-in-law Bandi's place, and then they could find a house to rent together.

On 19 May 1978, it was announced that all remaining prisoners would be released. That night there was a celebration in the prison complex. There was a performance of traditional Javanese comic drama (*ludruk*) by the Indra Pura ludruk group.

This time, the prisoners were to be released at the Regional Military Police headquarters on Jalan Sena in Medan. At seven in the morning dozens of trucks went in convoy taking the prisoners from Tanjung Kasau to the Military Police complex. Almost all the prisoners had family there to meet them. And then, the field in front was quiet, almost deserted, with just a few officials wandering around.

Wardik was alone. He had a knapsack with a few clothes slung over his shoulder. He was confused. The space was frightening, and he had no idea which way to go – north or west was all the same. He had once lived in Medan, the provincial capital of North Sumatra. And then, unexpectedly, he heard someone call his name. His brother-in-law Bandi, on his bicycle, was approaching. He propped up his bike. He did not know that Wardik had been released. Just that morning quite by chance he heard on the national radio (RRI) that there was to be a release ceremony of all prisoners that very morning.

'Right now, Brother, just come home with me. Then you can decide where you want to go. And if you don't want anything to do with your older sister, well, worry about that later,' Bandi said.

* * * *

Released from isolation, Wardik now felt more isolated than ever. He had a fear of crowds. After two days at his sister Yus's place, his brother-in-law Bandi took him to his sister San's place in Martubung. He stayed one night there. His sister's husband Mansyur told lots of stories about how busy they were now with their animals. The younger brothers and sisters Santo, Ambran and Subali helped out, but at the same time they were another burden. There were also the nephews and nieces, San's children, Agus, Maisih, Dinah and Jety.

Wardik ended up finding his friend Basiman who had been detained with him but released in 1974. He had opened a small wood-carving business, and he offered Wardik some work.

But not even one month passed before there were problems. When Basiman went out, it was his wife who was boss. Wardik could not stand her nagging and complaining and so he resigned. He still got some orders like making bed-head designs, which he could do at home. He also took the opportunity to go back to his village and visit his mother's grave.

On the way back to Medan after visiting his mother's grave, all the passengers got off the train at Medan station and Wardik got off last. He had nowhere to go. Didn't know which way to go. He walked along with his knapsack slung over his shoulder, containing just a few clothes and a pair of rubber sandals. Aimless, he ended up in front of the post office. In front of the post office was Merdeka Square, with an open pavilion. Wardik headed there. During the day he would look for work and at night go and sleep in the pavilion. There were many stalls in front of the post office, selling cigarettes, postage stamps, revenue stamps, newspapers and magazines. One morning he went over to the cigarette seller. Wardik had got to know him because he bought his cigarettes there every day. The seller got Wardik started selling newspapers and magazines at the railway station. He did that for two months.

One evening the train came in from Rantau Prapat and the passengers got off. While Wardik was busy selling newspapers, he heard someone call him. It was not his name that was being called, but the name of the newspaper he was selling, but he knew that voice well. 'Rohana!' he said. She was surprised, and did not recognise him. 'It's me, Wardik', he said. Rohana invited him to come and visit. So the very next morning he went over. After telling her his experiences and his current situation, he asked whether it would be possible to stay at her place for a while. Rohana and her husband Pardi agreed, as long as Wardik contributed to food costs.

Wardik then asked his older sisters and brothers-in-law to help find a friend of his, Zul Iskandar, who had also been detained. Zul had once told him that when he was released he could give him some gardening work. Prior to the 1965 incident, Zul had been a journalist for the daily newspaper *Harian Harapan*. He could write, sculpt and was very good at landscaping. The very next day Wardik was working alongside Zul, gardening. In the evenings he would go back to Rohana's place. When his friend Zul had no work to offer him, Wardik would find other odd jobs. The important thing was to give Rohana regular money for food.

He lived there with Rohana and her husband at the edge of the Sutomo complex for a year. Then he heard that there was an art studio offering work. He went over and was given a job and allowed to stay at the studio. The studio, called 'Sanggar Murni' was owned by Kamarudin Nasution. Even though the studio leaked when it rained, it was okay for Wardik who was happy not be dependent on others. He became calmer. But he did not forget Rohana, and sometimes went over and spent a night or two there.

Two years after his release, his older sister San started pressuring him to get married. Wardik always answered, 'You need savings to get married. I've got nothing at all'.

One day he had a chance meeting with a school headmistress and her husband, both middle-aged. It was late at night, around midnight, and he was on his way home from watching an outdoor film in the Kebun Pisang football field. The headmistress' car had broken down. Wardik went over and helped them. After cleaning the battery heads, the car started. They offered him money, but he refused to take it. They introduced themselves and the husband asked Wardik to visit them the next day. They lived at Sampali. As a result of this visit, Wardik was offered work landscaping the yard in front of the private high school (Perguruan SMA) where the woman was headmistress. They went over that very day to survey the yard, and Wardik said he would make a design.

The headmistress agreed to his design and the budget, and Wardik finished it all in one week. She suggested that the students help out with the planting as an extra-curricular activity. She also offered Wardik some work teaching painting at the school, and made him an honorary teacher. When he finished his teaching he still had to go to the studio and do his work there. When he did not have to teach, he would study art on his own.

Around this time, Wardik met a shy young woman called Elya Yuswita who lived at Sei Batang Serangan in Medan Baru, and the daughter of a policeman who had already passed away. After they had got to know each other for a while, they married. According to one of Wardik's friends, Juah Sembiring who lived at Binjai, if the mother of the young woman had not joined her husband, who was then working at Kisaran, she too might have been arrested, like Wardik, for being a member of a leftist organisation. This was one reason that Wardik decided to marry Elya.

Wardik told the story like this:

> On 29 February 1980, I got married. It was a very simple wedding, basically just a meeting of the two families. I had made a small wedding dias. There was the official solemnisation, yellow rice flour for confetti, and Arabic songs of praise. Supri and her husband Hendrik Napitupulu came, along with Anas and Rumandung. A week later I took my wife to a house I had rented for us in the village of Helvetia. So I became Elya's husband. And she became my wife.
>
> I continued with my work as honorary teacher and craftsman. Sometimes I would get extra work doing landscaping, fixing houses or building them, and if things were particularly good, renovating buildings. I had my friends' addresses, and would ask their children

to work with me. When Elsya was heavily pregnant, I gave up my honorary teaching work because having to spend three days there meant that I could not earn enough outside extra money. The teaching wages were minimal. So I explained the situation to the headmistress, and she was very understanding. Luckily, I got a substantial work contract that looked as though it had good prospects. My first child was born in November of the year of my marriage.

In early 1981, the headmistress came to visit me at home. She offered me a permanent teaching position. This was at the urging of the students and other teachers, and the wish of the headmistress herself. I told her how grateful I was. I knew why the students and teachers were encouraging me to become a permanent teacher. It was not just because of the extracurricular activities that I led, like art, marching band, scouts and swimming, but also because I could be a relief teacher when there were female teachers on maternity leave. The school would not have to hunt around trying to find teachers from other schools. When I was just a voluntary teacher, I often taught history and social studies for years one, two and three.

After the headmistress had left, I asked my wife Elya what she thought. I explained that my current work contract still had quite a while to go. But I could do the supervision of the workers after teaching at school. Particularly if my teaching duties were like those when I was just honorary teacher. She agreed with what I thought was the best solution.

So in early 1981, Wardik returned to the private high school, but now as permanent staff. The idea was that he would begin teaching after the papers for his official teaching contract came through. In 1996, in the second semester, Wardik signed a work contract with a contracting business building the Malibu housing complex near Polonia in Medan. His job was to coordinate and supply the labourers. Wardik decided to resign as teacher. He was never at ease anyway, because there had been the ministerial decree in 1981 from the Ministry of Home Affairs banning all former political prisoners from working as teachers, and even banning their children too. The sin was passed down to one's descendants.

In 1999, Wardik got a contract to build a ceramics factory. 'The salary was good. I got enough to build a simple four-roomed house. Three of the rooms were for my family. The fourth room, relatively large, was for friends from Padang Halaban who needed a place to stay when they came to Medan', Wardik said.

* * * *

Wardik has now [2010, trs] been married to Elya for eighteen years. In that time, his wife has given birth to four boys and one girl. Wardik has opportunities to meet up with his old prisoner friends when their children get married, or circumcised, or at other times. And they always have reunions at funerals, when one of their prison mates has gone to meet his Maker.

When news started going round that it looked as though Soeharto was going to fall, Wardik got into action. This is how he tells it:

> I began to think, I began to ask my friends who I thought knew a lot about these things. If Soeharto fell, then would they get back their land that had been confiscated? None of them could answer this. In order to get our rights restored, we needed to organise. We needed an organisation that would be our tool to fight for our rights. This was the beginning of what I had to do – get people whose rights had been taken from them, to organise.
>
> I had to go to Padang Halaban immediately. There I met Samiran, Sumardi and other friends. I told them that Soeharto was going to fall, and we needed to get prepared, I said that according to some activist students, it was only a matter of days before Soeharto would fall. If we were not organised, we could not get our rights restored. That's what I told them. Sumardi said that he still had some land titles and proof of ownership. He agreed to contact others and to try to get organised. As for what form the organisation would take, we would think about that later. Samiran said that it could be anything – like a monthly *arisan* group. We agreed on this. I returned to Medan on the night train.
>
> In May 1998, seven days before Soeharto fell, I held a circumcision ceremony for my third child at my house. All the friends I invited came. We all shared stories, telling each other what we knew about what was going on, and about those in power. We talked about the student movement that was going to occupy the parliament buildings in Senayan until Soeharto stepped down.

And on 21 May 1998, Soeharto finally stepped down. I immediately contacted my friends at Padang Halaban. They had made an organisation of farmers whose land had been confiscated under the Soeharto regime. It was a grouping of farmers from Padang Halaban and surrounding villages. They demanded the return of their land. Samiran was made head of the organisation. In Medan, I joined Agresu (Aliansi Gerakan Reformasi Sumatera Utara, Alliance of the North Sumatran Reformation Movement). The students and I went around drumming up awareness among the farmers that the New Order regime which had taken their land from them, had fallen. They had to unite, to oppose the tyranny of the authorities.

On 28 October 1998, the farmers' action began. Five thousand farmers, from the regencies of Labuhan Batu, Asahan, Deli Serdang and Langkat united in a march to the Governor's office and the regional government office. The demonstrators occupied their regional government building for the night. They said, as this was the house of the people's representatives, they had the right to stay in their own house. That night the farmers and students made an alliance of four farmers' groups from the four regencies that joined the demonstration. During the New Order, farmers' organisations were banned. The group was called Gerag (Gerakan Reformasi Agraria or Movement for Agrarian Reform). The student activists said that with the formation of Gerag, the farmers' struggle in those four regencies and in all the regencies in North Sumatra would now have the courage to stand up and no longer be afraid of the authorities.

Wardik continued enthusiastically.

The early years of the Reformation era were the years of action. These were the years of demonstrations. I joined whenever there was a farmers' demonstration. Sometimes friends from Padang Halaban came, at least one train carriage of them, to join the demonstrations in Medan. Some of our student activist friends got shot. At the demonstration at Tanjung Morawa, nine students were treated at the Elisabeth hospital. Two or three of them were shot in the leg, or bashed with sticks. At Langkat, the farmers' demonstration at Pancur Batu was overwhelming. So too were the demonstrations in the villages on the edges of the plantations in all the regencies in North Sumatra.

The farmers at Padang Halaban have continued their demonstrations right up to now, the current government of Susilo Bambang Yudoyono. And yet none of the land that was confiscated has been returned. As for the student activists that got us going, who knows where they are. They come about once every five years in the name of their political parties. They come to get votes for their parties and for themselves so they can sit as members of parliament, as representatives of the people, in Jakarta as well as at the province, regency and municipal levels.

But the Padang Halaban farmers keep on going, they never stop fighting for the restoration of their rights. There is a poem titled 'Stake' (*Pancang*) written by Astaman Hasibuan. It goes like this:

pancang itu bagiku
adalah janji yang kuyakini sampai hari ini dan nanti
pancang itu bagiku
adalah garis demarkasi
pancang itu bagiku
adalah senandungku

menapak matahari

To me, that stake
Is the promise I believe in
To me, that stake
Is the demarcation line
To me, that stake
Is the rhythm of my song

Walking towards the sun

Interviewers and transcribers: Astaman Hasibuan and Wardy.
Writer: Putu Oka Sukanta.

About the editor

Putu Oka Sukanta, born in Bali in 1939, is a writer and editor of fiction and non-fiction. He has written novels, poetry, collections of stories, and books about HIV/AIDS and traditional healing. His writing has also been published in English, German, and French translation. From 1966 to 1976 Putu was detained without trial because he was an activist with the leftist arts organisation LEKRA. He now lives in Jakarta, where he has an acupuncture practice, works to promote traditional medicine, and is active in programs for human rights and the prevention of HIV/AIDS. Putu is often invited overseas to present his writing and ideas. In 2012 he was awarded a Hellman/Hammett grant for commitment to free expression and courage in the face of persecution by Human Rights Watch, New York.